Zeal Unabated

This is believed to be the daguerreotype of Waghorn 'which he had done in Paris on his last return from Vienna' (Spring 1847) according to the *Liverpool Albion* of 14 January 1850. The present whereabouts is unknown.

Zeal Unabated

The Life of Thomas Fletcher Waghorn (1800-1850)

Andrew Ashbee

214, Malling Road,
Snodland, Kent
ME6 5EQ
e-mail: aa0060962@blueyonder.co.uk

Printed by TJ International,
Trecerus Industrial Estate,
Padstow, Cornwall
PL28 8RW
www.tjnternational.ltd.uk

ISBN: 978 0 9507207 8 4

CONTENTS

ILLUSTRATIONS

INTRODUCTION

The spark which ignited this account of Waghorn was the decision to hold an exhibition to commemorate the 200th anniversary of his birth in 2000, at the newly-opened Snodland Millennium Museum. Little was to hand locally apart from the actual presence of his house, his grave and the memorial in All Saints church. Research was required and I duly spent time at the Public Record Office, the British Library and elsewhere accumulating and checking facts, sufficient to be able to produce a 48-page pamphlet about Waghorn's life to accompany the exhibition. No sources were shown there and I determined that a properly documented account be attempted in due course. This is it.

I am treading in the footsteps of two earlier accounts: John K. Sidebottom, *The Overland Mail. A Postal Historical Study of the Mail Route to India*, 1948, and Marjorie Sankey, *'Care of Mr. Waghorn'. A Biography*, 1964, both published under the auspices of the Postal History Society. Sidebottom's fine book concentrates very much on the mails – his sub-heading is 'a postal historical study of the mail route to India', while Sankey's is a vivid and lively account of Waghorn's life, unfortunately marred by a complete lack of source references, particularly needed when querying and correcting some errors. Several of these found their way into Freda Harcourt's somewhat unkind Waghorn entry in *The Oxford Dictionary of National Biography* (2004); it has only been possible to amend the on-line version. Her conclusion that 'Waghorn had played no more than a minute off-stage part' ignores the fact that he was the grit in the oyster and that the incessant publicity of his travels and his cajoling and pleading ensured that communication with India and the Far East remained constantly in the eyes of the Government, the East India Company and the public.

My initial research was entirely dependent on searching original documents, including those at the National Archives (then the Public Record Office), the resources of the Oriental and Indian Office (now the Africa, Pacific and Asia Collection) at the British Library, and the Institute of Historical Research. How times have changed. The Internet has brought so much material into the home and it is now possible to search worldwide through sites like *The British Newspaper Archive, Trove, The National Archives of India*, and numerous others. Newspapers have proved a particularly valuable resource for this study. Not all are digitalised yet, but their practice of quoting from their contemporaries means that the net spreads wider still.

Throughout my research I have been in touch with several people who also have an interest in Waghorn and his exploits. Although Waghorn himself had no children, descendants of his siblings are proud of his endeavours. Most of these are in Australia, to which his sisters Ann and Sarah and his brother Edward all emigrated. Their own researches have added to the picture and I am grateful to them for willingly exchanging material. Three in particular were helpful in the early stages of this research: Mrs Robin Handley, Mrs Victoria Beer and Mr Edward Stock (the last two in England). It is not surprising to find that many Waghorn artefacts, including at least three portraits, went to Australia and some are still with the families there. But it is sad to learn that a case of Waghorn material on its way to England for legal reasons was sunk during the Second World War.

Another particular interest arises from the study of the postal stamps used in Waghorn's mails, so his name is well-known to philatelists. The postal aspect of Waghorn's scheme has been studied in depth by Sidebottom and his successors and I have not dealt with more than a skeleton of it here. Michel Houde has also written about Waghorn and the Post and he also kindly sent copies of material he has collected to add to the Waghorn archive at Snodland Millennium Museum. See the Waghorn section at <michelhoude.com>. The list of known covers in John Sidebottom's 1948 book has grown substantially since then and the Egypt Study Circle has up-dated it. The late Rudi Jeidel compiled an excellent CD of *The Waghorn Story* for The Philatelic Federation of South Africa which shows images of unique documents (as well as covers) in his collection, including what appears to be the daguerreotype of Waghorn taken in 1847. I thank the PFSA and the Egypt Study Circle for their help in trying to track down some of these. It is clear that Waghorn documents are coveted and collected by philatelists and have circulated among them for many years. Items from Sidebottom's pioneering collection continue to surface from time to time.

I am very grateful to the staff of all the institutions in which I have worked, or with whom I have corresponded, for their invaluable help. They are listed in the Bibliography. I am especially grateful too to Christopher Howick who has read the drafts of this book and who has offered most helpful advice on its content and structure.

In his day Waghorn aroused strong feelings and it is not easy now to assess how much he actually achieved. But his restless energy certainly drives his story and takes us vividly round the world of his day.

Abbreviations

APA	London, British Library: Asia Pacific and Africa Collections
KHLC	Maidstone: Kent History and Library Centre
MALSC	Medway (Strood): Medway Archives and Local Study Centre
NAI	Delhi: National Archives of India
NMM	Greenwich: National Maritime Museum
SHS	Snodland Historical Society
SMM	Snodland Millennium Museum
TNA	The National Archives

FOREWORD

THE BACKGROUND

In the 1820s a journey between England and India took a minimum of about three months. This was as true for news or a mail packet as it was for a person. The usual route was via the Cape of Good Hope on a sailing ship belonging to the East India Company. An alternative for mail was established some twenty years earlier with a ship from Bombay to Basra and then camels travelling overland to Aleppo and Constantinople. But this was always subject to marauding bandits. Also, in 1819 the East India Company began a regular service between Bombay and Cossier on the west coast of Egypt, crossing the desert on camels to the Nile and then sailing north to Alexandria. This was to avoid the south-west monsoon which prevented sailing ships from traversing the Red Sea for many months each year. The advent of the earliest steam ships in the 1820s seemed to offer a way towards solving the problems created by the monsoon. Steam funds were set up in India to explore the possibilities and money was promised to anyone able to speed journey times using new steamers. The first real attempt to replace sail with steam was made in 1825, when the *Enterprise* made a journey from Falmouth to Calcutta (round the Cape). Unfortunately it took 115 days rather than the 70 days target aimed at, so was deemed a failure and the ship was sold.

The development of steam services in the Mediterranean evolved in the 1830s. The Post Office had previously run an inefficient mail service to Spain and Portugal using sailing ships, but this had been replaced by the Navy and its early steamers. One problem was that steam needed coal and coal supplies had to be made available along all the routes. Between 1832 and 1834 Waghorn served on the Navy mail ships, giving him experience of steam, ports, and the workings of the mail system as far as Malta. Apart from the English the French had their own ships sailing from Marseilles, although the British remained wary of sending their mail through France. In 'races' to deliver the mail each nation claimed its own victories. Alexandria soon became part of the network as the Overland Route developed. To shorten the journey time the French eventually established a direct service between Marseilles and Malta, cutting out such intermediate stops as Genoa, Naples and Brindisi. This was in part to tackle competition by the Austrian Lloyd Company which had established an efficient service from Trieste to Alexandria.

The East India Company controlled all routes from India to the African continent. However, the Directors in England were lethargic in developing a steamship service to Suez, even though this might have eradicated the monsoon problem. They gave permission for the *Hugh Lindsay* to be built in Bombay and it made an inaugural journey from Bombay to Suez in 1829. But it was inadequately powered, with insufficient capacity for coal. Weighed down it took more than a month to make the journey. Furthermore the Directors were appalled at the cost of supplying coal to the various staging posts.

The name The Overland Route highlights the significance of that part of the journey between Alexandria and Suez. For passengers, the Bombay Steam Committee initially arranged for Hill & Company to set up rest-houses across the desert between Cairo and Suez, and hotels were opened in Alexandria, Cairo and Suez, all staffed by English personnel. Waghorn rather set his sights on speeding the mail 'Care of Mr. Waghorn' and gave priority to this, using camels on a route which did not go through Cairo. But with increasing passenger numbers he had to cater for their needs too and soon a successful joint agency was formed between Waghorn and Hill.

Steam may have been the new technology, but steamships were relatively slow—the 12 knots of merchant ships was considered a great advantage over the 8-10 knots attained by Navy vessels. This was before the advent of screw propulsion and when paddle-wheels and auxiliary sail was the technology employed. A journey from Alexandria to Trieste was estimated at five days. Another obstruction to travellers was the enforced quarantine at Malta or Marseilles, which usually took several days. Mail too was disinfected, all to combat the threat of the plague, although no travellers through Egypt ever succumbed to it.

Salvation came with the emergence of the P&O Company. In 1837 it won a contract to carry the mails to Spain and Portugal and in 1840 this was extended to Malta and Alexandria and the Eastern

Mediterranean with the further promise of a steam service from Egypt to India. The East India Company insisted on retaining its monopoly of the Bombay-Suez route, but allowed the P&O an alternative: Suez-Aden-Ceylon-Madras-Calcutta. New, larger, and more comfortable ships were built. In 1845 the P&O introduced a service from Point de Galle (Ceylon) or Calcutta to Penang, Singapore and Hong Kong. Late in life Waghorn agitated to extend this service to Australia, but died before it was created. He was also at the forefront of moves to extend the burgeoning railway network in Europe, but again was just too early for all the connections to have been made. Coach and horses was the alternative still in common use.

1

FAMILY AND EARLY LIFE

Thomas Fletcher Waghorn, according to his contemporaries, was a man of great courage, single-mindedness and unbounded energy. While this is certainly true, his courage and energy could turn to recklessness and his single-mindedness to obstinate intransigence. His impatience was legendary, as was his volcanic temper, so he was something of a flawed hero. George Smith, who as a boy knew him, wrote:

> 'Waghorn was a sailor-like man, short and broad, excitable in a high degree, and of tremendous energy … He had an unfortunate gift for quarrelling with people; his energy was unqualified by tact; his temper was explosive.'[1]

Yet these imperfections were often brushed aside by his friends and colleagues who realised that he had high aspirations and that his life was fully dedicated to the pursuit of these. The most famous account of him is the brief tongue-in-cheek description by William Makepeace Thackeray, in *From Cornhill to Cairo*:[2]

> The bells are ringing prodigiously and Lieut. Waghorn is bouncing in and out of the Court Yard full of business. He only left Bombay yesterday morning, was seen in the Red Sea on Tuesday, is engaged to dinner this afternoon in the Regents Park and (as it is about two minutes since I saw him in the court yard) I make no doubt he is by this time at Alexandria, or at Malta, say, or perhaps both. *Il est capable.*

---

1 George Murray Smith, 'In the Early Forties', *The Cornhill Magazine*, IX, No. 53, N.S., 577-585.

2 M. A. Titmarsh [William Makepeace Thackeray], *Notes of a Journey from Cornhill to Grand Cairo …*, New York, 1845, 146.

Mark Boyd came to know Waghorn during his own promotion of the colonization of Australia, and opens his reminiscence with these words:

> I knew the indomitable, persevering, and courageous Waghorn intimately. He was a good-hearted man, whose only failing was an excessive love of stimulants. 'You have made for yourself a great name,' I would say to him, 'and I wish to see you enjoy your honours for another quarter of a century; you have been blessed with a magnificent constitution, but it will soon break down unless you leave off.' The poor fellow's only reply was, "'Tis true, my good sir, but I cannot help it."

Sadly Boyd's prophecy came true and at the end of his life Waghorn's constitution finally gave way. What were these stimulants of which Boyd speaks? No other mention of them has been found, but one suspects opium or something similar, to which Waghorn may have become addicted during his time in the east. Opium was not restricted or regarded as dangerous in his life-time and was easily available in shops. It was often used as a recreational drug and was provided from sources in the Middle East and India. No doubt he felt its use helpful in his many hazardous and exhausting adventures, but how far it contributed to his general demeanour is impossible to say. The likelihood is that it enhanced traits which were present from birth, for he alone of his family seems to have sought adventure from an early age, rather than pursuing the routine of his father's trade of butcher.

The Waghorn Family

Genealogists have so far failed to find any conclusive record of Waghorn's father's birth, and some of their suggestions seem very wide of the mark. Marjorie Sankey led the search into these murky waters:

> Thomas Waghorn … was a butcher with a shop exactly opposite the Mitre [Chatham]. His wife had been a Miss Stedman, a descendant of the aristocratic Field family of The Hall, Ashurst Park, from an eldest son, who had been disinherited for marrying the daughter of a veterinary surgeon. This may be the foundation

of the legend of our Waghorn's aristocratic birth and fortune. The butcher Waghorn had had three daughters before the birth of their only son. Another daughter was born later.[3]

Following this line, a family descendant proposed that he might be the Thomas Field Waghorn, baptised at Teston on 7 October 1770, son of Hannah.[4] The date of this baptism tallies well with the elder Thomas's burial at St Mary's, Chatham, on 28 March 1826, aged 56, and no other Thomas Waghorn baptism has been found in this year. However, the marriage of Thomas Waghorn, a butcher from Chatham, and Ann Goodhugh of Snodland took place at All Saints church, Snodland, on 28 July 1794[5], demolishing the Sankey idea. In seeking Thomas's origins the trade of butcher seems to provide a lead.

An old view of Chatham High Street showing a few houses which were probably there in Waghorn's day.
(© Medway Archives and Local Study Centre)

3 Marjorie Sankey, *Care of Mr. Waghorn. A Biography*, Postal History Society, Special Series, No. 19, 1964, 5-6. Her list of Waghorn [I]'s family is very incomplete.
4 Hannah's child was illegitimate, the father's name presumably being Field.
5 This and other relevant entries are taken from the registers of All Saints, Birling; All Saints, Snodland; St Mary, Chatham.

It is intriguing to find two (and subsequently three) Waghorns trading as butchers in Rochester and Chatham and it seems worth investigating if there is any link between them. Apart from Thomas senior, there was a younger man, William, in Rochester High Street.[6] He was baptized at Otham, near Maidstone, on 17 January 1796, the son of Samuel and his second wife Ann (née Rose). He was of St Nicholas parish, Rochester, on 26 June 1821, when he married Ann Biggs, so presumably he had already set up his shop (a few doors to the west of The King's Head). They had eight children, one of whom, James, is well documented as an omnibus proprietor, and the family appear in the censuses. Samuel's two marriages at Otham were first to Margaret Bolton on 10 October 1785 (two children: Samuel and Elizabeth), and second to Ann Rose on 27 October 1794. This second marriage produced four children, of whom William was the eldest. Further investigation shows a baptism for Samuel on 29 July 1759, the son of another Samuel and Ann. No record of this marriage appears at Otham, so they must have come from elsewhere. Six children are recorded:

Mary	bap.	10 July 1757
Samuel	bap.	29 July 1759
Sarah	bap.	21 August 1763
William	bap.	26 January 1765
Thomas	bap.	12 October 1768
Edward	bap.	15 June 1771 (buried 22 October that year)

The occupation of Samuel I is not shown, but Samuel II was a butcher and it is possible the father was too. There seems a strong likelihood that Thomas the elder was Samuel II's brother. True the baptism date of 12 October 1768 does not conform with his stated burial age of 56, but there is only eighteen months difference and experience in many years of transcribing documents has shown that discrepancies of this magnitude (or greater) are commonplace. In those days there were no official records of baptisms, marriages or deaths other than the registers, so much depended on memory and mental calculation, either of which might prove fallible. No apprenticeships have been found for the family and they may have learned their trade from each other. If so, it is quite likely

6 I am grateful to Mrs. Robin Handley for information on this family.

that the elder Samuel taught his sons. Later William may have come under the wing of Thomas senior and, following his training, established himself in Rochester High Street. Eventually too there was Edward, Thomas I's son, another butcher, who on this basis would be William's cousin, trading first in Rochester and in later life in Melbourne.[7]

Ann Goodhugh's ancestors and relations on the other hand are well accounted for. The witnesses at her wedding were her father, John Goodhugh, and her brother-in-law, William Gorham. The Goodhughs had lived in Birling for several generations, while, on Ann's mother's side, the Fletchers were more attached to Snodland. A genealogical tree of Ann's family and the children of Thomas I and Ann appears as Appendix A.

Of those who survived infancy, the eldest, John (b.1795), became a slaughter-man and was still alive in 1821. Ann (1798-1889) married Robert Munday at Snodland in 1824. He became a licensed victualler in Rochester, but later seems to have spent several years in Cairo running Waghorn's hotel there. According to the biography issued by the firm of his business partner George Wheatley, Thomas Fletcher, the subject of this book, was born on 20 June 1800.[8] He took his second name from his maternal grandmother, while the next child, the infant James Goodhugh (1802-1804) was given that of his paternal grandfather. Mary Jane (1804-1883) lived un-married in the Medway towns throughout her life. Edward (1806-1868) became a butcher, eventually emigrating to Australia. Frances (1810-1848), seems to have lived with her uncle in Birling, perhaps acting as a housekeeper, while the youngest sibling, Sarah (1813-1887) married William Ransom, but also emigrated to Australia after William's death.

---

7 See Andrew Ashbee, 'Who was Waghorn's Father?', *The Clock Tower*, 7, (August 2007), 14-17

8 P.E.Clunn, *Lieutenant Waghorn, R.N., Pioneer of the Overland Route to India*, London, 1892 and 1894. (The latter edition is the one used here.) This birth date does not quite match up with information that Waghorn passed his examination for lieutenant in navigation '16 days before he attained 17'.

Chatham

It would appear that Thomas Waghorn senior was a man of some substance. By 1797, when he was aged 27, the Land Tax records show him as the owner of three houses, but occupying a fourth. According to Waghorn's later partner, George Wheatley, he 'held large contracts for the supply of the navy, though the speculation did not prove lucrative.'[9] No doubt the link was a means whereby his son's navy career could be initiated. On 30 June 1800 a terrible fire broke out in Chatham which destroyed a hundred properties. It began when sparks from a blacksmith ignited a shed full of cordage, hemp and oakum and spread along the High Street. *The Times* reported:

> Monday forenoon, between 11 and 12 o'clock, a fire broke out at a Wharf a little way above the Sun Tavern, Chatham, which raged with dreadful violence upwards of two hours; both sides of the main street are in one heap of ruins, from within three or four doors of the Sun Tavern to the Union Flag, and very few of the houses opposite that space, towards the new road, have escaped. [...][10]

The butcher was not affected and was one of the most generous contributors to the relief fund, donating £5. 0. 0. A second fire of equal devastation occurred on 3 March 1820, and this time he subscribed £1. 0. 0. to the relief effort.[11] In 1826 the address of the butcher's shop was 139 High Street, Chatham, and may have been his since the 1790s.[12] It is worth adding that in 1816 the butcher was declared a bankrupt and sold the three houses, his father-in-law John

---

9 George W. Wheatley, 'Some Account of the Late Lieut. Waghorn, R.N., the Originator of the Overland Route', *Bentley's Miscellany*, 27 (January 1850), 349-357.

10 *The Times*, 2 July 1800, 3.

11 William Jefferys, *An Account of the Fire [...] at Chatham ... June, 1800, [and] the money collected for the relief of ... sufferers*, Chatham, 1801; *ibid.*, *An Account of the Dreadful Fire at Chatham which happened on Friday the 3d of March, 1820*, Chatham, 1821.

12 Pigot & Co. Kent Directory, 1826-7, 603, where he is named as 'Thomas Wighorn'. Pigot's 1823 Directory seems to omit all butchers!

Goodhugh apparently providing support to enable him to continue in his trade.[13]

The Navy 1812-1817

Those who knew Waghorn frequently commented on his energy and enterprise. We can surmise then that for a young lad growing up in a butcher's shop in Chatham, the activity in and around the Royal Naval Dockyard and the presence of multitudes of sailors in the town promised an exciting future. He appears to have taken the earliest opportunity to join the service. His memorial in All Saints church, Snodland, states that 'He entered the Royal Navy at the age of 12 years, and served as midshipman in the "Bahama", under Captn. Wilson.' The muster lists for the *Bahama* at the time of his appointment have survived and show he joined the ship on 10 November 1812 as one of the dozen or so boys ranked as '3rd Class volunteer'. One is reminded that at this time not everyone joined the navy of his own free will, as the page that revealed this information about Waghorn had the heading 'Whence and Whether Prest or not'. This was a time when men might be kidnapped for service. Waghorn's age was mistakenly given as '13' in the initial entry, corrected to '12' in the next list two months later.[14] His place of birth too was consistently given as 'Rochester', not 'Chatham', in the book, but this again seems to have been an error which was remedied in later years.

13 He was declared bankrupt on 31 July 1816 and the houses and land were sold for £600 to another Chatham butcher, John Stiff, on 31 August (deed of sale in Snodland Historical Society Waghorn collection).

14 TNA: ADM 37/3918.

The Medway at Chatham, showing some of the hulks, of which the Bahama was one
(© Medway Archives and Local Study Centre)

The *Bahama* was one of the French ships captured by Nelson on 21 October 1805 during the Battle of Trafalgar. Now, captained by Henry Smith Wilson, she was moored at Chatham, serving as a prison for prisoners of war. The captain's log is particularly concerned with the supply of provisions and water, but also notes the escorting of prisoners to and from shore at various times.[15] *Bahama* was tied alongside an older hulk which was used as a store. By warrant of 4 May 1807 the ship's complement was 98 men (including the boys like Waghorn), but additionally had a large party of marines to help guard and escort the prisoners. On 8 April 1813, six months after joining, Waghorn was promoted from 3rd to 2nd Class Volunteer, but remained with the ship for a further six months only. To be moored constantly at Chatham was hardly the adventure he must have been seeking.

The *Tigris*, which had been in service for some years before, was commissioned at Chatham on 18 October 1813. It was shortly to set off on duty and on 3 November the captain's log notes 'Joined Mr Edmd Pretty, Mid., from *Irisistible* and Mr Waghorn from *Bahama*.' On joining Waghorn was made one of the four boys who were 'Volunteers of the 1st

15 TNA: ADM 51/2183.

Class' (additionally there were nine 2nd and twelve 3rd Class). The captain was Robert Henderson, who had a complement of 284 men and many marines under his command.[16] At Chatham the ship was moored alongside the hulk *Hasfruen* on the Medway until 24 December. The subsequent movements of the *Tigris* are summarised in Admiralty records[17]:

> 24 Dec.: arrived at the Nore; 1814: sailed for Spithead: 24 May: the Downs[18]: 25 May: Proceeded; 26 May: arrived at Spithead. 28 May: ordered to Cork; 31 May: sailed for Cork; 4 June: arrived at Cork; 8 June: sailed to cruise; 6 July: arrived at Cork; 7 July: sailed on a cruise; 26 July: arrived at Cork; 9 August: sailed on a cruise; 9 September: arrived at Cork; 29 September: sailed with convoy for Portugal and Spain.
>
> 1814, 14 October: arrived at Gibraltar with convoy from Cork; 22 October: sailed for Cork; 12 November: arrived at Cork; 7 December: sailed on a cruise; 26 December: arrived at Cork; 1815: 4 January: sailed on a cruise; 2 February: arrived at Cork; 1 March: sailed; 6 March: arrived at Cork; 12 April: sailed to cruise; 23 April: arrived at Cork; 3 May: sailed; 20 May: arrived at Cork; 31 May: sailed to cruise; 8 June: arrived at Cork; 16 June: ordered to Plymouth; 26 June: sailed; 30 June: arrived at Plymouth; 3 July: to follow Lord Keith's orders.
>
> (Channel) 2 July: sailed to cruise; 29 July: arrived at Plymouth; 23 August: paid off all standing.

Waghorn must have been taken ill towards the end of this duty, for when the *Tigris* arrived at Plymouth on 29 July he was discharged from the ship to Plymouth hospital. That same day the captain, having reached Plymouth Sound, noted seeing there the 'Bellerophon having Napoleon Buonaparte Prisoner on board'. With the crew discharged, the *Tigris* remained in Plymouth Sound for several months. Clearly Waghorn made a full recovery, for on 28 September 1815 the captain noted 'Volunteered Mr Thos Waghorn (volr 1st Class)'. He was still at Plymouth. But there is

16 TNA: ADM 37/5462, 5816-18 are the muster books for the *Tigris* to 1818.

17 TNA: ADM 7/560-561. The format of the original has been modified here.

18 A holding area for sailing ships sited between Deal and the Goodwin Sands, Kent, while they waited for favourable winds.

a further record that Waghorn was one of several men discharged on 1 March 1816 with two months advance wages (£3. 8s. 0d.). By order of the Admiralty the complement of the ship was being reduced, first to 260 men and then to 245 men from 21 April. However, Waghorn was one of those immediately re-commissioned the next day as a midshipman. On 19 April the *Tigris* was ordered to Barbados and set off on 1 May. Again there is an official summary of her movements:

> 10 July: Antigua; 29 July: Barbadoes; 6 November: Barbadoes; 9 Jan 1817: off Johnstone's Point, Antigua; 18 Jan: St Christopher; 20 Jan: sailed from St Christopher; 14 April: sailed for England from St Kitts; 24 May: arrived at Spithead; 4 June: to follow Sir Edward Thornburgh's orders; Portsmouth; 16 July: sailed; 26 July: St Helens; 30 July: sailed to cruise; 10 August: arrived at Spithead; 12 August: sailed off Brighton; 13th August: arrived in the Downs; 21 August: sailed; 24 August: arrived at Spithead; 30 August: sailed for Weymouth; 30 September: arrived at Plymouth; 10 November: sailed; 12 November: Weymouth Roads; 13 November: arrived at Spithead; 26 November: sailed for her station; 10 December: arrived at Spithead; 30 December: to be paid off; 13 January 1818: paid off.[19]

On 1 November 1816 (by which time the *Tigris* was moored in Carlisle Bay, Barbados) the muster lists record a promotion for Waghorn, although he remained a midshipman. The record shows he passed his examination as lieutenant 'in Navigation' on 23 June 1817, still identified as 'Midshipman of Tigris'.[20] Waghorn himself wrote:

> I was the youngest Midshipman who did not study at the Naval College at Portsmouth who ever passed as Lieutenant for Navigation. I did so before I was 17 years of age & had to leave the Service in October following, not having sufficient influence, on being discharged, to get another ship.[21]

19 TNA: ADM 7/561. Sankey, *op. cit.*, 12-14, adds some details of the time in the West Indies, including the effects of hurricanes and of Yellow Fever on the crew.

20 TNA: ADM 107/49.

21 TNA: ADM 9/58, written on 29 May 1846. He gives the date of his passing for Lieutenant 'for navigation only' as 1 June 1817.

The obituaries published at Waghorn's death note that '16 days before he had attained 17 he passed in navigation for lieutenant:—the youngest midshipman that had ever done so'.[22] Quite why he was allowed to take the examination before he had completed the required six years as a midshipman is unclear; this technical infringement returned to haunt him later on, because the authorities used it to deny him the promotion to lieutenant he sought. Unfortunately for him, with Napoleon in captivity, the war against the French was at an end, and the Navy was shrinking. Instead of the hoped-for commission an Admiralty order discharging him from the service took effect on 25 October 1817. Presumably he left the *Tigris* while she was at Plymouth. Accounts of Waghorn's life state that he immediately found a merchant trading ship and took the position of Third Mate on board. Records suggest it was not so immediate. The account given below shows that the ship was the *Thalia*, of 357 tons, commanded by Captain James Ballingall. This was licensed by the East India Company on 15 April 1818 for a voyage to Fort St George and Fort William (Calcutta), with Liverpool as the port of clearance; the journey perhaps gave Waghorn the idea of employment in the East India Company and in 1819 this was realised.

After Waghorn's death, Captain Ballingall recalled the circumstances of the return voyage:

> On the return voyage from Calcutta, the *Thalia* put into the Cape of Good Hope, and found there another ship, also on her homeward voyage, belonging to the same owners. Capt. Walker, the captain of this ship, having died on her arrival at the Cape, the first mate succeeded to the command. The second mate, not understanding navigation, was unqualified for the office of first mate, and the captain applied to Captain Ballingall for one of his officers to fill the vacancy. Capt. Ballingall being highly satisfied with the acquirements and good conduct of Mr. Waghorn, recommended him for the appointment; and he was appointed accordingly. Mr. Waghorn was at this time only nineteen years of age, and by the energy of his character and good conduct, had thus recommended himself on his first voyage in a merchantman to the office of

22 *Kent Messenger and South Eastern Intelligencer*, 22 January 1850.

> first mate of a ship larger than the *Thalia*. He did his duty to the satisfaction of the captain, and on being discharged from the ship on her arrival at her destination in London, he returned to the East Indies, and embarked in the pilot service.[23]

Captain Edmund B. Walker commanded the *Lady Banks*, 414 tons, which was licensed to leave London for Calcutta on 6 February 1818, so presumably had preceded the *Thalia* to India.[24] The *Calcutta Journal* shows that the *Lady Banks* left Calcutta for London on 19 November 1818, to be followed by the *Thalia* sailing to Liverpool on 9 December, so Waghorn is likely to have reached London quite early in 1819.[25] But it is not until 20 October that year that the Court Minutes of the East India Company

> Resolved that Mr. Thomas Waghorn be appointed as Volunteer for the Bengal Pilot Service, and that the Committee of Shipping be requested to take necessary measures accordingly.[26]

23 *Illustrated Australian Magazine*, Vol. 2 (1851), 46-7.

24 The dates of arrival of both vessels have not been determined.

25 British Library, Asia Pacific & Africa Collections [APA]: SM155 (microfilm): *Calcutta Journal*, November and December 1818.

26 APA, B/160.

2

BENGAL AND BURMA

'Thos Waghorn Volunteer for the Pilot Service' was among the passengers who set sail from the Downs in the *Astell* on 14 January 1820, bound for a new life in the employ of the East India Company.[27]

The *Astell* was commanded by Captain Francis Cresswell, and his log of the journey has been preserved.[28] It notes a generally trouble-free passage of nearly six months duration. Main events were a death and burial at sea 'with the usual ceremony', the cancellation of Divine Service on one Sunday because the weather was too 'unsettled', and several trials and public punishments meted out to prisoners. The numerous prisoners on board spent much time tediously picking oakum, while from time to time tradesmen were 'employed as necessary'. Picking oakum was a normal and unpleasant punishment for prisoners (and the poor of a parish), involving separating the strands of rope which were then used for caulking ships – making them watertight by driving the strands between the timber planks of a vessel.

In his lecture at Bath 28 years later, Waghorn recalled 'being, in 1818, becalmed on the equator for fourteen days on a sailing voyage to India, and was, altogether, 122 days out of sight of land,' citing this as a factor leading him towards his determination to take up steam navigation.

On 1 June 1820 'At ½ past 8 A.M. Saw a Pilot Schooner at Anchor in Ballason Roads and at ½ past 10 Mr Hudson Branch Pilot came on board and took charge of the Ship.' The passengers, including Waghorn, 'left the ship at the New Anchorage [Calcutta] June 2nd 1820'. Waghorn's appointment as 'Volunteer, First Class' in the Bengal

---

27 *East India Register and Directory, 1821*; *Calcutta Annual Directory, 1821.* William Astell (1774-1847), after whom the ship was named, was a director of the Company. Waghorn fell out with his son John Harvey Astell later on.

28 APA: L/MAR/B/12 G.

Pilot Service is recorded as beginning that same day.[29] Unfortunately the papers relating to his appointment do not appear to have survived, but in London he would have had to provide a certified copy of his baptism and to have signed an agreement similar to the one below:

> I [*Thomas Fletcher Waghorn*] being appointed a [*Volunteer for the Pilot Service*] on the [*Bengal*] Establishment, in the Service of the United Company of Merchants of England trading to the Eastern Indies do swear, that I will be true and faithful to the said Company, and will faithfully and truly execute and discharge the Trust reposed in me, to the utmost of my skill and power
>
> So help me God
> [Sworn: (date)][30]

In 1820 the Bengal Marine Establishment had seventeen sailing ships whose prime responsibility was to guide vessels into and out of the Hoogly river and Calcutta and other ports in the vicinity. Some too were engaged in surveying duties. Each brig had a Commander (a branch pilot), two First Mates, two Second Mates, six Volunteers (acting as leadsmen) and 36 native seamen. The officers and senior crew were all Englishmen in the employ of the East India Company. Their annual salaries were graded: Master (£270); First Mate (£156); Second Mate (£60); First Class Volunteer (£60); Second Class Volunteer (£30).

Waghorn's position was thus a relatively humble one in the hierarchy and remained unchanged until 27 May 1828, when he was promoted to Second Mate. Although he is listed in the 1820 directory of the Marine Establishment, his name is not associated with a particular vessel there, perhaps because as a new-comer he had not then been assigned to one. However, the Company's records give him as 'on leave to England' on 28 February 1821.[31] The reason for this visit so soon after taking up his new post is not known, but Sankey notes without quoting a source that he 'applied for special leave "To proceed to England on account of his private affairs"', adding 'Waghorn's request

29 APA: L/MAR/8/11, 1820.

30 Specimen text from APA: L/MAR/8/1.

31 APA: L/MAR/8/11, 1821. The *East India Register and Directory, 1822*, p.198, gives this date as 28 Feb. 1820.

was granted "without prejudice to his promotion in the Pilot Service, but during his absence he is not entitled to any pay"'.[32] He requested to withdraw his application to visit England,[33] but evidently went ahead with the journey. 'Mr T. Waghorn, Pilot Service' arrived again in Calcutta in May 1822 on the *Belle Alliance*, commanded by Captain William Rolfe.[34] The return voyage to India had not begun well: the ship, having left harbour in December 1821, was then forced to ride out a storm off Portsmouth on the 28th.[35] On his arrival Waghorn was attached to the Marine Establishment brig *Henry Meriton*, then assigned to surveying duties, and the following year he was attached to the *Cecilia* and later to the *Eliza*.[36]

Very soon after his return, Waghorn married:

> Thomas Fletcher Waghorn of Calcutta, Bachelor, a Volunteer in the Pilot Service of the Hon[ble] Company, and Elizabeth Bartlett of the same place, spinster, were married at St John's Cathedral in Calcutta aforesaid by License this Eleventh Day of June in the year of our Lord One thousand eight hundred and twenty-two by me Dan[l] Corrie, Senior Chaplain at the Presidency of Fort William. In the presence of James Fielder, John Mills, John Higgins.[37]

His bride was aged just seventeen. She was the daughter of William and Ann Bartlett, born on 28 March 1805 and baptised in St John's cathedral on 8 July 1805. Edmund Bartlett, appointed as First Class Volunteer in the Pilot Service on 15 November 1820 (aged fourteen) appears to have been Elizabeth's brother, so quite possibly the match arose from an acquaintance between him and Waghorn. A John Bartlett, appointed as Volunteer on 4 May 1823, seems to have had a different ancestry, but Thomas Bartlett (born 1809 and appointed

32 Marjorie Sankey, *'Care of Mr. Waghorn'*, 19. She assumes that he cancelled the visit since he -would have had to pay, but the next evidence suggests he made it.

33 National Archives on India [NAI], 1821, O.C. 13 January, no. 39.

34 *Calcutta Annual Directory*, 1823.

35 *The Times*, 30 December 1821.

36 *Calcutta Annual Directory, 1823 and 1824 editions.* APA does not hold the 1825-30 editions.

37 APA: N/1/12, f.153.

Volunteer on 6 November 1824) was another son of William and Ann.[38]

The First Burmese War

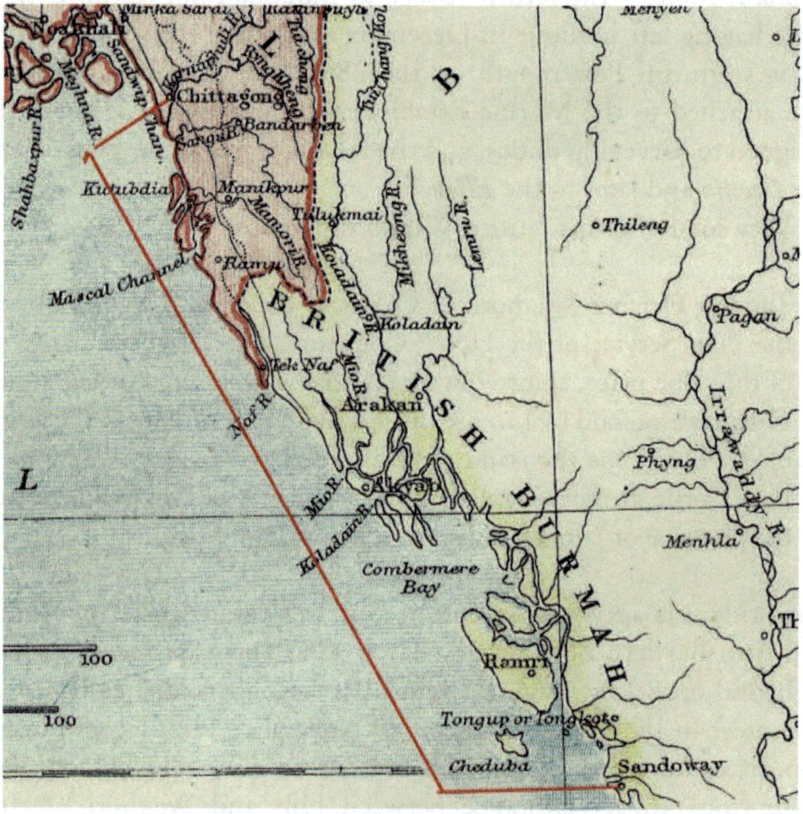

The Burmese coast where Waghorn spent the war. Arakan, Akyab, Ramri and Cheduba are all places where he was active
(Courtesy of Snodland Historical Society)

38 Burials at the North Park Street and South Park Street Burial Grounds in Calcutta include numerous Bartletts. Of particular note here are Edmund, late Branch Pilot, who served 35 years and died on 17 June 1813 aged 48 years 7 months; and William junior, son of William, Branch Pilot, born 7 Sept. 1798 and died 21 Sept. 1816. A Frances Ann, wife of William [senior], born 4 January 1778 and died on 19 March 1815, had thirteen children and may have been the mother of Elizabeth.

Relations between the British in India and the Burmese deteriorated during the later eighteenth century as the latter seized parts of Siam, the kingdom of Araccan, and other neighbouring areas. This posed a threat to the eastern frontier of the dominion controlled by the East India Company, but attempts by various British envoys to mediate proved unsuccessful. On 24 September 1823 a force of 1000 Burmese seized control of a small island called Shahpoori on the arm of the sea called the Tek Naaf between Chittagong and the Araccan. The English guard on the island was overrun, and some were killed. This was the start of a larger confrontation between the Burmese and English forces in the area. The Burmese also advanced into Bengal and although at first rebuffed by the English both here and at Shahpoori, the conflict continued and expanded. In the meantime the new governor-general of India, Lord Amherst, made preparations for war, resolving to send an expedition up the Irrawaddy to capture Rangoon. Major-General Sir Archibald Campbell commanded the expedition, with Commodore Grant (and later Captain Marryat[39]) in charge of the naval forces. War was declared on 5 March 1824.

Sir Archibald Campbell (1769-1843) arrived at Rangoon in May 1824 at the head of 11,500 men, capturing it on the 11th. His first attack on Dagon Pagoda at Kimendine was repulsed, but he succeeded on 10 June. In July he despatched a force under Col. H. F. Smith to Pegu, which stormed the pagoda at Syriam on 4 August, but heavy rains caused severe disease and interrupted operations. In November he was besieged in Rangoon; reinforcements arrived and he stormed the stockade of Kokein on 16 December. Campbell left Rangoon on 11 February 1825 and marched along the banks of the Irrawaddy accompanied by about 40 gun-boats. They were repulsed at Donabew on 7 March, but stormed this successfully on 1 April. Campbell entered Prome on 5 May and established his headquarters there. More disease and death affected his men during the rainy season. Eventually he advanced to Ava between November 1825 and February 1826, where the Burmese concluded a peace treaty on the 24th.

Accounts of Waghorn's life state that he volunteered for active service in the conflict and took command of the Honourable East

---

39 Apart from his naval career, Frederick Marryat became a writer; his most famous book is *Children of the New Forest*, published in 1847.

India Company's cutter, *Matchless*, for two years and six months, that he took part in five battles in Araccan and the Irrawaddy and was wounded in the thigh. There are several large published accounts of the conflict[40], but, with one exception, neither the *Matchless* nor Waghorn is mentioned and generally we can only guess at his movements. The main reason is that the *Matchless* was a small gun-boat in a large flotilla. The following ships were listed as being under Commodore Hayes's command in Arracan:

> The *Vestal*, Bombay Cruizer, The Honourable Company's Surveying Ships Research and Investigator, the Armed Brigs *Helen*, *Henry Meriton*, *Planet*, *Sophia*, and *Assearghur*. The *Trusty* Ketch, and Steam Gun-vessel *Pluto*. Ten Gun Pinnaces and eight divisions each of ten Gun-boats, each carrying a 12-pounder carronade, besides Transports and Mug and country boats. Besides the crews of the vessels and boats, they carried a Flotilla Marine, about 600 strong.[41]

Yet according to Clunn's biography

> Waghorn was attached to the flotilla of the Arracan division of 1,800 men, which left Chittagong in 1824, and after serving in that expedition in various departments, was appointed to command the Matchless cutter on a survey, and in that service received the commendation of the Naval Commander Sir John Hayes, and the Military Governor-General Morrison. During the war he was appointed by them to act at all points where peculiar dangers and difficulties demanded the presence of rare courage and enterprise. The history of that war, 1824 to 1827, contains abundant testimony to the valuable public service he rendered; but it should be recorded as an illustration of the indomitable pluck of the man, that he

40 Henry Horace Wilson, *Documents Illustrative of the Burmese War*, Calcutta, 1827; London, 1852; Sir Henry Havelock, *Memoir of the Three Campaigns of Major-general Sir A. Campbell's army in Ava*, Serampore, 1828; John Marshall, *Narrative of the Naval Operations in Ava during the Burmese War*, London, 1830; F. B. Doveton, *Reminiscences of the Burmese War 1824-5-6*, London, 1852. George William Vittalli de Rhé-Philipe, *A Narrative of the First Burmese War 1824-26*, Calcutta Military Dept., 1905.

41 H. H. Wilson, *op. cit.*

> planted the first gun on a hitherto inaccessible rock at the mouth of the Arracan river, by hoisting a 12-pounder from the deck of his ship to a perpendicular height of 220 feet; and it still serves as a landmark for ships entering the river. It is to this day well known as "Waghorn Rock". The subject of our sketch remained at the scene of action when nearly all the other officers had been compelled to return invalided, so that he became eventually senior naval officer, and was left in command of the coast from Chittagong to Sandoway, some 300 miles, with a force of 3,000 men under him.[42]

Evidently Waghorn was actively involved in the action early in 1825. A report dated 5 February, written by Captain Hardy at Ramree harbour to Commodore Hayes, notes the failure of a military venture at Ramree:

> The sergeant and six privates of His Majesty's 54th Regiment, on board the Hon'ble Company's armed cutter Matchless for their health, volunteered to serve on this occasion with our marines under Lieutenant Bell ... I regret to say one of them fell, and one was slightly wounded ... Previous to this attack with the military, we had, with a party of seamen and Marines, under Lieutenant Wyndham, several skirmishes with the enemy, and had succeeded in defeating them in two separate attacks, and in taking and burning two of their villages, strongly defended by five hundred men sent from Ramree for the purpose. I reconnoitred the creek under a smart fire, and gave the Lieutenant-Colonel the result of all my observations, and also every professional information connected with the service. Enclosed is a return of our killed and wounded; our boats suffered from the enemy's shot. I further beg to acquaint you, that the ships and vessels under my orders at Cheduba, have been actively employed on the enemy's coasts and possessions since I took command.
>
> The cutter Matchless is now going into Cheduba Creek, to undergo repairs and caulking, after which I intend examining Chandwah, and

42 Clunn, *op. cit.*, 2-3. Clunn's source for the episode concerning the gun was perhaps a letter to *The Times* from a W. P. Andrew, who mentioned it in the edition of 15 March 1884, 5 and he also drew upon the certificates and letters quoted in Waghorn's 1829 pamphlet, summarised later in the chapter.

> some of the creeks on the eastern side of Ramree Channel, that are said to lead into the Irrawaddy, unless called up to Arracan ...[43]

A further account of this skirmish appears in *The Times*, quoting despatches of 28 February, and including the following:

> The troops destined for the attack were embarked on the *Francis Warden*, and the gun boats. The *Planet* took the European artillerymen. The whole got to the creek, which is about 28 or 30 miles from the entrance of the river, or harbour, on the 2d of February; when a reconnaissance took place in the boats of the frigate. About three miles up the creek it was found to be staked across in two places—the first very slightly; but the second in the strangest manner, and on these latter the boats could not make the smallest impression: beyond the stakes were a breast-work, and stockades, with a fortified hill in the area. On the 3d, at daylight, the whole of the troops proceeded up the creek in the Matchless cutter—the *Fletcher* ketch—and ten gun-boats, together with the boats belonging to the *Hastings*, *Warden*, *Henry Meriton*, and *Planet*, the latter vessel bringing up the rear, so soon as there was water enough for her to cross the bar. The force consisted of about 500 sepoys [private infantrymen], 46 artillery, and 50 of the crew of the *Hastings*: they carried with them four pieces, two of which only, however, were landed, and two howitzers, which, owing to the bad landing, could not be got on shore. The landing was covered by the vessels and boats; ...[44]

Matchless is not mentioned in the list of ships involved in the attack on Chamballa Stockade on 22 February, so may still have been under repair. All this suggests that Waghorn's main duties were on the coast and somewhat further north and separate from Campbell's attack via Rangoon to Prome and Ava.

The story of Waghorn's involvement in the conflict is fleshed out by a number of documents which he printed in a pamphlet: *Steam Navigation to India, by the Cape of Good Hope. Mr. Waghorn's (of*

---

43 Rhé-Philipe, *op. cit.*, 244.

44 *The Times*, 15 September 1825, 2.

the Bengal Pilot Service) Documents and Papers relative to the Steam Communication to India, by the Cape of Good Hope, etc. [1829]. He gave May 1824 to January 1827 as the length of his time in Burma and included copies of 'Certificates and Letters of my Services in the late War, sent by Charles Lushington, Esq. Secretary to the Bengal Government, in January, 1827.' Clearly these were intended to show him in the best possible light when appealing for support from the East India Company for his proposals to establish steam communication between England and India; although unsolicited, they vividly show his zeal and enterprise throughout the conflict. In summary:

(a) Lt. Col. Thomas Murray, 40th Regt. Bengal N. I. certified Waghorn's service with the flotilla and command of *Matchless* on the Ramree and Cheduba stations in 1825.

(b) In a letter dated 25 November 1825, Brigadier General I. M. Morrison, commanding at Arracan, recommended Waghorn for the post of superintendent of flat-bottomed boats if it remained vacant, noting that in a journey from Arracan to Calcutta, 'although suffering at the same time under periodical returns of fever and ague, [he] never for an hour allowed himself to rest, when exertion was called for'. He noted that at the time Waghorn 'discharged the duties of first officer of the Honourable Company's ship *Research*.'

(c) He piloted the East India Company's vessel *Nerbudda*, safely over the bar from Akyab to sea 'when the Captain of the ship refused to do so' in August 1826. Inclement weather had made it necessary that the *Nerbudda* be freed from the harbour to replenish the sea provisions laid in for the troops on board. Sankey quotes an official letter from the Senior Commissioner in Arracan to the Vice President in Council in Calcutta which suggests the feat had not gone un-noticed :

> As the approach to Akyab by Sea is very intricate and as there will be in all probability a great number of vessels coming … I beg to recommend that a Pilot with a small cutter be attached to the Port … and accordingly suggest that Mr. Waghorn, who is intimately acquainted with the navigation and has proved himself materially useful … be attached under the Civil Power to the Port as Pilot.

The plea was rejected. Calcutta replied that

> Government has already approved of the return of Mr. Waghorn to his own Duties in the Pilot Service, and we consider it very expedient that no exception be made to the general rule which should be sanctioned on this head in regard to Pilots.[45]

(d) A letter from the Commandant's Office at Sandoni [Sandoway?], dated 22 November 1826, commends Waghorn for 'your very great assistance to me on many occasions (particularly on the removal of the Mungdoo depot)'.

(e) Another from the same place, dated 28 November, is addressed to Waghorn as commanding the *Matchless* again, from Lt. Col. J. L. Stuart and begins: 'As I shortly expect to leave this coast, where your services have repeatedly come under my notice, during the last ten months, I feel it but justice to express my conviction that you have, on all occasions, evinced the most laudable exertions to promote the public service whenever you have been employed. …'

(f) R. Hunter, Commissioner, writing at Arracan on 8 January 1827, shows that Waghorn was already intending to visit Europe: 'Sir, On your approaching departure from Akyab, preparatory to your proceeding to Europe, I think it but justice to express to you the satisfaction I have derived from your unremitting exertions in every department in which I have had occasion to communicate with you. Your establishing the flag staff on the Passage Rock [NB there is no mention of the gun], and the activity displayed by you in finding new crews, at a very reduced rate of pay, for the flat boats transferred to the salt department, have met with my entire approbation …'

(g) H. J. Vardon, Commander, at Calcutta, on 24 January 1827, wrote to Waghorn, then commanding the cutter *Mellis*: 'Dear Sir, Having seen your arrival notified in the public papers I take the earliest opportunity of returning my sincere thanks for your unremitting attention during our endeavours to get out of the Arracan river last

45 Sankey, *op. cit.*, 28 and 30; NAI, 1826, 19 October, No. 18.

August; and more particularly, during the gale when we lay aground off Akyab.

(h) Finally, John Hayes, as Commodore at Fort William, Calcutta, summed it all up on 1 February 1827: 'These are to certify that Mr. Thomas Waghorn, Second Mate in the Pilot Establishment of this Presidency, has obtained leave of absence to proceed to England on his private affairs. Mr. Waghorn has obtained a favourable character in his station; he was employed throughout the Burmese war in charge of different gun vessels, during which he manifested great zeal and activity, and the several commanding officers, under whose orders he acted, have testified to his praiseworthy conduct, and useful service.'

At home Waghorn's father had died and was buried at St Mary's, Chatham, on 6 September 1826. It may be that Waghorn needed to return to England to help sort out the family's affairs, but it is also clear that his thoughts had already turned to the prospect of establishing a steam service for mails between England and India. The journey provided a welcome opportunity for him to outline his scheme to the appropriate authorities and it seems very likely that the letters of appreciation listed above were part of his plan to establish his credentials with them.

3

MAILS TO INDIA BY STEAM

When Samuel Bevan wrote *Sand and Canvas*[46], an account of his time in Egypt, he dedicated it

To
Thomas Waghorn, Lieut. R.N.,
who by his own energy, and indefatigable
exertions, succeeded in establishing the Practicability of
the Overland Route to India, sacrificing his time and
fortune in divesting the Egyptian portion of that route of
its various discomforts; facilitating by the aid of
steam the passage of the Mohmoudieh
and the Nile; and rendering safe, and
even agreeable, the once
dreaded desert …

This is indeed a precise summary of why it is Waghorn rather than any other person who is remembered in connection with the Overland Route to India. He was not the first, nor initially the most enthusiastic promoter of the route, but earlier attempts to set it up were beset with problems which had to some extent been resolved when he came on the scene. In particular he was a leading figure in putting the final part of the jigsaw into place, especially the trek across the desert from Cairo to Suez. Some of his contemporaries were less than happy that it was Waghorn's name only which was attached to the Overland Route. One in particular was Commander John Wilson, the first to sail a steamship from Bombay to Suez, and he published what can only be described as a hundred-page whinge in which he did his best to discredit Waghorn, making him out

46 Samuel Bevan, *Sand and Canvas, a narrative of adventures in Egypt, with a sojourn among the artists in Rome*, London, 1849. See below, Chapter 9.

to be little more than a charlatan and opportunist who was prepared to jump on any bandwagon and take the credit for all developments of the Overland Route.[47] To be fair to Wilson, he *was* the first to sail a steamship from India to Suez and consistently advocated the route via Egypt when Waghorn was still enamoured of the traditional one round the Cape. At the time Waghorn had virtually no experience of steam navigation, whereas Wilson had, and consequently Waghorn's views on the performance of steam ships were largely guess-work, as Wilson shows. Yet it was Waghorn who had the tenacity and energy to bombard governments in England and India, the Navy, the East India Company and mercantile traders with pamphlets and letters, to speak at public meetings, to travel the globe and to put money into the venture. He was undoubtedly a good self-publicist and it is not surprising that it was his name which was known rather than that of Wilson, who was operating exclusively from India to the Red Sea.[48]

East India Company House, Leadenhall Street
(© Guildhall Library, London)

47 John H. Wilson, *Facts Connected with the Origin and Progress of Steam Communication between India and England*, London, 1850.

48 Wilson did send an account of his pioneering journeys in the *Hugh Lindsay*, which were published in the appendix to the Report of the Select Committee on Steam Navigation, 1834.

Routes to England from India avoiding the journey round the Cape

Normal communications between India and England were around Africa via the Cape of Good Hope. Nevertheless, during the latter part of the eighteenth century various alternatives were tried. Lord Wellesley, Governor of India, established a fortnightly service of East India Company ships between Bombay and Bussorah [Basra] in the Persian Gulf. From there the Company's Resident supervised Arab carriers, on camels, to Aleppo in northern Syria. Tartars then carried the despatches between Aleppo and Constantinople.

In 1794 George Baldwin negotiated a treaty allowing the free navigation of British ships in the Red Sea and the free landing of goods, passengers and mails in Egypt. For sailing ships there were difficulties in using this route. For several months each year the south-west monsoon prevented ships sailing between Bombay and the Red Sea. In the event, this proved a difficulty too for the first steamers, which were not built with sufficient strength to withstand the sustained tensions created by battling against the monsoon. At the time these problems were compounded by political instability in Egypt and outbreaks of plague, which resulted in quarantine regulations.

For some three centuries Turkish pashas had given weak and corrupt government to Egypt and warring factions of Mameluke chiefs eventually attempted to establish independence from the Ottoman Empire. In 1798, however, Napoleon captured Alexandria and soon put the country under French rule. This lasted a mere three years, for in 1801 the British gained control and restored the country to the Porte—the administration of the Ottoman Empire. In 1805 an Albanian soldier Mehemet Ali became pasha, quickly building economic prosperity and political stability. He reigned until 1849 and Waghorn's friendship with him was a key element in the successful setting up of the desert route. However, by 1819 the East India Company had established a regular service between Cosseir [Quseir] (on the Egyptian coast of the Red Sea) and Bombay. From Cosseir travellers proceeded west across the desert to Ghenna [Qena] by camel and then down the Nile to Alexandria.

While Mehemet Ali's stabilising control over Egypt was an important factor in this, so too was the emergence of steam navigation in the 1820s, which could overcome many difficulties previously caused by contrary winds. The first steamers were small and confined to river navigation, like the *Diana* which had impressed Waghorn with its performance during the Burmese War. But the Atlantic had been crossed in 1819 by the *Savannah* and steam service on the long route to India seemed well worth investigation. A first report on the idea was presented to the House of Commons in 1822 by a group of entrepreneurs and with some financial backing assured a Lieutenant J. H. Johnson was sent to India to sound out opinion there. Mr. Mount Stuart Elphinstone, Governor of Bombay, and Lord Amherst, Governor of India were among those who gave support and 20,000 rupees was promised to anyone who could establish by 1826 a service of two return journeys per year at no more than 70 days for each single voyage. Wilson also notes the enthusiasm of Mr. Greenland, then Secretary of the Marine Board of Calcutta, and later of the Calcutta Steam Committee.

Not unnaturally there were concerns about the safety of steam at sea and among the records of the East India Company are numerous printed pamphlets of the time explaining and demonstrating steam engines. Lieutenant Johnson was convinced that sea-going steamers (still with sails) were viable. Through his efforts a further £8000 was raised from subscribers and on his return the steamship *Enterprise* was built in England. The ship was of 500 tons, had two 60 horse-power engines, with copper boilers extending across the ship, and seven furnaces, each seven feet in length. Under Johnson's command the *Enterprise* left Falmouth on 16 August 1825 and arrived at Calcutta on 9 December, a journey of 115 days. This compared very unfavourably with the East India Company's sailing ships which could do the same trip in 90 days, and fell far short of the 70-day target, so the experiment was deemed a failure. The *Enterprise* was sold to the Government for £40,000 and she spent her time mainly on duties around India.

The 'Enterprise' enters Madras
(© National Maritime Museum, Greenwich, London)

Waghorn's first plan for a steam service between India and England

Nevertheless, Waghorn viewed the journey of the *Enterprise* with interest and later stated that he 'had his attention first turned to the question of steam navigation, on board the *Enterprise*, as a pilot, in 1826', at Arracan. There he met Johnson and the two men held fruitful discussions about the possibilities of steam navigation.

In spite of his lowly standing it was not long before Waghorn set out his first scheme to carry mails by steamer between England and India. Written in Calcutta on 1 February 1827, it was endorsed the same day by the resident Chief Secretary, C. Lushington, for the attention of the East India Company in London.[49] He noted that Waghorn's plan 'merited the Court's encouragement'. Waghorn left for England on the Friday (6th), carrying the letters with him:

---

49 NAI, 1827, 1 February, No. 71; *Ibid.* No. 69 is Waghorn's plan for the small steam vessel to be built in England.

Service by Steam.

C. Lushington, Esq. […]
Sir,

From your high situation I am induced to solicit your introduction to bring my plan before His Excellency the Vice-President in Council. I proceed on Friday to London for the purpose of building, on the model of a Leith Smack, a Vessel—burden from 200 to 220 Tons—for the sole purpose of a Dispatch Mail Packet to sail from Falmouth with the Government Mails and private letters to Madras and Calcutta.

I possess the connection immediately on my arrival, to build and fit any Vessel ready for sea, with the exception of the Engines, only requiring an introduction through the means of His Excellency, the Vice-President in Council to the kind consideration of the Hon'ble Court of Directors for them.

The Vessel to be cutter rigged, with the Mast to go on a swivel for striking when head to wind. Vessels rigged in this way lay from one point to one and a half nearer the wind than those square rigged.

Certain restrictions will be necessary in order to carry coals sufficient for the Engines, which I at present calculate to be two 25 Horse Power Engines, and the consumption of Coals will be 4 Tons per diem at the utmost, allowing we continually steam, which for a Vessel of 200 Tons will be 50 days' Coals.

The restrictions to ensure immediate despatch are:– We do not carry a single Passenger, have not a single Cabin, except a small one on Deck for Nautical purposes. The Commander myself to live on Deck with the Crew included, 16 Hands only. We carry no live Stock or Lumber of any kind, but a sufficient quantity of preserved meat will be got to ensure the health of the Crew; consequently we have the means of stowing everything for the Crews subsistence on the Decks of the Vessel at leaving Falmouth, and as the Coals are consumed so we shall find comfort below.

About 30 Tons of Coals will be stowed in as many Iron Tanks, that as the Coals are used, so the Vessel if requiring ballast, can fill with Salt water, and as the Engines will communicate with the

Tanks so we can pump it off at pleasure when the wind is light. A Vessel built outside Clinker and inside Carvel must sail faster, and there can be no doubt, as the model will be attended to for Steam and Sails, that when we have a wind we can always outsail other Vessels with our sails only. Two Brigs will be despatched to the Cape, with instructions to have sufficient hands to put the Coals on board in a few hours, which will be the only detainance on the Voyage, and should we be fortunate to the Cape, of course we do not stop at all. My object in bringing this to the notice of the Vice-President in Council is that I may gain an introduction through him of my plan, and that the Hon'ble Court will go to the expense of purchasing the Engines for the Vessel. I do not despair of completing the passage within the 70 Days allowed for the premiums of the Steam Committee of Navigation in India; in fact, all who now know my plan seem convinced it must succeed. I have therefore to solicit your earliest application on my behalf to His Excellency on the above subject, as I have only a few hours left before I join the Ship, which is now on her way down the River.

[…] Thomas Waghorn
1st February 1827 Bengal Pilot Service

N.B. The Mails and letters to be carried in large Copper Tank tinned inside, with sliding cover to it from Deck.

N.B. I beg leave to add various letters addressed to me while serving the Flotilla and Pilot Service.[50]

Having arrived in England in June 1827, Waghorn soon wrote to Francis Freeling, Chief Secretary to the General Post Office of Great Britain, forwarding the details of his scheme and the accompanying testimonials which had by then been delivered to the East India Company:

50 TNA: POST. The letters mentioned in the final note are those recorded above and published in *Steam Navigation to India …*

Sir,

I have the honor to address you for the information of Lord Montague, the Postmaster General of Great Britain on the subject of expediting the Public Dispatches and Private Letters by a Steam Mail Packet, to sail on steam from Falmouth in England to Madras and Calcutta in the East Indies.

I arrived in England about a month since (June 1827) and had a "letter on Service" of Introduction from the Chief Secretary, C. Lushington of the Bengal Government by order of the Vice-President and Council these to the Hon'ble the Court of Directors of the United East India Company. From which introduction I confidently expect the Honourable the Court of Directors will do me the service to present me with the Engines for this important undertaking; if so I intend (should I be patronized by the General Post Office) immediately to build and fit a Vessel solely for this purpose under the following restrictions, viz., To carry no Passengers, no Cargo, no live Stock, etc., etc., but simply to have the Vessel to carry Coals only and the Public Dispatches and private letters. I am sanguine I can so arrange the Voyage to perform it out and home in Six months and fifteen days, stoppages included, from the day of leaving Falmouth to the day of our arrival again from India. My object in bringing this important subject to the attention of the General Post Office of Great Britain is that as such an undertaking must benefit the best Interest of both India and Great Britain, that after I have obtained the Engines from the Hon'ble the Court of Directors of the East India Company, the General Post Office, receiving all Emoluments, etc., arising from such Dispatches and Letters being thus conveyed Forty days quicker to India and again the same time in coming from India, will in some part arrange how I am to be remunerated for the Vessel's expences in the accomplishing so National an undertaking.

I have the honor to forward the correspondence I made to the Government in Bengal with Certificates, etc., transmitted by them and a recommendation to the Hon'ble the Court of Directors by which I expect the grant of the Engines which is half the outfit, hoping I have not intruded on your valuable time.

I have the honor to be, Sir
with respect

Your very humble and obedient servant
London   Thomas Waghorn
July 30th, 1827   Bengal Pilot Service
My Direction is
Thomas Waghorn
Hoboro, near
Rochester, Kent

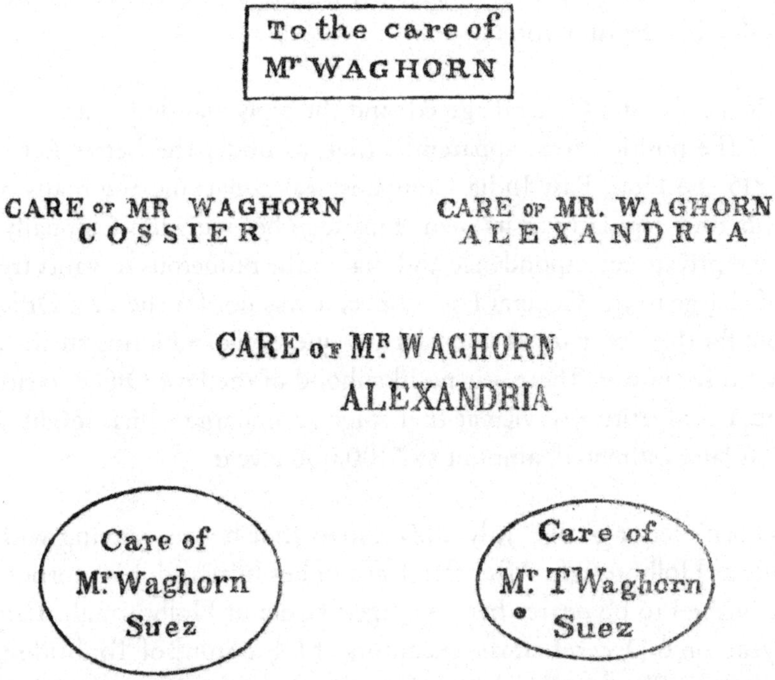

Some of the cachets found on early mail using Waghorn's service (drawn by John K. Sidebottom)

In the first of several dismissive letters concerning Waghorn's scheme and the use of steam vessels, Freeling advised the Postmaster General:

We can have nothing to do with the Establishment of Steam Vessels to India, and consequently cannot 'patronize' the undertaking of this gentleman. It appears to be a wild scheme to fit a Vessel for so long a Voyage with Engines of the Power of 50 Horses only, which is not more than we employ upon the Voyage between Dover and Calais.[51]

I presume the only reply can be that this Department cannot pledge itself to any particular course of proceeding contingent upon the success of an Experiment, and that the question appears to be one exclusively for the consideration of the East India Company. 3 August 1827.[52]

John Sidebottom, who pursues the dealings with the Post Office in considerable detail, wrote:

> The Postmaster General agreed, and the reply was duly sent.
>
> The position was, apparently, that, as under the Letter Act of 1815 the Hon. East India Company was conveying the mails by this time regularly in its own ships together with the Company's own private correspondence and that of the numerous servants free of charge to the General Post Office, it was not for the Post Office but for the Company to consider any question of adopting steam as a motive power. There was no likelihood of the Post Office setting up a competitive service at that stage at a charge which might, it was later estimated, amount to £100,000 a year.

Waghorn's letter of 30th July 1827 shows that he was staying with his family at Holborough. After the death of her husband, his mother may have wished to be nearer her own aged father at Holborough. Later in the year, on 6 December, the executors of John Stone of Tonbridge sold to 'Thomas Fletcher Waghorn of the Bengal Pilot Service in the East Indies, gentleman', the forge and house with one acre at Holborough,[53] while around the same time, no doubt also during Waghorn's visit to

51 TNA, POST, quoted in J. K. Sidebottom, *The Overland Mail. A Postal Historical Study of the Mail Route to India*, Published for the Postal History Society, Allen and Unwin, 1948.

52 *Ibid.*, 18-19; other Freeling-Waghorn letters are on pp. 29-33.

53 KLHC: U2102/T.34.

England, John Goodhugh passed ownership of Island Cottage to his grandson. A widow, Ann Fielder, was living there at the time, but some time after the death of her son Richard in October 1827[54] she seems to have moved out of the village and Ann Waghorn became the occupant of Island Cottage.[55]

As we shall see, Waghorn's optimism that the East India Company would back his scheme was largely misplaced, although the Company was eventually forced into some action by the Government. It did agree to provide two fifty H.P. engines for any boat acquired by Waghorn, and several directors appear to have offered some private financial help. Waghorn then appealed for the support of the general mercantile public in London, Liverpool, Manchester, Glasgow and Birmingham, before making his departure for India via the Cape.

Waghorn seeks backing for his plan in India

Waghorn's arrival in Calcutta was reported on 5 June 1828 and he immediately set about forming a Steam Navigation Fund to oversee trials for the route.

He placed his proposals before the subscribers to the Fund on 30 July and began by reminding his audience that in the previous year he had travelled to England with a recommendation from the authorities in India to the Directors of the East India Company that his plan should be encouraged. He had concluded that steam power was not yet sufficiently developed to allow vessels to carry cargo or passengers. Space and weight requirements of the coal needed meant that 'all hope of profit must be sacrificed'. He re-iterated the points he had made in his plan to the East India Company, although the size of vessel had now increased to 280 tons, and reported that he had consulted eminent engineers while in England. One of these

> Mr. Gurney, the inventor of the steam carriage, [promised] that ere I reach England he will have succeeded in perfecting an engine

54 Buried at All Saints, Snodland, 'from Holborough' on 8 October.

55 Land Tax records (drawn up twice-yearly) show Waghorn as owner from 1828—succeeding John Goodhugh—and Ann Waghorn as occupant from 1830, succeeding Ann Fielder.

> that will enable me to carry forty-days coal, consequently if that be the case I should only have to wait once on the passage; by that time he will have demonstrated the perfect safety of the high pressure engine on his improved principle. …
>
> The vessel will start from Falmouth with the mails for Madeira, Cape, Isle of France [Mauritius] and India, no passengers, no cargo, but simply letters and parcels – letters 4s. each and parcels the same charge, by the ounce, for which charge the sanction of the Authorities, both here and at home, I would apply for.

Having mapped out his places for coal supplies, Waghorn estimated the initial capital required at £12,000, exclusive of the cost of the engines. Taking the number of letters brought out by the *Undaunted* frigate as a criterion, he calculated that the receipt, for letters only, out and home, would amount to £4,137.

At the meeting Mr. Prinsep, Secretary of Government, had suggested that Waghorn could not succeed in bringing the vessel out to India via the Cape in less than eighty-five days, whereas letters could be conveyed from Calcutta to Cosseir in twenty-nine days and thence to Cairo in two days and finally to London in twenty-three days, a total of just fifty-four days. Captain Johnson spoke on the reasons for the partial failure of the *Enterprise* in making her voyage to India within the time allocated. He said he knew Waghorn as 'an individual of persevering industry and unshaken self-possession in the hour of danger'; and he considered that 'if any person could carry the project into effect, it would be Mr. Waghorn.' He felt convinced that a vessel of the right type would make the voyage in seventy days; but, at the same time, he was certain she would never pay the necessary expenses. He felt that Waghorn's proposed specification was wrong in terms of weight, because the vessel would be too heavy at leaving port, and he thought it would be necessary to have a further coal depot to counter this. Waghorn listed people from whom he had received encouragement, but he acknowledged that the Postmaster General 'would not pledge himself to any measure regarding my plan' and the East India merchants too were cautious, although several 'tendered me their support to the extent of £500 each, if I would myself make the experiment.' He also admitted that 'The assistance of the Hon'ble Court and the sums tendered me by the East India Agents in London, will not form a sufficient sum for the purpose I have in view', so he appealed to his audience to award to him the balance of the Fund they had already created so that he could put his scheme into practice. He further promised £1000 of his own money to show he believed that the risk of failure was small.[56]

Waghorn continues his search for supporters of his scheme

To further the project Waghorn applied for permission to return to England on furlough for two years keeping his rank, but with no pay.[57] He again sailed for England in October 1828, with introductions organised by the Committee of the Steam Navigation Fund to officials in Madras, Ceylon, Mauritius, the Cape, and St Helena. He addressed meetings at each place.[58] The first was held at Madras on the 4th of October, 1828 'at the request of 12 Gentlemen of the Presidency', the proceedings of which were summarized in the local press.[59] Waghorn's plan had been circulated beforehand and its approval by the Calcutta merchants at their meeting had been acknowledged. The Madras merchants were then requested to add to the fund before a deadline of 14 January 1829 so that, assuming 'no speculation promising greater or equal success' had been received, the plan could be put into action.

The meeting was under the chairmanship of Sir John Hayes, who had served with distinction in the Burmese war and had noted Waghorn's valour in it. Therefore, he was very supportive. Postal rates were an obstacle which Waghorn had to try to solve to his own satisfaction, since they would be a source of income in his steam venture. So among the documents was a letter from the Secretary to Government in India showing acceptance of postal rates which Waghorn had proposed and which were set out as an appendix to the proceedings.

The chief secretary to the Bengal government, Charles Lushington

---

56 Printed. Quoted in full from a copy in his own collection by J. K. Sidebottom, *op. cit.*, 20-24.

57 NAI, 1828, 7 August, Nos. 47-48.

58 Madras: 4 October; Mauritius: 15 November; Cape of Good Hope: 20 December; St Helena: 8 January 1829.

59 *Ibid.*, 24-28.

(later MP for Westminster) arranged for letters from Lord Combermere, then Vice-President in Council—the Governor-General being away on tour—to the East India Company in London, advocating Waghorn as a fit and proper person to open steam navigation with India via the Cape of Good Hope.[60] Waghorn himself was the carrier. Once back in England, in April 1829, he pursued the project and attempted to raise funds by addressing public meetings in London, Liverpool, Manchester, Glasgow and Birmingham, but these produced only a lukewarm response. Wilson remarks that on arriving in England Waghorn 'at once addressed himself personally, or in writing, to many influential men, both of the Home Government, the Navy, Parliament, the Court of Directors, and the leading men and associations among the mercantile community in England interested in the trade with India, and … the conductors of the leading London papers.'[61]

Waghorn also found that the Post Office continued to be hostile to the idea of carrying the mails in steamships, and the East India Company Directors, except for John Loch, were against it, in spite of all his efforts. The Directors did go so far as to approve the necessary steam machinery for one vessel. So contrary to his hopes, Waghorn was forced to bide his time. When giving evidence to the Select Committee on Steam Navigation in 1834 Waghorn provided further details of the scheme:

> A steam committee having been formed in India some years previous, had a sum of money at their disposal, some four or five thousand pounds, which they gave me for the purpose of expending it in the build of a steam vessel, to put these two 50 horse power engines in, but that fund was not sufficient; I repaired to Liverpool again, and the merchants there then undertook to build me a vessel, and take all the responsibility, provided I would make over to them the four thousand odd hundred pounds and the steam engines: I

60 The texts of letters in support of Waghorn and details of his speeches are printed in *Steam Navigation to India, by the Cape of Good Hope, Mr Waghorn's accounts and papers relating to Steam communication with India* [London, 1829].

61 Among the 'influential men' was the Duke of Wellington, who refused to support Waghorn's scheme: University of Southampton, Wellesley papers, WP1/1018/3 (9 docs. Dated 1829) and WP1/1156/14 (2 docs., 1830)

consented to that, and came back to London for that purpose. I am sorry to say that a part of this money was lodged in the hands of Rickards, Macintosh & Company[62], and a dividend has been received and sent back to India.'

A first Indian exploration of the Red Sea route, 1828-9

In the meantime it would seem that apart from the messages carried by Waghorn on behalf of the Committee of the Steam Navigation Fund, Sir John Malcolm, the new Governor of Bombay, had also despatched his own courier, Major Barnwell, who travelled to Egypt rather than round the Cape and who arrived at Alexandria on 23 December 1828. John Barker, Consular-General in Egypt, was at the centre of developments. Barker had been acting as consul in Egypt since 28 June 1826, having previously been based at Aleppo in Syria.[63] Aleppo was on the well-established route overland from Bussorah (Basra), via Baghdad and the Euphrates so Barker had opportunity to assess the merits of this journey against one using the Red Sea. His son later wrote: 'we shall find that he gave the preference to the Syrian one'.[64] Nevertheless his correspondence with several interested parties shows something of the tug-of-war between the opposing factions of those in India hoping to set up the steam route via Egypt (not the Cape) and those in London who showed absolutely no enthusiasm for the scheme, as well as his own diplomatic impartiality in the matter.

> [23 December 1828] Major Barnwell is this instant arrived, and will sail as soon as the wind will permit for Marseilles with the dispatches for England.
>
> There is a plan set on foot by a late Governor of Bombay, and warmly seconded by the present one, for establishing two steam vessels on each side of the isthmus of Egypt, for the purpose of accelerating the transmission of dispatches to and from India; and from an official report which I have this moment perused, it is

62 Who went bankrupt.

63 He was not formally appointed as Consul-General until 30 June 1829.

64 Edward B. B. Barker, *Syria and Egypt under the last five Sultans of Turkey*, London, 1876 (reprinted New York, 1973), ii, 122.

> calculated that thirty four days would be the average time occupied in a voyage by this route from London to Bombay. Three hundred miles is the distance on each side which, at only eight miles an hour, may be traversed in thirty-one days. The remaining three days are allowed for the dromedary's journey from Alexandria to Suez. The dispatches by this route would of course be less time on the way in time of peace, when they would be conveyed across the Continent to Marseilles, or to one of the ports of Italy.
>
> It is thought that three or four steamers would be able to convey dispatches to and fro regularly every month, and that a great part of the expense would be defrayed by a heavy postage on private letters and the sums that passengers would be disposed to give for the advantage of a quick conveyance. The plan was suggested so long ago as the 31st May, 1823, but it seems now to have obtained the Hon. Company's approbation, and that it will soon be put into execution.[65]

Optimism that the scheme was imminent came from Captain Moresby, one of the East India Company captains, to whom Barker replied on 12 May 1829:

> I am glad to perceive that you are of opinion that the steamers that are destined to convey the Company's correspondence between Bombay, Cosseir, and Suez, are competent. I shall await the arrival of the first passengers by the steamer, in order to learn from them what difficulties they met with, and. their opinion of what could be done towards removing them for the benefit of future travellers.[66]

However, the East India Company itself was horrified by the estimated costs of providing coal for steamships for this route. Barker wrote to Barnwell again, following the latter's return to India:

> Soon after your arrival in India you will have had the displeasure to learn, what was officially communicated to me on the 18th June, a week after you quitted England, that it is not the intention of the Court of Directors to adopt any measure of this description.

---

65 *Ibid.*, ii, pp. 123-4, letter dated 1 September 1829.

66 *Ibid.*, ii, pp. 124-5.

> That dry paragraph alludes to the hopeful plan of Sir John Malcolm and his gallant brother. It appears the Company has been appalled by the estimate of the enormous expense that would have to be incurred in the sole article of coal, and in its transport to its depôts in the Red Sea. I suppose, however, the steamer will be sent, as proposed, for one trip to Suez in the month of November next.[67]

Barker's son noted: 'The *Thetis* had brought (on board a consort) 125 tons of coal to Cosseir. The Court of Directors, who had written to Mr. Barker when he proposed to them the steam navigation by the Red Sea, "that it was not a matter of his competence," etc.; were now urged on by the Government (who had the transmission of the mails at heart), and were prevailed upon to send Mr. Barker a list of eleven questions on the subject to answer.'

Waghorn's journey to India via Egypt, 1829-30

Soon Waghorn heard that the steamship *Enterprise* was to make an experimental voyage from India to the Red Sea and he immediately offered to go to meet it as a courier. He had some encouragement from John Loch, then Chairman of the East India Company, who told him to 'go and make a sailor-like report on it.' Furthermore, his offer was taken up in October 1829 by the President of the Board of Control,[68] Lord Ellenborough, who ordered him to proceed to India through Egypt, taking important dispatches for Sir John Malcolm, Governor of Bombay, whilst at the same time reporting upon the practicability of the Red Sea route. One advantage of this official journey was that Waghorn was provided with a courier's passport. Again he reported to the Select Committee on Steam Navigation:

> I went the journey and was delighted with it, the greatest difficulty I met with and the most exposure, was in crossing the Alps, and not any difficulty, as I had conceived, in Egypt. Upon the strength

67 *Ibid.*, ii, p. 125.

68 The Board of Control was the government department in charge of Indian affairs.

> of my passport, I was offered a guide of armed men through the country if I wished it. ... The British Consul, Mr. Barker, asked from the Pacha whatever I required to make the journey.

Waghorn left London on 28 October, crossed from Dover to Boulogne 'where he bought a carriage and posted all the way to Trieste, where he had to wait several days for a passage to Alexandria, which he at length obtained in a Spanish ship.'[69] Arriving at Trieste on 8 November, he had accomplished the 1,242 mile journey in eleven days, not the nine and a half days he told the Select Committee. Sailing from Trieste to Alexandria and his meeting with Barker on the 28th to deliver the eleven questions from the Court of Directors took nineteen days. Barker subsequently reported to various people:

> (a) to Rear-admiral Sir Pulteney Malcolm, 8 December 1829.
>
> Dear Sir,— Mr. Waghorn informed me that the Court of Directors had offered £1,000 to the proprietors of the steamer *Superb*, to come to Alexandria and convey the dispatches expected by the Enterprise to Marseilles, but that £1,500 was demanded for that service; whereupon the Court resolved on sending him by way of Trieste with their duplicates for India, and leave me to forward those coming from India as best I could.[70]

> (b) to Sir Robert Gordon (Envoy to the Ottoman Empire), 10 December 1829.
>
> Dear Sir,— "Mr. Waghorn presented me with a string of eight questions, as a paper that was put into his hands, on the moment of departure, by Mr. P. Auber, Secretary to the Court of Directors, for the purpose of their being submitted to me. I enclose herewith for your Excellency's information, a copy of said paper, together with my answers thereto, annexed.
>
> Eleven questions on the same subject have been put to me by the Board of Control, dated 22nd October last; to which I will reply as soon as I can collect the necessary information to enable me to answer them.

69 *Calcutta Magazine and Monthly Register*, 4-6, (April-June 1830), 321.
70 *Ibid.*, ii, 128.

> It is evident from these questions that the plan in contemplation by the Board of Control is not confined to the transmission of dispatches across the Isthmus, but to journeys of travellers; the passage money of whom, it is hoped, may go a great way towards defraying the expense of the enterprise.[71]

> (c) to Alexander Turnbull, (Consul at Marseilles), 15 December 1829.
>
> I am anxiously awaiting the receipt of dispatches from India which left Bombay on the 15th of last month, for Suez, and are therefore fully due.
>
> The Samarang is here under waiting orders to carry the dispatches to Corfu. I think it probable that the long contemplated project of a communication by steam vessels on both sides of the isthmus will be carried into effect in the course of next year.[72]

A rival scheme proposed by R. W. Taylor

It turned out that Waghorn was not the only one anxious to set up quicker communication between Britain and India, for the Board of Directors of the East India Company had been persuaded by a Mr R. W. Taylor that he could provide them with a fine steam ship service. Taylor too headed for Alexandria and a meeting with Barker, arriving before Waghorn.

On this Barker writes;— ALEXANDRIA, 12th Nov., 1829.

> We cannot get away from Alexandria: we still hope nothing will occur to prevent our setting out for Rosetta in a few days. We have been detained these few days past by the arrival here of a Mr. Taylor, brother to Major Taylor, the East India Company's Resident at Bussorah, a person who has distinguished himself in the steam navigation line. His object in coming here is to proceed to India for the purpose of making some arrangement with the

71 Barker, *op. cit.*, ii, p. 127.
72 *Ibid.*, ii, 128-9.

Governor-General of India, for carrying into effect an enterprise of a most gigantic nature. It is no less than to ply between London and Alexandria, touching at Gibraltar and Malta, four steamers, the least of which, of 550 tons, to carry from 40 to 50 passengers. To begin to sail in August next, and afterwards to follow every fortnight, the 1st and 15th of every month.

On the other side the Isthmus of Egypt there will be employed six steamers of the same dimensions, to ply between Calcutta and Suez, touching at Madras and Bombay, and to sail the first in August next, and so to follow that one will arrive at Suez every fortnight. Passengers to be booked through, all the way to and from India; and to be furnished with the necessary accommodations and subsistence in their journeys across the desert, between Alexandria and Suez.

There are already prepared the necessary steamers, which are twelve in all, two being to replace such as may become disabled by accidents. The British Government in India engages to come to the aid of the Company with certain facilities for the first two years, on condition that afterwards their dispatches shall be carried free. Lord Aberdeen, it is said, patronises the enterprise, and promises that in time of plague the Board of Trade shall recognise certificates of officers, to be expressly appointed, that the "caravan" of travellers has had no communication with infected places, in order to exempt ships and passengers from quarantine regulations.

The distance from London to Gibraltar is nearly 1,000 miles; from Gibraltar to Malta, 1,100 miles; from Malta to Alexandria, 800 miles; from Suez to Mocha, 1,200 miles; from Mocha to the island of Socotra, 650 miles; from Socotra to Bombay, 1,350 miles: in all, from London to Alexandria, 2,900; and from Suez to Bombay, 3,200 miles. The mean rate of going is reckoned at 230 miles in every twenty-four hours, so that the voyage from Malta to Alexandria will be performed in three days and a half.[73]

Barker's son recorded:

---

73 *Ibid.*, ii, pp. 129-131.

> The East India Company's brig-of-war *Palinurus* also arrived at Cossier for the purpose of taking soundings, in December 1829.

On the 24th December he wrote to his brother-in-law to this effect:-

> "I make no doubt the Government will compel the Directors of the East India Company to carry the steam navigation plan into effect. Government has expressed great anxiety on the subject of those questions, and took extraordinary precautions that no delay should take place in my receipt of them.
>
> "An East India Company's man-of-war arrived at Suez on the 18th inst., in 100 days from Bombay, and brought twelve tents for the use of the passengers expected by the Enterprise. It was sent to take soundings and make a chart of the Red Sea."

Barker had long known R. W. Taylor's father at Bussorah and perhaps this acquaintance led him to confide in the son regarding Waghorn's plans. On 28 November 1828 he wrote to him at Cairo from Alexandria:

> Dear Sir,— "Mr. Waghorn arrived this afternoon, and will set out to-morrow evening for Cairo, on his way to Suez, there to embark, by order of the East India Company, on board the *Enterprise.*
>
> He has brought me a letter from the Secretary, Mr. Auber, dated the 28th October, recommending him to my attention in furthering his object of proceeding to his destination. Mr. Waghorn is charged with public dispatches for the Presidencies in India. He has talked to me, not at all in confidence, of a plan of establishing a steam vessel to ply between England and India for the sole purpose of carrying letters, bullion, newspapers, periodical publications, etc.; and the Company has promised to give him, or rather lend him, two engines of 50-horse power, as an encouragement to engage him to persevere in the undertaking. The Indian Government has sanctioned his tariff or tax on letters and packages from India; and he has been promised, as he assures me, that an Act of Parliament will settle the same rates on letters to India.
>
> He has also been charged by the Company to give them information of the means of transporting their correspondence

> by steam navigation by this route. I said above that Mr. W.'s conversation with me was not confidential; yet I beg you will not let him understand that I have addressed you on the subject.
>
> Believe me to be, truly, etc., JOHN BARKER.[74]

Edward Barker continued:

> Mr. Waghorn met Mr. Taylor at Suez. Mr. Taylor had been sent by the Court of Directors, but he had also in view the speculation of a steam company on his own account; but when he found the Red Sea route taken by the Government of India, he transferred his plans to the river Tigris, where a steam company was started.
>
> Mr. Waghorn was also sent on the part of Directors, but with very little encouragement, for the Company had no wish for the success of the scheme. He got more from the Government. Mr. Waghorn made several voyages between England and Egypt before the so-called Overland Route' was finally adopted.
>
> More than once after dinner Mr. Barker used to say to him, "Waghorn, don't be too sure of success. I wrote about this long ago, but the Court of Directors won't have it."[75]

Thus on 29 November Waghorn set out from Alexandria, proceeding by donkey the 33 miles to Rosetta, then 150 miles by boat to Cairo and 72 miles by camel to Suez, where he arrived on 8 December, having experienced a three-day delay en route. Waghorn had been provided with letters of introduction to the governors of Suez, Cosseir and Jiddah to facilitate his journey. The ill-fated *Enterprise* had been ordered to meet him there two days earlier, but unknown to him had broken down between Bengal and Bombay, so did not appear.

The next day he sailed for Cosseir in a local boat, arriving on the 13th. Five days were spent there. His obituary notes: 'As he had important government despatches, Lieut. Waghorn had no resource

74 *Ibid.*, ii, pp. 133-4.
75 *Ibid.*, ii, pp. 134-5.

except to return to England, or go on in an open boat down the Red Sea. He preferred the latter as a matter of duty, and sailed down the centre of that sea, without chart or compass, the north star being his guide by night, and the sun by day. Suffice it to say that he arrived at Jiddah, 620 miles, in six and a half days, and there first learned that the *Enterprise* steamer had broken her machinery ... and was not coming.' Clunn adds that between Cosseir and Jiddah 'some of the Arab crew mutinied; Waghorn, however, was not to be baulked; he produced his pistol, and threatened to shoot the first man who persisted in his refusal to proceed.' Waghorn himself published an account of his journey: *Particulars of an Overland Journey from London to Bombay by way of the Continent, Egypt and the Red Sea*,[76] and summarised his journey in his statement to the Select Committee for Steam Navigation in 1834, but made no mention of his adventures navigating from Cosseir to Jiddah, other than to say it was the same boat he had used to get to Cosseir.

Having reached Jiddah on 23 December Waghorn was forced to wait another eighteen days before he was able to board a local vessel for Bombay. During the delay he had a recurrence of the fever caught during the Burmese War, but eventually he was able to transfer to the East India Company's ship *Thetis* at sea, which had made the journey as a substitute for the *Enterprise*, and which took him there, arriving on 21 March 1830. The journey had taken 145 days in all, but 55 was Waghorn's interpretation of the actual time excluding stoppages.

The log of the East India Company ship *Benares* mentions the journey in passing:

> 11th Oct. 1829, sailed for the Red Sea. Reached Jiddah in November; laid there awaiting authority from Turkish Government. Surveying the harbour and environs. January, 1830. Lieutenant Waghorn arrived from England with despatches (first overland mail) also Mr. Taylor, merchant, from Liverpool on same object.[77]

Taylor had set off seven days before Waghorn and in the various parts of the journey was the quicker of the two, although both men met at

76 Privately printed, 1831.

77 Low, *op. cit.*, ii, 72. This is Low's summary rather than a transcription from the original.

Cairo on 5 December and finished their voyage at the same time in the *Thetis*. Waghorn noted later that he had met Taylor once in London, but that the latter had become a bankrupt when Taylor had proposed and invested £12,000 in his own scheme for the Overland Route using a combination of steam-tugs and sailing vessels. Even Commander Wilson thought this un-viable. Taylor's journey, exclusive of stoppages, was timed at 46 days.

Waghorn too was dismissive of the plan:

> … on his arrival at Bombay, to my great astonishment, he insinuated that he was the agent of a grand steam-company, that would immediately introduce twelve steam- vessels in the Red Sea communication, if the Bombay community would pledge themselves to send their letters by them for two years: it was to me most unaccountable, how they could gulp down his nonsensical bombast about "coals to be used without smoke," "conveyances across the desert, to be drawn by camels, as easy as sedan chairs," this said novel conveyance to have *lateral* springs—a *spring* I must confess I never heard of—for the comfort of the ladies; for the gentlemen he described No. 1 on one side the Isthmus, the same in every respect as No. 1 on the other; all this, aye, and more luxuries and comforts than ever ran in any one's head but his own. Will it be believed that all this was explained at a public meeting at Bombay, to which the *ladies* were especially invited?
>
> All appeared satisfactory except the parties' names who were to embark in the said undertaking, which Mr. T. hoped would not be expected from him, and which, he said, he was bound in honour (clapping his hand on his breast) to keep secret. I was present at the meeting, which not joining with me in insisting on knowing who were to pay for this immense undertaking, broke up after many flowery speeches and thanks to Mr. I. W. Taylor.[78]

Waghorn placed an advertisement in the *Bombay Courier* dated 10 April 1830, assuring readers that he was not connected with any scheme of steam navigation except that which he had advocated in

78 *Particulars of an Overland Journey …* , 23-24.

1828. On 17 April, four weeks after his arrival in Bombay, he spoke at a public meeting, still advocating the Cape route, while Taylor of course continued to favour the Red Sea passage. They both proceeded to Calcutta for another meeting on 24 June[79], when Sir John Hayes again spoke in Waghorn's support. At this time the proprietors of the Calcutta Steam Fund gave Waghorn 10,450 sicca rupees to cover expenses he had incurred.

While Taylor favoured the Red Sea route, Waghorn was still assuming journeys would be via the Cape. On his return journey Taylor resolved to explore an alternative one from Bombay via Baghdad and the valley of the Euphrates. Leaving Baghdad around September 1830, his party reached Mosul in northern Iraq, but was attacked by tribesmen soon after and Taylor and two English companions were killed.[80]

The *Hugh Lindsay* makes a pioneering voyage to Suez

Meanwhile other events were occurring. Sir John Malcolm's suggestion that the Red Sea should be properly surveyed had been put into action in 1829. On 20 March 1830, the day before Waghorn and Taylor had reached Bombay, the East India Company's new steamship *Hugh Lindsay* left the port, in the hands of Commander John Wilson. Even while she was still under construction, he had volunteered to sail the vessel to Suez:

> I was the staunch assertor that the Red Sea route was the one which must become, through the means of steam, the high road to India, and I was stimulated by a desire to be the first steam navigator of the Red Sea.

The voyage was not without difficulties. In the words of Charles Low:

79 The *Calcutta Magazine and Monthly Register*, vols. 7-9 (July-September 1830), cv-cxvi reports the meeting and correspondence. 'Mr. Waghorn' sailed from London in the *Sir Thomas Munro* on 1 January 1830, reaching Madras on 26 May and Calcutta on 31 May.

80 On Taylor, see John S. Guest, *The Euphrates Expedition*, London, 1992, 15-22; also the account in *Calcutta Magazine and Monthly Register*, 4-6 (1830), 319-323.

The *Hugh Lindsay* was a steamer of only 411 tons, with two eighty horse-power engines, built to carry five and a half day's consumption of coal, and drawing eleven and a half feet of water, while she was required to perform a voyage of 3,000 miles, of which 1,641 were across the Indian Ocean to the first coaling station at Aden. To enable her to effect this long flight, she took on board sufficient coal for eleven days, for which purpose more than two-thirds of the space abaft, intended for accommodation, and also half of the forehold, were filled with coals; this, together with stores and provisions for the voyage to Suez and back, no less a distance than, 6,000 miles, increased her draught of water to thirteen and a half feet, and it is certain her safety would have been seriously imperilled had she encountered bad weather. Previous to undertaking the voyage, a collier brig, laden with 600 tons of coal, under convoy of the *Thetis*, had been despatched to the Red Sea, so that a supply was ready stored at Aden, Jiddah, and Suez. The experiment was a triumphant success; Aden was reached on the 31st of March, the whole distance having been covered under steam alone, and the *Hugh Lindsay* arrived with only six hours' consumption of coal in her bunkers. Commander Wilson called at Mocha to deliver despatches and at Jiddah for coal, and arrived at Suez on the 22nd of April, having been thirty-two days and sixteen hours, including stoppages. … On his return voyage Commander Wilson called at Cosseir, Jiddah, and Mocha, and reached Bombay on the 29th of May. It appears from the *Hugh Lindsay*'s log, that the voyage to Suez was accomplished in twenty-one days and eight hours, and the return to Bombay in nineteen days and fourteen hours. The total time occupied in the passage there and back was seventy days, but the preceding was the time she was actually under steam, during which she traversed 5,928 miles, being at the average rate of somewhat less than six miles an hour; a surprising result, when we consider that she was two feet deeper in the water than was intended by her builder, and consequently was much out of trim. For this achievement Commander Wilson received the thanks of the Bombay Government.[81]

---

81 Low, *op. cit.*, i, 527-8. See John H. Wilson, *Steam Communication between Bombay and Suez, with an account of the Hugh Lindsay's four voyages*, Bombay, 1833, for a full account of the journeys and the difficulties encountered.

On 31st May, after his return, Wilson sent a report on his journey to the East India Company.[82] He acknowledged the difficulty with having to load so much coal, but suggested this could be overcome if engines of *c.*25 hp were employed. He felt that one coaling stop at Aden should then be adequate, so as not to prolong the journey by further coaling at other ports. He recommended that the route via Cosseir be retained although this took 24 hours longer than one via Suez: in his view it was otherwise equal to Suez for convenience and would allow passengers to see something of the splendours of ancient Egypt on their journey.

Waghorn resigns from the East India Company

Waghorn determined to further his cause by returning again to England. In September 1830 he left Calcutta in the *James Pattison*, reaching England in January 1831. He was dismayed to find that the Court of Directors refused to provide the two promised steam engines and further that he could not overcome an Act of Parliament which restricted the postage on a letter to 2d. He wrote in his pamphlet:

> as this conduct of Mr. Astell [Chairman of the Court of Directors of the East India Company] totally disgusted me, I came to the resolution of resigning the Company's service; and, in so doing, I stated in my letter that I did it the better to further the object of steam navigation between England and India.

Although his resignation is dated 29 July 1831 in the East India Company records, it must have been submitted earlier; on 1 July the Company secretary wrote to him at 39 Cornhill:

> Sir,
>
> The Court of Directors of the East India Company have considered your letter stating your wish to retire from the Bengal Pilot service in order that you may be the better enabled to promote the object of Steam Navigation between this Country and India, and requesting that the Court will furnish you with a Document

82 APA, E/1/176, 257-61.

> expressive of their satisfaction with your conduct and services and also that they will grant you some pecuniary reward.
>
> In communicating to you the Court's acceptance of your resignation, I am commanded at the same time to inform you that whilst the Court acknowledges the zeal which you have evinced for the service, they are under the necessity of declining to grant to you upon your retirement any pecuniary allowance.
>
> I am further to apprise you that the Court cannot encourage any expectation that you will be employed by them in the promotion of Steam Navigation to India.[83]

Not surprisingly this response did not please Waghorn, who made a further application, but this too was rejected on 18 August:

> The Court of Directors of the East India Company have had before them your letter soliciting a reconsideration of your case in the hope that with reference to the Testimonials accompanying your application, and under the circumstances you have represented, the Court will grant you some pecuniary assistance; and I am commanded to inform you that the Court are under the necessity of adhering to the decision already communicated to you.[84]

It is extremely doubtful that we can trust Waghorn's own account, full of bravado, which Mark Boyd induced him to tell to dinner guests for their entertainment:

> He [Waghorn] often lunched with me, and it was a treat for any of my country friends to meet so great a lion, and if his time, theirs, and my own permitted, I generally led him into a little sketch of his own career for the information, and not, improbably the amusement also, of my visitors, for I knew the precise chord to touch. … [There follows a brief account of Waghorn's career.] … Waghorn worked his way home from Bombay up the Red Sea, making, himself master of many important details. At this point, of his narrative Waghorn's pulse always rose, his

83 APA: E/1/267, No. 1648.

84 *Ibid.*, No. 2020.

countenance became rubicund, and the table never failed to receive a tremendous blow from his fist. 'Gentlemen,' looking round at each of my guests, 'you shall hear—Mr. Boyd knows it well—how I was treated for bringing Bombay within twenty-six days and eight hours of the capital of England. I went to the India House, and asked if the Chairman was in his room. He was. I sent my name and was received. I handed my letter of introduction from the Governor-General to the Chairman. He read it, placed it on the table, and was about to resume his writing, but thought better of it. I waited patiently, when the Chairman addressed me as follows:—"Mr. Waghorn." " Yes, sir." "You are, I find, in our service in India." "I am, sir. I am one of the Honourable Company's pilots." Are you in bad health, Mr. Waghorn?" "I am in perfect health, sir." "Well, then," said this Chairman of the East India Company, "Mr. Waghorn, take my advice, and return to your duties in India, for I have to inform you that I, as Chairman of the Honourable Court of Directors, am quite satisfied, as heretofore, with sending our letters and despatches to India by the Cape of Good Hope, and receiving, our replies by the same route." He then resumed his pen, telling me his time was much occupied, and that he had given his decision. I then said, "I assure you, sir, the Governor-General looks upon the plan I had the honour of submitting to him most favourably, and the last words, on my taking leave, which his Excellency was pleased to address to me after my full explanations, were, that he was convinced the Overland Route could be carried out." What answer did I get from this enlightened Chairman? "I take a different view, as representing the Court of Directors (pronounced with great emphasis), leaving Lord William Bentinck to entertain what opinion he chooses; for, as I have already said, our postal communication, as conducted viâ the Cape of Good Hope, is all that the authorities in Leadenhall Street, require. I must now request that our interview ends."

'I left the Chairman's room instantly, and, not forgetting the reception I had met with on my entrance, I was determined my departure should not be forgotten, for I gave his door such a precious slam (a stronger word was used) as to be distinctly heard through the corridors of the building. I hurried to one of the hall-porters, and asked for a sheet of paper and a corner from which the poor tabooed Bengal pilot might address a few lines to the mighty lord of Leadenhall Street. My letter was short and as follows:

"'To John Harvey Astell, Esq., M.P., Chairman of the Hon. East India Company.

"'Sir,—I this day resign my employment as a pilot in the Hon. East India Company's Bengal Marine Service, and have the honour to remain,

"'Your obedient servant,

(Signed) "'Thomas Waghorn."

Without even asking the porter for an envelope, and the ink still wet, I rushed back to the chairman with my letter. "There, sir, is my resignation of my position in the Company's service; and I tell you, John Harvey Astell, esquire, Member of Parliament, and chairman of the Hon. East India Company, that I shall stuff the overland route down your throat before you are two years older." I then dashed out of his room, slamming the door even more violently than I had done five minutes previously. That is the way, gentlemen, a poor devil is served who has the good of his country at heart.

'I have still something to tell you; for, after the treatment I received at the India House, I should immediately have presented myself at the Board of' Control; but my feelings were so exasperated, that, I required a couple of days to calm them down. I then repaired to Cannon Row, where I soon discovered that an arrow had been sped from the quiver in Leadenhall Street which had reached the Board of Control before me, as, from the whispering and staring that went on in the outer chamber, I much doubted whether I should ever see the inner, where sat the Minister for India. However, after deep consideration, I was told that Sir John Hobhouse could see me. What a piece of condescension in a well paid Minister of the Crown.' I was received with extreme frigidity, the key-note, sounded in Leadenhall Street, had obviously been re-echoed in Cannon Row, for if Harvey Astell was rude and offensive, Sir John Hobhouse was doubly so. After handing in my letter of introduction from the Governor-General, I recapitulated all that had passed between Lord William and myself, as well as communicating my own observations as concisely as possible on the general question of the overland route, but without making any impression on the Right Hon. Baronet, who seemed to view its unimportance as Mr. Astell had done. In his remarks Hobhouse so grossly insulted me, that the only return I could make in hurriedly leaving his presence, was striking my own body in a manner which I was informed afterwards was extremely distasteful to the President of the Board of Control, affording me, with not a few others I can assure you, intense satisfaction and great amusement, and I hope I may now include you in the number. My revenge, gentlemen, on these men was seeing my plans carried out., and in being enabled to say, "*There, behold another route to India, besides the Cape of Good Hope.*"[85]

85 Mark Boyd, *Reminiscences of Fifty Years*, London, 1871, 270-4.

4

1831-1835

The 'Firebrand' steam Navy vessel
(© National Maritime Museum, Greenwich, London)

As early as 2 June 1831 Waghorn had again become a midshipman in the Royal Navy, serving on the *African*.[86] The circumstances are again set out by Waghorn himself:

> After a lapse of 14 Years from October 1817 to 1831 during all which times I was employed in the Rivers of India, Egypt, and the Red Sea, 3 years of it commanding East India Companys armed Vessels in the Arraccan War, I was induced by late Admiral Sir Thos. Hardy, then Managing Lord, to again become a Midshipman at the age of 31, in order to get a knowledge of Steam Navigation. I passed for Lieutenant for Seamanship

86 TNA: ADM 35/4532.

> in 1832 & was promised my promotion on doing so, but only received it 11 Years afterwards …[87]

'Mr. Thomas Waghorn, of the *Firebrand*, steamer' was one of three Midshipmen found 'duly qualified in seamanship' on board the *Victory* in Portsmouth.[88] The *African* was one of five paddle steamers ordered by the Admiralty Board in 1824 and was completed at Woolwich the following year.[89] These ships were of 295 tons and about 110 feet long and in addition to their 100 nhp steam engines they had a schooner rig for sails. *African* was at Woolwich when Waghorn joined her, but a heavy swell on 8 June caused a collision in which the paddleboxes were 'carried away', while on the 11th the 'safety valve gave way'.[90] Nevertheless, by the use of her sails she remained active in towing vessels down river and in transferring men between ships. After a journey to Plymouth and back she 'took Steam Vessel *Firebrand* in tow after being launched' to Woolwich for fitting out. Other duties took her to Chatham and Margate and on 26 August she received the Duchess of Kent's luggage for Cowes. This was delivered and the Duchess with Princess Victoria hitched a ride to Ryde on 3rd September. Twice more, on 21 September and 25 October she was called to move the *Firebrand*.

Having served as midshipman on *African* for some six months, on 15 January 1832, Waghorn transferred to the *Firebrand*, now almost ready for active service. With her companion, the *Flamer*, *Firebrand* was to be used for experiments with new machinery. Compared with the *African*, *Firebrand* was of 495 tons and 155 feet in length, the engines producing 140 nhp. The ship had a complement of 39 men, two boys and two engineers' apprentices. During his time on board Waghorn would indeed have gained experience of the workings of a steamship, but equally to the point the *Firebrand* regularly made trips to the Mediterranean, transferring mails and sometimes passengers from ship to ship, or port to port. He could see at first hand a system of distributing and forwarding mails and become acquainted with many

87 TNA: ADM 9/58, dated 29 May 1846.

88 *Maidstone Gazette*, 23 November 1841.

89 For information on *African* and *Firebrand* see David K. Brown, *Paddle Warships. The Earliest Steam Powered Fighting Ships 1815-1850*, London, 1993.

90 TNA: ADM 51/3048 is the log book for 1831-2.

of the Mediterranean ports served by both merchant and naval vessels. The various journeys made by the *Firebrand* during Waghorn's service can be reconstructed from the log-book[91]:

> In dock being fitted out at Woolwich until 22 February 1832; 23-26 February: to Falmouth; 9 March: sailed; 15 March: Cadiz; 16-17 March: Gilbraltar; 21-22 March: Galita; 23-26 March: in Quarantine Harbour at Malta; 27-29 March: Corfu; 1-2 April: Quarantine Harbour at Malta; 8-9 April: Gibraltar; 10 April: Cadiz; 17 April to 4 May: at Falmouth.[92]
>
> 11 May: Cadiz; 13 May: Gilbraltar; 19-20 May: Malta; 23-24 May: Corfu; 27-28 May: Quarantine Harbour at Malta; 4-6 June: Gibraltar; 7 June: Cadiz; 13 June to 2 July: Falmouth.
>
> 7-9 July: Tagus [Lisbon]; 14 July to 12 August: Falmouth.
>
> 18-20 August: Gibraltar; 23 August: Algiers; 26-27 August: Malta; 29 August: Patras; 30 August to 5 September: Corfu; 8-11 September: Malta; 17-19 September: Gibraltar; 20 September: Cadiz; 26 September to 11 October: Falmouth.
>
> 16-18 October: Tagus and Lisbon; 20 October: Oporto; 24 October: Falmouth; 30 October: Plymouth dockyard; 1 November: Portsmouth.

On 10 November, prior to the fitting of new engines, all the crew, including Waghorn, were paid off. A principal reason for Waghorn's service was so that he could serve sufficient time to enable him to become a fully-fledged lieutenant (his previous service prior to 1817 had not quite notched up the required six years). Wilson notes that he had achieved his 'pass for a superior grade' during his service, perhaps indicated by the fact that from 6 September 1832 Waghorn was named as 'Mate'.

In giving evidence to the Select Committee on Steam Communication with India in 1837, Waghorn recalled that three years before he was 'in

91 TNA: ADM 52/3986.

92 The return journey is also recorded in the *Times*, 20 April 1832.

a steam vessel at sea in a gale of wind, where power was useless, because we should have gone down head first; in this case it was His Majesty's steam-ship *Fire Fly*, in a gale of wind in the Bay of Biscay'.[93] *Fire Fly* was launched at Woolwich on 29 September 1832, but was only completed in 1834. She was 550 tons, and larger than both *African* and *Firebrand*. However, a search of the muster lists and log-book provides no trace of Waghorn, although the *Fire Fly* did make a journey from Falmouth to Malta and back in September-October 1834 and there were strong winds and seas on the outward journey.[94] But this is contradicted by George Wheatley's assertion that it was in October 1835 that Waghorn embarked on board the *Fire-fly* steamer and placed himself at Alexandria.[95]

With East India Company ships now established in the Red Sea, the most difficult and dangerous part of the journey was that across the desert. As we have seen, in the 1820s the route was from Cosseir to Ghenna and then up the Nile to Alexandria. Suez was not yet a part of it.

Perhaps drawing on his new experience of Mediterranean routes and practices of dealing with the mails, it appears that Waghorn at last transferred his allegiance from steam navigation via the Cape to that via the Red Sea. He immediately put all his energy into advocating the benefits of the latter, having already published an account of his 1829 journey: *Particulars of an Overland Journey from London to Bombay by way of the Continent, Egypt, and the Red Sea* (London, 1831).

News reached him that the *Hugh Lindsay* was to make a journey to Suez in January 1833 and return to India on 1 March and he immediately wrote to likely persons offering to take letters to meet the ship. However, a Mr. Harcourt at the India Office advised him that after all the *Hugh Lindsay* might not appear since the journey had been planned without official sanction by the East India Company. Waghorn was forced to cancel his offers, but the setback proved a blessing in disguise, for the East India Company were seen by many to be unnecessarily dilatory in withholding support for a mail service using steam navigation and the Overland Route. Numerous complaints were made through the press. Waghorn met the Right Hon. Charles

93 *Report of the Select Committee on Steam Communication with India* (1837), pp. 12-13.

94 TNA: ADM 37/9105 (Muster books) and ADM 51/3171 (Captain's log).

95 Wheatley, 'Some Account ...' p. 349.

Grant on 12 January 1833 who advised him that 'it must be done by a private company ... draw out a plan.' Waghorn did so, and presented it to Grant three days later. Wilson disparagingly remarks that in spite of Grant's enthusiastic acceptance that it said all that needed to be said, there was in fact little detail. The proposal was for one company overseeing the mails from England to Alexandria and another from Suez to India. (Presumably Waghorn himself was expecting to supervise the mails from Alexandria to Suez.) Wilson notes that Grant 'advised him [Waghorn] to go and lay it before the public in India, and say that he had told him to do it.'

So Waghorn set out for India in February 1833, but was delayed a long time in Mocha, finally reaching Bombay on 12 July after a journey of four and a half months. Here he published another fourteen-page pamphlet, proposing a single steamer service from Bombay to Suez, with a coal depot at Socotra. This scheme was not approved at Bombay, nor at Calcutta, where Waghorn arrived around the end of August. The Steam Fund there also failed to endorse an alternative proposal to that of Waghorn when it refused to lease the *Hugh Lindsay* for the service. They gave Waghorn 4,000 sicca rupees as further expenses. According to Wilson, Waghorn left Calcutta for Suez, via Madras and Bombay, with the intention of staying in Egypt. Having arrived in Bombay, however, he purchased a yacht, the *Rob Roy* of about 25 tons, and in mid-December set sail for Suez, accompanied by Mr. Hyslop, formerly a purser in the East India Company. 'On the way up ... when a little to the southward of Judda [Jeddah], the vessel grounded on one of the shoals, and stuck fast.' They were rescued by an East India Company ship and towed into Jeddah. There the damaged yacht was sold and the Englishmen continued in a native boat to Suez.

Instead of remaining in Egypt as originally planned, Waghorn continued to London. He appeared twice to be questioned by the Select Committee on Steam Navigation—on 7 and 9 July 1834.[96] On the way home he made an important contact:

> I got a personal introduction on the 3d of April last, to the Pacha of Egypt; at which introduction the Pacha's minister explained to

96 His interviews are printed on pp. 208-16 and 229-232 of the *Report of the Select Committee on Steam Navigation*, 1834.

> me, that the Pacha was ready to throw open Egypt so that British merchants might trade through it.[97]

The published report of the Select Committee contained several resolutions. They agreed that 'communication with India by means of steam vessels' was important and had been tested successfully over five seasons, although so far as the Red Sea route was concerned the south-west monsoon months from June to September needed further trial. It was hoped that the 'very great expense' could be materially reduced and decisions taken as to whether Bombay or Calcutta should be the point of communication.

Of equal concern was a decision whether the Euphrates route would be a better proposition than the Red Sea route:

> It appears from the evidence before the Committee, that it would be practicable [to sail]between Bombay and Bussorah during every month of the year.
>
> The extension of the line of the Persian Gulf, by steam navigation on the river Euphrates, has not been brought to the test of experiment; but that it appears from the evidence before the Committee, that from the Persian Gulf to the town of Bir, which is nearer to the Mediterranean port of Scanderoon than Suez is to Alexandria, there would be no physical obstacles to the steam navigation of that river during at least eight months of the year; November, December, January, and February, being not absolutely excepted, but reserved for the results of further experience.
>
> There appear to be difficulties on the line of the Euphrates from the present state of the countries on that river, and particularly from the wandering Arab tribes, but those difficulties do not appear to be by any means such as cannot be surmounted, especially by negotiations with the Porte, Mehemet Ali, and the Chiefs of the principal fixed tribes; and that this route, besides having the prospect of being less expensive, presents so many other advantages, physical, commercial, and political, that it is eminently desirable that it should be brought to the test of a decisive experiment.

---

97 *Ibid.*, p. 231.

It was pointed out that the difficult months for the Red Sea route were June-September and for the Euphrates between November and February, so in combination the two could keep communication open throughout the year.

> That the expense of this experiment by the 'Euphrates' has been, by an estimate which the Committee has subjected to the examination of competent persons, stated at £20,000, which includes a liberal amount for contingencies, and the Committee recommend that a grant of £20,000 be made by Parliament for trying that experiment with the least possible delay.

The House of Commons duly granted £20,000 towards the exploration of the Euphrates route with General Francis Rawdon Chesney in charge. Here was a threat to Waghorn's dream of a steam service via the Red Sea. To counter it he petitioned the House of Commons against the Euphrates route and the expense of exploring it, at the same time trying to enlist support from Lord William Bentinck[98]. The petition was presented by Joseph Hume M.P. on 23 July 1835, although there is no mention of it in *Hansard.*

> To the Honorable the Commons of the United Kingdom of Great Britain and Ireland, in Parliament assembled.
>
> The humble petition of Thomas Waghorn of Snodland in the County of Kent
>
> Sheweth
>
> That, your Petitioner has been, ever since the year 1827, employed by the Bengal Steam Committee, to aid their endeavours to obtain a permanent Steam Communication between England and India; and that your Petitioner was in January 1834 employed by such Committee to come to England on their behalf, to further that object, which met the approbation of the late Governor General of India, Lord William Bentinck.

98 University of Nottingham, Portland Collection, Pw Jf 2167. The letters, making the same points, are Pw Jf 2166 and 2168.

That, in the month of June 1834, a select Committee of your Honorable House was appointed, to investigate the subject, with the view to its adoption and that such Select Committee, after hearing competent Evidence, reported (inter alia) "That the Red Sea route was wholly favorable for eight months of the year certain, for such Steam Communication, the remaining four months of June, July, August and September, being left for the results of further experience, also that it was expedient that measures should be immediately taken for the regular Establishment of Steam Communication from India by the Red Sea."

That the Euphrates route was also recommended for trial, and upon the report being brought up, a vote of money to the extent of £20,000, was passed by your Honorable House, to be expended in exploring the last mentioned route.

That your Petitioner humbly submits, that the difficulty of the passage of the Euphrates, is now demonstrated by the fact, that Captain Chesney, (who has sailed for the purpose of exploring that route) has taken out a double diving bell boat, with mining Apparatus, for the purpose of blasting rocks, and of overcoming the other obstructions anticipated; and that your Petitioner is informed, and believes, that the course contemplated to be pursued by Captain Chesney, is to drop slowly from Bir down the Euphrates, with the Iron Steamers, preceded by Arab Boats carrying Coals, with light gigs leading the way by sounding the depths of the river.

That the United Prayer of England and India, is for a rapid Steam Communication, and that your Petitioner humbly submits, that object cannot be effected by a Channel which requires the apparatus taken out by Captain Chesney to open it.

That it is a fact, established by the Evidence, taken before the Select Committee, up to the time the report of that Committee of your Honorable House was made, no Englishman had ever been the whole course of the Euphrates, from Bir to the mouth of that river; whilst, on the other hand, your Petitioner is informed, and believes, that Lieutenant Burnes got, within the present year, from Falmouth to

Bombay, by Steam, via the route of the Red Sea, in 56 days including all stoppages.

That your Petitioner has ascertained that the navigation of the Red Sea is a straight line up its centre, for a distance of 1180 miles. That, with respect to its depth of water, there is sufficient for 50 Steamers abreast of each other, to proceed up or down, and that the Channel, in its narrowest part (the Straights of Jubal) is two miles broad.

That the statement of its being navigable for the 8 months specified in the Report, is placed, beyond question, by the fact, that, since March 1830, the "Hugh Lindsay" has been up and down 6 times by Steam, and the "Forbes" once, without encountering any accident or obstruction, altho' those Vessels were not built for the purpose of being employed on that Sea: further than this, His Highness the Pasha of Egypt, has publicly signified his intention to construct a rail road from Cairo to Suez, at his own expense, to show his co-operation with British interests in this truly important undertaking.

That altho' the sum of £20,000, voted by your Honorable House, was positively stated to be a sufficient sum for exploring the Euphrates, with liberal allowance for contingencies yet your Petitioner is informed and believes that sum has already been exceeded by £5,000, altho' in point of fact the expedition has not yet left Bir.*

That altho' such Select Committee resolved that the effective trial of both lines (those of the Euphrates and the Red Sea) would open a certain communication with the Mediterranean in every month of the year, changing the line of the Steam Vessels on both sides, according to the Seasons, Yet your Petitioner humbly informs your Honorable House, that no steps whatever have been taken to establish a communication with India by the Red Sea route.

Your Petitioner therefore humbly prays, that your Honorable House will forthwith take into consideration, that part of the Resolutions of the Select Committee, of June 1834, which relate to the Communication by Steam with India, via the route of the Red

> Sea and resolve upon such measures for establishing such Steam communication as your Honorable House shall deem expedient.
>
> *That your Pet^r believes that if the select Committee had known that diving bells & Mining apparatus were requisite at all, they w^d not have made any grant for the Euphrates route.

The Euphrates Route

Travel to India via the Euphrates was established in ancient times and the *Foreign Quarterly Review* of 1837[99] in assessing the relative merits of the Euphrates and Egyptian routes gives an account of a number of sixteenth century travellers from Bir to Baghdad. As with later explorers all had problems with navigating the river shallows, rapids and sunken rocks and all were attacked by wandering tribes of Arabs. The *Review* concluded that

> even under the most favourable circumstances [...] the navigation of the Euphrates has never been an upward but only a downward navigation. The vessels were constructed only for a single voyage; the rapids in the high flood and the shallows in the low flood of the river, preventing a return. Its traffic must remain physically and morally restricted.

We are quite willing to admit that, provided a canal or railway-communication could be accomplished between the Orontes and the Euphrates, the comparison between the two routes would become more equal.

Travellers felt that while Mehemet Ali was in charge, it would be possible to overcome the problem of banditry on the route, but a weak ruler would fail to control the marauding bands. A further problem was, as Chesney wrote, that it gave 'the easiest possible route for a Russian force to threaten India'.

In spite of Waghorn's protestations Chesney's expedition had gone ahead. It met with considerable difficulties, crowned with disaster

---

99 *Foreign Quarterly Review*, Vol. XVIII, No. XXXVI, 342-392.

on 21 May 1836, when one of the expedition's two ships, the *Tigris*, sank during a storm with the loss of twenty men.[100] The other, the *Euphrates*, struggled on and reached Basra from Bir after 91 days. Then followed indecisive criss-crossing of letters between London, India and the expedition, a voyage up the Tigris to Bagdad (which went well), another to the higher reaches (which did not) and the eventual cessation of expedition activities. The last was a caravan taking the survey leader Captain James Escourt to England. At Alexandria the party picked up Waghorn, whom Escourt disdained:

> as he is a vulgar sort of fellow, he saw in us, his opponents, & with no very friendly feelings. He was civil however, tho' there was always a lurking disinclination towards us.[101]

The *Morning Post* clearly suspected that the relationship would be tetchy:

> Mr. Waghorn, the indefatigable promoter of the route to India by the Red Sea, was also in Malta … where he arrived in the same steamer with Major Escourt and the Euphrates expedition. These gentlemen had, therefore, the very best opportunity of discussing the merits of their respective undertakings, and we hope the fortuitous meeting was not lost to the grand object each has in view; for no doubt each had much information to communicate to the other, and a temperate comparison of their experiments must have been interesting and curious.[102]

Escourt's description of Waghorn as 'a vulgar sort of fellow' raises again the perception that he was not from the upper classes. During his life many saw this as a factor counting against him.

> Sir James Graham has refused Mr. Waghorn's request to be appointed (even nominally) a lieutenant of the navy; yet Mr. Waghorn is about to venture himself and property for the country's good, in the

100 John S. Guest gives a full account of the whole enterprise in *The Euphrates Expedition*, London, 1992.

101 Gloucester Record Office, papers of General J. B. Estcourt (D 1571), letter from Estcourt to father, 7 May 1837.

102 *The Morning Post*, 31 March 1837, 5.

> attempt to shorten the passage to India. What a pity Mr. Waghorn had not been the ninety-ninth cousin to Earl Grey, or the toad-eater of a Whig nobleman. Would such a man have asked twice in vain?[103]
>
> I may venture to infer that the Lieutenant is not a member of any noble family, or, ere this, for his important services, promotion and some honorary distinction would have been conferred. Are our gallant sailors and soldiers still destined to waste their energies, as Napier would express it, "under the cold shadow of the aristocracy!" Heaven forbid. The rising spirit and intelligence of the people equally forbid. The subject is not unworthy of a powerful pen.[104]

Waghorn grew up in Chatham, with its naval dockyard, its poor, and its seedy side to life.[105] In his biography Clunn mentions Waghorn's time spent acquainting himself with the Arabs, something which a person from the upper classes would not have attempted, but which served the more lowly Midshipman in good stead when establishing his company. An article in *Parbury's Oriental Herald* praised Arab schools 'and Mr. Waghorn acknowledges that he felt himself "far, far beneath them in education"'.[106] Two extracts from newspapers highlight contrasting attitudes. A passenger in transit, describes the arrival in Alexandria and the first real taste of the East:

> The Arabs themselves, notwithstanding the numerous public baths, are exceedingly filthy—it is always advisable to keep the lower classes at arms length. This, together with the reflection from the heated sand is no doubt the cause of opthalmia, from which all, more or less, seem to suffer—they get so thick-skinned or become so accustomed to their tormentors the flies, that they seldom take to trouble to brush them off,—and little naked piccaninies are often so covered with them, that there is not room for a penny piece all over their bodies.
>
> … half-naked donkey boys, yelling, shouting, and pushing for a

103 *Royal Cornwall Gazette*, 16 February 1833, 2
104 *The Times*, 11 November, 1845, 7, letter from 'P' of Hull, dated 8 November.
105 On nineteenth-century Chatham see Brian Joyce, *The Chatham Scandal*, Rochester, 1999.
106 *Parbury's Oriental Herald and Colonial Intelligencer*, vol. I, 110.

> fare—sedate Arabs and Turks, turbaned and slippered, stroking their beards, and walking with the utmost composure, casting slight and contemptuous glances at the Franks, the general name for Europeans—the swarthy water-carriers and fellahs—men and women, slightly covered with a blue calico shirt, the former often naked, with the exception of a blue rag round the loins ... If you cannot secure a seat in the gaudy two-horsed 'bus, allow yourself to be perched on the nearest donkey—from this majestic elevation do not scruple to lay about you with a good stick (the only method of insuring respect, or even peace). ... Before taking [a donkey], scruple not to use your stick well on the backs of the various little grinning suitors, and you will generally be able to choose a good one; the same forcible reasoning may be judiciously administered during the ride, should the animal fall down or the driver attempt any imposition. Backsish, backsish, Ingelese—(money, Englishman, money)—is their continual cry, and is only to be silenced by blows. Poor Waghorne, I found, held a high rank in their estimation. He would often have bonfires, and whole sheep roasted for them.[107]

Waghorn's empathy with the donkey boys went further and perhaps his sympathetic treatment of them was one reason why he was able to gain a particular friendship with the Pasha:

> Next to his extraordinary influence over Mehemet Ali (from whom he once obtained the forfeited lives of seventeen natives, and out of whose own pipe he was permitted to have a whiff on another occasion—an unprecedented honour), there were two of his Oriental exploits of which Waghorn was particularly proud. The first was inveigling the Arabs employed in the transit across the desert into breeches, instead of the more picturesque napkin round the loins; and the second was playing cricket in the square of Grand Cairo, with the assistance of the donkey boys and dromedary drivers of the City of the Caliphs, drilled for the purpose.[108]

107 *Sydney Morning Herald*, 9 February 1858, 2: an article headed 'A month in Egypt, via Marseilles and Malta.

108 *Liverpool Albion*, 14 January 1850, quoted in *The Maitland Mercury and Hunter River General Advertiser*, 1 June 1850, 3.

Waghorn himself raised the subject in his lecture given and printed at Bath:

> … on the third occasion when I went to Egypt, to establish British means of transit through the country, many of the English merchants at Alexandria even deemed it impossible, telling me that I could not then speak Arabic, therefore, they asked, how was it possible to get on with the Arabs of the desert? My reply was, to teach them English would be my method, and British influence and money would do the rest. The wanderer or robber of the Suez desert was then in the state he had been for centuries. See, then, what I have been enabled to do. They are now paid according to their knowledge of the English language, and get places of trust accordingly—the once robber of that desert is now its protector, and I know no better class of men to deal with than they. They respect us in return more than any European nation, for they call all other nations "Franks", but we English they have a name for, and they call us the "Inglisé".[109]

Nevertheless all the time Waghorn ran his agency in Egypt he gave the senior positions to the English, but once Mehemet Ali took charge he systematically replaced them with his own native people.

Family matters

Waghorn was away from Calcutta when his young wife died. This was on 8 March 1834 and she was aged 28 years, 11 months and 7 days according to the register of St John's cathedral.[110] Waghorn can have seen relatively little of her during their twelve-year marriage, for the Burmese War and his subsequent travels to and from England meant that he was often absent from Calcutta. There is no record of her travelling with him. Nine months later, on 8 December, he married a second time. His new bride was Harriet Martin, daughter of the

109 *Lieutenant Waghorn's Lecture at Bath*, H. E. Carrington, Bath, 1846, 7-8.

110 APA: East India Register N/1/40/f16. The burial was at 'Calcutta', but none of the printed lists of English burials there mention it, so the grave is probably unmarked.

miller at Holborough in the parish of Snodland. Next door was Island Cottage, which he had bought in 1827 and where his mother Ann now lived.[111] The marriage took place at All Saints church, Snodland, as part of a double ceremony with his sister Sarah and her groom, William Ransom of St Mary, Rotherhithe.[112] His brother Edward and sisters Ann and Mary Jane (and surely his mother too) were all present as witnesses. Waghorn's grandfather, John Goodhugh, had died a week earlier on 2nd December, but was not buried until 4 January 1835.

Holborough: Island Cottage on the left, home of Waghorn's mother; the water mill, home of Harriet Martin in the centre; and his grandfather John Goodhugh's house in the foreground.

Between 1802 and 1837 James Martin is recorded as a tenant

111 KHLC, U2102/T34, dated 6 December 1827, is a title deed from the executors of John Stone of Tonbridge, transferring Island Cottage to Thomas Fletcher Waghorn 'of the Bengal Pilot Service in the East Indies, gentleman'.

112 Apart from the entry in the parish register, the marriage licences of the two couples are extant in the parish archives now held in the Medway Archives and Local Study Centre, Strood: P342/2/6 and P342/2/4 respectively.

occupying the water mill at Holborough, after which it passed to his son, Edward.[113] Harriet, daughter of James and Elizabeth Martin, had been baptised at the neighbouring parish of Birling on 27 September 1801, shortly before the family's move to Holborough mill.

On 23 December 1834, a few days after the marriage of Harriet to Waghorn, her father James made his will, leaving £100 to her. In time Edward too bequeathed her money, but clearly was troubled that this might be seized by Waghorn. To his friends Thomas Matthews of Snodland, farmer, and Richard Postans the younger, late of Punish Farm, Snodland, he left all property upon trust, they to dispose as they think proper and to pay from the income £100 a year 'to my sister Harriett, wife of Thomas Fletcher Waghorn, for term of her life, for her own absolute use and [it] shall not be subject to the control, debts, or engagements of her present or any future husband.'

It must have been during one of Waghorn's visits to England that a story recounted by Harold Stedman took place:[114]

> Walking in the country many years since, the writer casually met a very old man whose home had, at a former period, been at Birling. He remembered the Goodhughs and related the following incident. During a winter of severity, considerable distress was experienced by many of the villagers. Waghorn, home from abroad, paid a visit to his grandfather Goodhugh, who, at the time, was from home. Nevertheless, in order to give relief to the needy, he ordered the best bullock in the farmyard to be slaughtered and distributed among them; somewhat to the chagrin of his grandfather on his return home.

---

113 James was an executor to his brother, Edward, a blacksmith of West Malling, who died on 25 June 1829, and who then owned property in Brook Street, Snodland (will: TNA: PROB 11/1764, f.718). One of Edward's daughters married into the Norton family, which included Silas, a lawyer who (as noted below) acted for John Goodhugh among others. James's son Edward, baptised at All Saints, Snodland, on 21 October 1812, continued at the mill until his death in 1847. On Holborough mill, see Michael J. Fuller, *Snodland and Holborough Watermills*, Snodland Historical Society pamphlet No. 9, Snodland, 1998.

114 Newspaper cutting, *The Chatham News?* Exact reference untraced.

Stedman's letter has some inaccuracies of time and place; it is likely that the event took place at Snodland rather than Birling. John Goodhugh and his wife had inherited from her family what was then called 'Gilder's Farm' in Holborough and which in later years was farmed by the Goodhugh's son James. The Goodhughs had lived in Snodland since the 1770s. John (the grandfather) died on 2 December 1834, having made his will on 22 November 1831. Thomas Fletcher Waghorn was named as one of the executors, together with his uncle James (John's son) and Silas Norton, a gentleman lawyer from West Malling. All the Waghorn grandchildren were among the beneficiaries:

£50 to Mary Jane Waghorn
£150 to Edward Waghorn
£25 to his nephew, William Higgins of Snodland, schoolmaster
all household goods, implements, plate, linen, china and glassware to be equally divided between his son James, grandson Thomas Fletcher Waghorn, and granddaughters Ann Munday and Mary Jane Waghorn.

His son James to receive 'my watch and the Seal, Keys and Chain thereto appending and also my pair of Gold Studs marked with my Initials.'

Thomas Fletcher Waghorn to receive 'my silver pint tankard'.

The executors to put £1,000 in trust, to be put out for interest, 'for the benefit of my daughter Ann Waghorn for and during the term of her natural life', and after her death to whichever survive of the four granddaughters, Ann Munday, Mary Jane Waghorn, Frances Waghorn and Sarah Waghorn in equal parts.

The rest of the personal estate to be divided between James Goodhugh and Thomas Fletcher Waghorn.

'I give and devise all that Smith's forge and the two Messuages … adjoining with the rights, members and appurtenances thereto belonging situate at Snodland … and now in the several occupations of the Widow Phillips and Thomas Huggins unto my two granddaughters

Ann Munday and Mary Jane Waghorn as tenants in common.'

'I give ... those two Messuages ... with ... appurtenances ... situate at Snodland ... and now in the occupation of Edward Hawks and John Baker unto my Grandson Edward Waghorn.'

'I give ... those two messuages ... with ... appurtenances ... situate at Snodland ... now in the several occupations of Mrs Southgate and William Phillips and also all those two messuages ... with ... appurtenances ... situate at Snodland ... and now in the occupation of the Churchwardens and Overseers of the Poor of the Parish of Snodland, the one called the old poor house and the other the new poor house ... and also all that my newly erected Messuage ... with the Garden as now endorsed, rights, members and appurtenances thereto belonging situate at Snodland aforesaid and now in the occupation of John Moore unto James Goodhugh, Thomas Fletcher Waghorn and Silas Norton upon trust' (with rents of £40 per annum) to my son John Goodhugh for life.[115] Any profits are to be paid in insurance against fire and tempest. After John Goodhugh the younger's death, the Southgate, Phillips and Moore houses are to descend to Sarah and Frances Waghorn; the New Poor House to Edward Waghorn; the Old Poor House to Thomas Fletcher Waghorn.[116]

'I give all that ... Farm House with the Barns, Stables, Outhouses, Edifices and Buildings, Yard, Garden and several pieces of land [c.23 acres in Snodland] occupied by William Burgess and commonly called ... the Mill Stream Cottage and the rest of my real estate' to James Goodhugh.[117]

A letter written by Ann Munday to Silas Norton from Australia on 25 January 1865 notes that following James Goodhugh's death[118]

---

115 It appears that John Goodhugh the younger was handicapped in some way.

116 Nos. 207-12 and 270-2 on the Snodland Tithe Commutation map.

117 Nos. 154, and 375-8 with associated fields on the Snodland Tithe Commutation map.

118 He was buried at Birling on 1 October 1864.

> The Farm at Holborough containing 23 Acres of land House &c was left him for his natural life only. After his decease to my departed brother Thos Waghorn; as he has left no heir, it now belongs to Edward Waghorn ...[119]

According to an account by 'E. Edwards', it appears that following their marriage Thomas and Harriet Waghorn set up home in Rochester:

> A brother of Waghorn's kept a butcher's shop in the High Street of Rochester in 1836. At that time Mrs Waghorn, wife of the lieutenant, lived in a small cottage at St Margaret's. I remember her very well as a comely, matronly woman of about 40 years of age. She had no family.[120]

Perhaps it was the same house (11 Boley Hill) occupied by Mary Jane in later years. However, during this period Waghorn wrote some letters from Snodland, so it is possible that they lodged with his mother or Goodhugh or Martin relations.

---

119 I am indebted to Mrs Robin Handley for a photocopy of the letter which belongs to a descendant of Ann Munday.

120 *Notes and Queries*, 6th series, vii, 218. As noted on p. 12 the High Street butcher is named in contemporary directories as William, but he was the son of a Samuel Waghorn and born at Otham, Kent, on 17 Jan 1796. Possibly Samuel and Thomas senior were brothers, but proof is lacking. The writer may have meant Edward Waghorn, whose butcher's shop was in St. Margaret's parish.

5

DEPUTY CONSUL IN EGYPT

Waghorn was becoming impatient that his entitlement to become a lieutenant was still ignored.[121] Nothing daunted he wrote to the premier. Sir Robert Peel, from Liverpool on 5 February 1835:

> Pray your acceptance of the inclosed pamphlet; its object is [to] place India one half nearer to England.
>
> The writer of it most respectfully solicits to be presented to the rank of Lieutenant in H. M. Navy, being eligible for that rank since Sept 1832.[122]

He was also frustrated that the work of the Select Committee on Steam Navigation had not been acted upon. He himself left London for Egypt in October 1835 to establish a private agency at Cairo for the conveyance of passengers and mail. It was on 21 December that, according to Wilson, Waghorn first 'set his foot on board a steamer on the waters of the Red Sea, … more than five years after the *Hugh Lindsay* made her first voyage in 1830, and after she had made seven voyages up the Red Sea.' The two men met. Wilson records 'He told me, among other things, that the London houses in the East India trade at this time gave him each a salary.' Waghorn offered to carry the mails across the desert for Wilson, but the latter spurned the idea, saying that it would be quicker to leave the Arabs to do the job themselves rather than be slowed by an interfering Englishman.

121 The *Royal Cornwall Gazette*, 16 February 1833, was among newspapers which indignantly reported that 'Sir James Graham has refused Mr. Waghorn's request to be appointed (even nominally) a lieutenant of the navy; yet Mr. Waghorn is about to venture himself and property for the country's good, in the attempt to shorten the passage to India.'

122 British Library, Add. MS 40413, f.348. No doubt the pamphlet was *Steam Navigation to India, via Egypt and the Red Sea*, Liverpool, 1835.

Waghorn seems to have remained in Egypt until he returned to England in the spring of 1837.

Two letters from him are known to have been sent from Cairo to Mr. P. Stewart of Smith, Elder & Co., his London agents, at this time[123]:

9 April 1836:

My dear Sir,

I hope you have made all right about the bills for £50 drawn by me in January payable about this time. There is an old account that Messrs. Alexanders have against me of some years' standing which the Steam Navigation Committee ought to pay and not me, but as I am responsible I must pay; it is not more than £70 or thereabouts with interest. I am sorry to say Mr. Kerr seems annoyed I have changed my channel, but in private to you I could do no less, being under pecuniary obligation to Mr. Ransom, who is the guarantee to my various debts, except the lot to Mr. Kerr, which I have now asked him to guarantee. It is far, very far, from my intention to draw bills either on you, or Ransom, if I can help it.

Have the kindness to pay Mr. Ransom in future, to whom I am much in debt, but I have property in England, embarrassed it is true, but upon the whole, I (am) far from being on the wrong side, if I die to-morrow. I write this to you in a plain friendly manner; after a year or so, I shall be beyond all this, my expenses for living in Egypt amount only to £150 a year.

I will never encroach beyond that in what you could deem improper, or intrusive.

26th July, 1836

My dear Sir,

I go on to Mocha … This letter is specially to tell you that … I intend to draw a bill on you for £70 … which will be due about 2nd Nov. It is more than likely, even at that time, you may not have funds to cover it, of mine, but I trust you will honor it, as I give my

123 Formerly in the collection of John K. Sidebottom and quoted in his book *The Overland Mail*, pp.113-114. I have not been able to ascertain the present whereabouts of these letters.

> honor not to draw on you again till I know its payment is covered by funds of mine in your hands.

Many accounts of Waghorn's life state that he received a large legacy. John Sidebottom, for instance, writes

> 'He came of a wealthy landed stock and his father left him a large legacy – said to have been between £40,000 to £50,000. This he spent [...]'

No evidence has been found to substantiate this claim and it seems unlikely. More probably an extra '0' has slipped into the figures, which should read £4,000 to £5,000. Thomas Waghorn senior was a butcher and hardly likely to amass or inherit even such a sum—and was a bankrupt in 1816, as noted earlier No will by him has been traced. John Goodhugh on the other hand was quite affluent and the legacies recorded above suggest that this is a realistic amount for Waghorn to have inherited from him (maybe some of it as property rather than cash). His mother of course outlived him.

In 1836-7 Waghorn was active in setting up a network in England to support his agency for the transfer of mails. He urged his Liverpool agents to advertise his success in speeding the mails:

> ...the January letters from England to my care for India (arrived here at noon on the 27th ultimo) having *sailed before sunset on the 30th ultimo,* twenty-four hours earlier than the arrival *in Cairo* of the post-office mails to India, forwarded through the B. Consulate.

He goes on to explain to the merchants the regulations he and they faced:

> As *parcels* have already come to my care from England for India by this route, I must beg you will take note that my charges are merely for the despatch of same to Suez or to Mocha, as occasion may require: besides which, articles of any description of merchandise, valuables, &c., whether intended for *private use* in India or not, are subject here to a transit duty of 3 per cent., and as the custom-house officers may insist upon *their right* of opening them, the parties

sending them ought to write me, with an invoice or list of their contents, and specification of their value, for my government here, in paying the duty, which I will afterwards write you to recover from the parties sending these packages. I should wish to know if insurance has been effected in England, or if they wish it; there are companies here to take the *risk* of carriage by water to Cairo, and by dromedaries from Cairo to Suez, and by sailing vessels from Suez to Mocha. Impress upon your friends, at the same time, that little or no *actual* risk is incurred; and I have no doubt they would insure on far better terms in England for the whole distance, when expressed "*forwarded through my agency*".

I trust to see the number of letters from your city [Liverpool] considerably increase, as the unprecedented despatch I have accomplished can only be obtained by foot messengers relayed every half hour between this [Alexandria] and Cairo. I find the weight and bulk of newspapers a serious inconvenience, and request you will limit the number as closely as you can, without refusing them altogether.

Parcels, of course, cannot have the same despatch as letters—in the first place, my letters leave Alexandria one hour after the arrival of the steamer-consequently, before I could possibly get parcels through the custom-house, and then, if of any weight or size, parcels must go to Cairo by boats, and therefore will only reach Suez in time to go off with my letters by the steamer following that which brings them.

Pray excuse the trouble I am giving you, and believe me, respectfully, gentlemen, your most obedient servant, THOS. WAGHORN.[124]

Within the year his firm was in full operation, with agents in major cities:

Mr Waghorn has now brought into full operation his arrangements for the RAPID TRANSPORT of Letters and Packages, and the Conveyance of Passengers from Alexandria to Mocha, and from Suez to England, and Letters and Parcels passed from England to India by this means in from 47 to 85 days.

124 *Manchester Courier and Lancashire General Advertiser*, 28 March 1836, 2.

Dispatches for India through this medium must be addressed "To the care of Waghorn, Alexandria"—presented for registration to one of the undermentioned parties, before five o'clock on the last day of the month—a charge agreeable to the annexed seal paid—and then transmitted, *post paid*, by that evening's mail, in time for the Falmouth steamer, which sails on the third of each month.

MR. WAGHORN'S CHARGES	£. s. d
Single letters, weighing less than one ounce	0. 2. 3
Double letters, ditto, ditto	0. 4. 6
Letter containing more than one enclosure, ditto	0. 6. 9
Letters weighing one ounce, whatever the contents may be	0. 9. 0
For every quarter of an ounce above that weight	0. 2. 3
Newspapers each	0. 0. 4
Parcels not containing letters or newspapers per lb weight	1. 0. 0

Further information may be obtained from, and letters
Registered with-

Manchester	Mr. T, W. Winstanley, solicitor, 20 Brown-street
Liverpool	Messrs. D. and T. Willis
Birmingham	Messrs. Broomhead and Thomas
Glasgow	Messrs. Thompson and Stirling
Falmouth	Mr. George W. Wheatley, Church-street
London	Messrs. Smith, Elder and Co., 53, Cornhill[125]

On 5 May 1837 the *Times* reported that 'Mr. Waghorn, in addition to his present arrangements for expediting the transfer of the Indian mails via Egypt, is about to place a vessel of his own in the Mediterranean, to ply constantly between Marseilles and Alexandria—an instance of zeal and enterprise which deserves to be well rewarded.' This was the 'yacht *Lady Emily*' of 156 tons whose first voyage was advertised for 12 June. The first French steamers had also inaugurated their rival service on 11 May. In June too the London Overland Registry Office was opened at 34 Cornhill and Waghorn soon transferred himself there from 71 Cornhill, while George Wheatley moved from Falmouth to be the chief factotum in the new office. The Directors of the Manchester Chamber of Commerce each subscribed a 'small sum' as a testimonial

125 *Manchester Courier and Lancashire General Advertiser*, 11 February 1837, 1.

to thank Waghorn for his efforts.[126] In London, at the suggestion of George Larpent, chairman of the East India and China Association, a piece of plate, valued at 100 guineas, was presented to Waghorn; the *Times* reported that 'among the subscribers appear 20 of the first names in the city connected with the East India trade.'

On 13 June Waghorn again gave evidence before a Parliamentary Select Committee—the first to do so since he planned to leave for Egypt the following day. One of the main problems in establishing a route for steamships was the ever pressing need for coal. It was imperative that depots were established at convenient intervals where coal could be stored to supply ships in need. Waghorn was called to give his opinion, which in the event was contradicted by a fellow expert, Lieutenant Wellsted, all neatly summarised by Charles Low:

> Lieutenants Waghorn and Wellsted were examined before the Committee regarding the question of the most suitable coal depots, and, while the former stated that "Mocha is the best place that can be found in the Red Sea, and the only depot required," and "the place for everything," Lieutenant Wellsted gave his opinion, "most decidedly, that Mocha cannot be made a station, for during nine months of the year the southerly winds blow with such violence that you can only communicate with the shore at intervals, and it is an open roadstead." Again, in opposition to Waghorn, who declared that the harbour in Camaran Island, about thirty miles to the northward of Hodeida, is "good for nothing," and "altogether useless," having a bar across the entrance all round, Wellsted said that "the best station between Socatra and Suez is Camaran, which is a good harbour, is partially susceptible of cultivation, and that there is not any difficulty in the navigation into the harbour, the width of the channel being a mile and a half." Both these officers spoke from actual observation and experience, Waghorn, as he stated, having been at Camaran "dozens of times," and Wellsted having been professionally employed for three years in surveying the Red Sea.[127]

126 *Ibid.*, 177 February 1837, 4.

127 Low, *op. cit.*, ii, 74. Waghorn seems to have been proved right as Mocha became the station.

Wilson too pointed out other inconsistencies in Waghorn's evidence:

> Previous to giving his evidence before this committee, Mr. Waghorn handed in a written statement, self-laudatory as usual, and commencing somewhat inconsistently, by stating that he was to quit England the next day for Egypt, via Marseilles, "encharged by the East India Company and the Board of Control, in that quarter, for the establishment of steam communication between England and India, by way of the Red Sea;" yet concluding with complaints that his services were unheeded by His Majesty's government, stating that he was going out in debt, and at the same time, praying that the committee would embody his past and present labours, in their proceedings, and hand them in to the House of Commons. In reference to this statement, Sir John Hobhouse, President of the Board of Control, and a member of the committee; when subsequently himself giving evidence before the committee, made the following observations:—"Let me remark, also, in reference to what was stated by Mr. Waghorn, that his services had been overlooked by His Majesty's government; that the present Board of Admiralty have declined to promote him to a lieutenancy, in consequence of certain rules of service, which had induced two former Boards of Admiralty to come to the same conclusion. At the same time, the King's government have, in conjunction with the Court of Directors, shown every disposition to acknowledge the merits of Mr. Waghorn. The Court of Directors have, in the first place, given him a sum of money for his past exertions; and they have, in conjunction with the India Board, now given him the appointment of deputy-agent and superintendent of the India mails in Egypt; and, in compliance with his own request, they have moreover advanced to him a year's salary."[128]

On 6 June 1837 Waghorn wrote to Sir John Cam Hobhouse (1786-1869), President of the Board of Control, offering to take dispatches to Alexandria.[129] There is too another (undated) letter probably written prior to this:

---

128 Wilson, *op. cit.*, 62-3.

129 British Library, Add. MS 36468, f. 161.

Sir John

It is requisite that you get on, at the Foreign Office about getting me D[eput]^{y} Consul of Egypt & also ask Lord Minto[130] to make me a L^{t} in the Navy which rank I have been many years intitled to.

I shall pay no attention to any other person than yourself The Chan^{r} & Lord William about other question. I'm ready to go off with Dispatches via Marseilles whenever you like – I should say on the day or 2 or 3 after you detail your plan to House of Commons. A note to 71 Cornhill will always get to me.

I am Sir John
Your most faithful serv^{t}
Thos Waghorn[131]

Waghorn's appointment as East India Company Packet Agent in Egypt, and Deputy Consul subordinate to Colonel Patrick Campbell, was made on 7 June, although on the 13th of the month he told the Select Committee that he had only gained the post 'a few hours' earlier. Campbell had been Consul in Egypt since May 1833, in succession to John Barker. Before he left England Waghorn had submitted to the East India Company a plan with costs for 'Steam Navigation with India'.[132]

On 4 May Waghorn proposed immediately placing the *Hugh Lindsay* steamer between Suez and Mocha [Yemen] and the *Atalanta* and *Berenice* steamers between Mocha and Bombay. Five thousand tons of coal each should be delivered to Alexandria, Mocha and Bombay, costing £35,000 in total. A 'small Iron Tug Steamer and Flat for the Nile for the purpose of passing Coals, Mails and Passengers between Alexandria and Cairo' would cost £6,150 according to Maudsley & Co.. Waghorn would locate an Englishman at each of the stations at Alexandria, Cairo, Suez and Juddah at an annual salary of £250 per person. The total estimated cost was £42,150. Waghorn continues:

General Remarks. The Crew's Pay & Expences of the small Steamer for the Nile I would undertake. I will also convey the Coals from

130 Sir Gilbert Elliot, 1782-1859, First Lord of the Admiralty.

131 British Library, Add. MS 36468, f. 318.

132 University of Nottingham, Portland Collection, Pw Jg 367.

> Alexandria to Suez at £2 per Ton – I will also convey them to Juddah at £1 p^{r} Ton more. I will also build coal sheds at each of the four places placing these sheds under charge of the four agents at Alexandria, Cairo, Suez and Juddah – in fact with guarantee that in case steam breaks down in the Red Sea not only will I send people to repair the Vessel from Cairo, but will send on the Mails regularly to and from Mocha rapidly till she was repaired – All this I will do and much more provided I receive a liberal Salary from the Court of Directors as well as their authority to incur just and proper expenses, they addressing a Despatch to the Pacha of Egypt that they seek for me his firman [written authority] – by which I will get all the facilities of his extensive territory.

In a follow-up letter dated 29 June Waghorn drew the attention of the Directors of the East India Company to the French Government's intention to establish a steam service between Marseilles and Alexandria every ten days, beginning on 1 June 1837. He repeated the details of his plan outlined above, suggesting the E.I.C ordered the movements of the *Hugh Lindsay*, but left control of the *Berenice* and *Atalanta* to the Bombay Government. He continued by setting out his own requirements:

> I have only one favor to ask, viz. I beg and pray The Ho^{ble} East India Company will never employ me again if they think that I have the slightest idea as to my own emolument in it, because I can tell them conscientiously I have not. I can appeal to their Gov^{ts} in India and the People there. For this assertion who all know I have not, else is it likely that I should have regularly sent on their own Packets during the time I have been in Egypt without the slightest remuneration as yet from either the East India Company or its Gov^{t} as the annexed copy of certificate from the Consul General of Egypt sheweth.
>
> All I want is Authority from the Court to incur the necessary expences between Alexandria down to Mocha having under me an Englishman at each of the following places, viz. at Alexandria, Cairo, Suez and Juddah.
>
> With respect to Mocha a Military resident should be sent there immediately under whose authority I could be placed, the above Englishman being under mine.

> Nothing more is wanting except an application from the East India Company to solicit His Highness Mahomet Ali of Egypt, that I possess his firman at the solicitation of our Gov^{t} throughout the line, with which I will not only place the Coals from Alexandria to Suez but be always moving between Mocha and Alexandria inspecting and regulating the matter as it should be. [...]
>
> With respect to the more comprehensive Plan which is now in Progress between the Govern^{t} and the Company all the foregoing will not in any way interfere in the slightest degree – on the other hand it becomes a part of it when that comes into operation in a more comprehensive way. [...]
>
> For myself all my energies, my zeal, or my faithfulness are at the disposal of The Honble Court of Directors whom I have served most faithfully and am ready to do the same again at their bidding.

By 13 July Waghorn was in Alexandria and by the 24th of the month in Cairo. An exchange of correspondence between Waghorn and Campbell continued until 28 November[133] and shows that the relationship between the two men became increasingly strained: Waghorn's impetuous and impatient attempts to set up an infrastructure for the Overland Route, and the consequent need to expend money on this, were met with caution on Campbell's part. Quite naturally Campbell was not prepared to authorise major expenditure without permission from his superiors in the Company and was constantly imploring Waghorn to be economical in all his activities.

No sooner had he arrived in Egypt than Waghorn sent to Campbell a copy of the ideas he had put to the East India Company regarding the Overland Route. It is dated 14th July and falls into several sections, all dealing with the personnel required in maintaining the route and in particular the oversight of the mails. It is typical of the thoroughness with which he considered all aspects of the venture.

The system between Alexandria and Suez and vice versa. 'The best course', according to Waghorn, 'is:

1st. The immediate appointment of English Packet Agents at Alexandria and Cairo, whose duties should be the speediest possible transmission of letters and despatches; the reception and transit of

133 All the letters from both men are in British Library, APA, R/19/1.

coals between these places; as well as assistance to Passengers going to or coming from India by this route. For the transport of mails, the purchase of four mules is requisite between Alexandria and Cairo, and four dromedaries between Cairo and Suez, the maintenance of which animals, with the Arabs encharged with them will be £20 per month.

I now go to the transport of coals; the Agent at each place should receive or send the coals in charge of his janissary, to prevent waste and fraud; and whatever the expenses of their transit is, those Agents should pay, subjecting their payments to reduction if deemed necessary by Col. Campbell, and this, Sir, is the best check upon the Agents with regard to all due economy.

Camels can be hired for the first 2000 tons to Suez, and afterwards Col. Campbell can report whether the purchase of fifty camels for the constant purpose of passing them from Cairo to Suez, will not be more economical, my own opinion now is, it would be so, tho' the time for doing it should be postponed until the arrival in Egypt of the Iron Steam Boat for the Nile, and this, Sir, appears to be the whole that is requisite between Alexandria and Suez.

Explanation regarding expense of No. 1:

Packet Agent at Alexandria in full of all personal allowances whatever	£250
Packet Agent at Cairo in full of all personal allowances whatever	£250
For Janissaries (one to each Agent, at £50 ea.)	£100
Purchase of Four Mules £20 ea.	£80
Purchase of Four Dromedaries £10 ea.	£40
Maintenance of four Mules and four Dromedaries with their Drivers per month at £20 for the eight	£240
Annual Expense of Agents, Janissaries, Mules, Dromedaries, Drivers between Alexandria and Suez	£960
Extra: Coal shed at Cairo	£100

P.S. The probable charge of Coals between Alexandria and Suez is 35/- per ton until the Iron Steam Boat arrives and then this will reduce to 25/- per ton.

Prior to the arrival of the *Hugh Lindsay* Waghorn suggested the following arrangements between Suez and Mocha:

> 1st. I propose to send mails monthly by the native boats up and down the Red Sea, hired for such purpose, from Suez to Mocha, these mails to be so taken in charge by a Maltese messenger. Boats for this purpose can be hired from time to time at Suez or Mocha, such messengers being in these boats will ensure the quickest possible dispatch either way. I therefore propose four Maltese messengers for this purpose.
>
> 2nd. English Agents to be invested with the authority of Vice-Consuls, are required at the following places, at Suez, Juddah, and Cosseir, and until the arrival of the Military resident at Mocha, and Agent or Vice-Consul will be required there, who can afterwards return and take up some duties at Cosseir, each to be allowed a Janissary, and thus will be established the best system between these places, on the most economical basis, and this, Sir, appears to me the whole that is required between Suez and Mocha.

Explanation regarding Expense of No. 2.

Packet Agent or Vice Consul at Suez in full of all personal allowances whatever	£250
Packet Agent or Vice Consul at Jiddah in full of all personal allowances whatever	£350
Packet Agent or Vice Consul at Cosseir in full of all personal allowances whatever	£200
Three Janissaries, one to each £50 ea.	£150
Annual Expense of Agents, Janissaries in the Red Sea	£950
About £150 per month will be required for the hire of Native Boats to take Mails from Suez to Mocha and vice versa	£1800
Four Maltese Messengers to go on in these Boats from these places £60 each	£240
	£2040

Both these charges of £2040 will cease on arrival of the *Hugh Lindsay* in the Red Sea.

This Agent to be stationed at Mocha till the arrival of the Military resident there, and then return to his proper station at Cosseir.

No. 3. Messengers to and fro between London and Egypt.

I have the honor to report that my final opinion that by the means understated the India Board, and India House will always have quicker and later intelligence to and from Egypt than can possibly be obtained thro' the medium of the Post Office, an object I humbly think is of great importance to both of these Departments, the more valuable, when it is shewn that the Confidential Despatches thus sent, will not meet the eye of any of the French Authorities.

I am of opinion that six messengers/Maltese/ ought to be entertained for this service, at salaries of £120 each, in full of all allowances, except their travelling expense, each messenger to leave London regularly on the 6th day of each month, via Marseilles from Alexandria, where they will arrive on the 26th of that month, leaving again on the 28th of same month with return Despatches for Malta, where those Despatches would arrive on the 4th of the next month, and there go through the ordinary quarantine rules, next day go on to London, without being subject to any French inspection at all. At Malta, 2, out of the six messengers to be always in Practique, to take such Despatches on to London, the messenger who brought them going into quarantine there. And in due course get Practique to go on from Malta with next despatches from Egypt. By this plan the quickest possible means of passing confidential Despatches between Egypt and England is secured, but should any important Despatches arrive, and no messenger happen to be at Alexandria, there will be no difficulty in hiring a provisional one for such purpose, tho' this is a contingency that need hardly be calculated upon. I know of no better plan than the above.

Explanation regarding Expense of No. 3	
Six Messengers £120 ea.	£720
Twelve journeys from London to Marseilles at £10 each journey and twelve times back again to London	£240
Twelve second class passages from Marseilles to Egypt at £14.7 each and twelve passages from Egypt to Marseilles at £14.7	£344.8

Whole expense of six messengers between London and Egypt annually	£1304.8
Messengers leave London inside per Mail for Dover at 8 p.m. 6th day of each month £1. 10	
Steamer to Boulogne from Dover	10. 6
Coach fare to Paris	£1. 15
Malle Post from Paris to Marseilles	£6. -. 10
	£9. 16. 4

It is necessary to secure the Malle-Post that a monthly place be ensured from the French Post Master General for the eighth evening of every month.

P.S. The Chief Secy at Malta will be the most proper person to select these Six Messengers despatching four of them as second class passengers to you in London and keeping the other two at Practique in Malta.

It is some indication of the slowness of communication at that time that it was not until 28 October that written opinion on these matters was received in Egypt from the East India Company's Board of Directors. They agreed to all expenses in items 1 and 2, except for the coal shed at Cairo, and hoped the £2040 would only be required for a short time. They dismissed out of hand the whole of item 3.

On 24 July Waghorn asked Campbell for authority to purchase two mules and two dromedaries and to incur charges for the service between Suez and Mocha. He offered to submit relevant accounts every three months. He also suggested that a Maltese, Fortanatus Revestre, be appointed as messenger, subject to subsequent approval by the East India Company. With all this Campbell was generally supportive except that he argued for three rather than four Maltese messengers in the Red Sea and after further correspondence Waghorn agreed to this.

It appears he had previously suggested to the East India Company that they provide sacks, weighing machines and shovels for movement of coal in Egypt and the Company had already accepted tenders for delivery of 2000 tons of coal to Alexandria. Much of the official correspondence in August and September concerns arrangements concerning coal and discussion of whether similar stocks should be held at Suez, Cosseir, Indola and Mocha. Early in August Waghorn was poorly, perhaps from a recurrence of the fever he had caught during the Burmese War, and on the 10th his assistant Henry Levick had to write:

> I am directed by Mr Waghorn to acknowledge the receipt of your two letters dated 7th and 8th inst., and beg to say that at this moment Mr Waghorn's health is not sufficiently re-established to enable him to return to business or to write to you.

Waghorn had recovered by the 15th, when his next letter was written. A letter on its way from India to London had missed the steamer at Alexandria, but 'a box of letters to the care of "Mr Waghorn"' had arrived there 'with some days to spare'. As well as his duties as Deputy Consul Waghorn maintained his private agency for conveying mail; indeed he was reprimanded later in the year for imposing charges which Campbell felt were out of order. In this Campbell was supported by the East India Company, who wrote to him and expressed

> displeasure at his [Waghorn] having incurred for [conveyance of mails from Mocha to Bombay] a heavy amount of charge not warranted by his instructions and not called for by the necessities of the public service. This step was the more reprehensible as having been taken in direct opposition to your judgement.

Campbell pressed Waghorn for the prompt repayment of an advance of 2500 dollars which he had made to him towards setting up the native boat service and associated work, but on 6 October Waghorn acknowledged that this would have to be deferred until the end of the year. The following day he was negotiating a place for a coal depot:

> I was this morning at Shoubra with the "Sheik of roads" who said that the spot a little beyond the Pacha's Palace at Shoubra would be better than between there and Boulake for our purpose. I have adopted his opinion and selected one, and this evening am going to the Pacha to get his permission in writing for the said spot.

He would also ask for permission to buy camels to carry 200 tons of coal there and requested an assistant to oversee the coal work.

Further letters to Campbell were written on 9 October. In the first he suggested the appointment of John Norton as English Agent at Suez, on a provisional basis until the East India Company could rule on the matter, and requested other English Agents for Judda, Cosseir and Mocha 'the native agents being useless'. In the second he reported that the Pasha had given permission for the purchase of the camels, continuing:

> Respecting the Coal Magazine, His Highness ordered me to give him a Plan in writing for the spot fixed on, and that he would have it erected at his own expense, thereby to show how faithfully he went with the views of H. M's Gov^{t} and the Honble Court of Directors as to the steam object thro this Country.

He enclosed a copy of the plan for Campbell's information, which was to be submitted to the Pasha that evening, and stated that the camels were to be purchased at the government price. Typically he included a break down of requirements and cost:

> The Persons required to be attached to the Cairo Agency for receiving and dispatching Coals to Suez and everything connected therewith.
>
> Current dollars *per mensam*

a) One Magaziner	30
b) One weigher	8
c) One Janissary	13

> Amounting to £127-10 per annum
>
> a) to be wholly and solely in charge of the Magazine and everything belonging to it and to supervise the weighing of coals in and out of the magazine.
> b) to weigh the coals
> c) to take letters and attend the loading and unloading of Boats and Coals to prevent breakage and waste of coals
> NB each to pay their own donkey hire

At this point Campbell asserts his authority and effectively breaks with Waghorn. In a letter of 11 October he refuses Waghorn his request for an assistant—a dragoman—to supervise the movement of coal, unless and until this could be authorised by the East India Company. Waghorn was to make a copy of all his transactions with the Pasha and was not to take any action without first consulting Campbell. Furthermore Campbell would decline the Pasha's offer to build the coal depot.

Waghorn was furious and replied at length on 16 October[134]:

> Sir,
>
> I have the honor to state that your letter of the 12th Inst. has been duly received.
>
> On receipt of it I had only one course left, which was, writing to the Governts & mercantile Communities of both England and India, exonerating myself from the result of your late refusal of the Pacha's offer, and valuable gift to the Steam Object, as a Depot in Cairo would have been for Coals on the way to Suez.
>
> The Steam Object thro' this country should not have been treated in a political point of view, as you have done; it should have been treated by you, as a general object, to which the Pacha's aid was of the most vital importance, and that he had a right also to give that aid; because his own interests were interwoven with it as well as H. M. Govts and the Honble Company's. Whereas you have treated him with Contumely.[135] For, by your refusal of the Pacha's most valuable offer you have slighted if not insulted him, and can you continue to think that thus slighted or insulted you have the power in yourself to do without his aid and assistance in Egypt, when you will know that thro his orders only, sufficient camels could be got at any reasonable price, and these (if, without such orders we could get them at all) we should have to pay doubly,

134 A 'true copy' of this letter, signed by Waghorn, was sent to Lord William Bentinck: University of Nottingham, Portland Collection, Pw Jg 369.

135 i.e. in an insulting and contemptuous manner. As a senior English civil servant Campbell did not treat the Egyptians as equals, whereas Waghorn worked among them and gained their trust as a friend.

perhaps trebly for, as well as for everything else requisite for the Steam Object.

Sir, you had before you the most gratifying point of benefitting the Steam Object by evincing to help, and aid, that of Mahomet Ali's to its fullest extent, and this you have altogether slighted by your incorrect idea of false dignity towards your Authorities; the which, have led you to treat that man's offers with contumely who had it most in his power to aid, to benefit and secondly to economise the object in all its bearings in this country; and I must say the true dignity of Her Majesty and the Court of Directors would have been best upheld, in accepting the Pacha's offer in the same gracious manner that it was made, and if either Her Majesty's Ministers or the Court, had no wish to accept the obligation of such favors, either, might have courteously sent a present beyond the value of such favor, and this should have been the course I would have pursued instead of that you have chosen, which will marr and defeat all future hopes of economy to the Steam Object in Egypt, which can only come from and continue to it thro the Pacha; and I candidly avow I consider you have done more harm by the unfortunate course you have adopted, than aught else could happen to the Steam Object; however, I shall endeavour by every means in my power to rectify your refusal of Mahomet Ali's offered aid thereto, untill I be assured by Mr Sec^y^ Melvill you have adopted the proper course.

Sir, it is with much regret that I feel it impossible to continue longer than the answer from Mr Sec^y^ Melvill to my letter of the 16th Ins^t^ under your orders in the Steam Question in my public capacity. Still I take this opportunity of thanking you for many personal civilities.

Campbell replied the next day, but stood his ground with dignity:

... The good of the service to which you declare yourself so much devoted, is the feeling that prevents my noticing the rather harsh tone which c[h]aracterizes the general style of these communications ... You say that no Dragoman, Jannissary, or Storekeeper had been allowed you for the proper dispatch of business, and that the assistance of such officers is indispensable to you ... [Campbell here inserts a quotation from an earlier reply to Waghorn:] 'I could

> not consent to any permanent establishment of that nature until I had more specific instructions from the Honble Court' …

but he had agreed to allow a temporary arrangement. On the Pasha's offer he refuted Waghorn's views and accused him of acting above his station:

> The question is simply and purely of a political nature and in this line of duty, I cannot allow you in any way to interfere. A reference to the Instructions you received in your being appointed to your present situation … will convince you, sir, that it was never meant to give you any political duties to perform, and that therefore by your so doing you are actually exceeding the limits of your Mandate, in a delicate matter; a matter indeed of much consequence and importance … and it is my most pressing direction that you will refrain from all similar interference's in future … Should at any time, my views on public points unfortunately differ from yours, I must be permitted to act upon my own judgement at the same time that I shall always forward to the Honble Court of Directors any suggestion that you may offer to me, with my own opinions thereon for their approval or dissent. …

Further difficulties had greeted Waghorn in these months. At the end of September one of his menial servants, Edmund Francis, accused him of reneging on the original contract between them, which Francis said was made on 15 May, and which had been superseded by another on 2 June, stating that he was 'violently assaulted by him [Waghorn], discharged and turned out of the House.' Francis was employed to bottle wines, to serve at table when required, and to travel with the horses between England and Egypt. From the papers submitted to the Court hearing he felt Waghorn was not keeping to the terms of the contract and that he should be entitled to a promised pay rise, to travelling expenses and to damages for the assault. Waghorn, for his part stated that Francis was an unsatisfactory servant and he did not think it right to pay all that was asked. The only contract was the one dated 2 June: the earlier one was just a draft. It is clear that the assault arose through Waghorn's impetuosity: Francis returned around eleven o'clock after an evening out. Waghorn considered this too late, since the rest of the household had retired to bed, and appears to have had a heated exchange of words, expelling Francis from the house, perhaps striking him (although there were no witnesses to this) and certainly pushing him downstairs. Statements from various persons were supplied to the Court (chaired in Cairo by the Vice-Consul) and proceedings went against Waghorn. On 28 October he was required to pay £25 for Francis's annual salary (not the £50 which Francis was demanding), £25 for his travelling expenses and £5 for the assault, together with all the costs of the case.[136]

More was to follow. On 16 November Henry Raven claimed that Waghorn owed him 3746.25 piastres for various expenses in boat-building and the like which Waghorn had authorised him to arrange. Some of the charges Waghorn refuted and recorded them as 'unjust expense' in the list submitted to the Court. Again he lost, although the costs of the case were shared between plaintiff and defendant. Evidently no lasting harm was done, for Raven, having commenced in the employment of Waghorn's rival, Hill, later joined Waghorn's establishment following Hill's death and was still working for him some years later when Samuel Bevan described the operation of the Overland Route.[137]

The Hon. E.I.C. steam ship of war 'Berenice'
(© National Maritime Museum, Greenwich, London)

136 TNA: FO 841/3, No. 6.
137 TNA: FO 841/3, No. 8. See below for Bevan's account.

It is not clear when Waghorn officially left the East India Company's service, but his last filed letter as Deputy Consul is dated 28 November. Nevertheless he remained in Egypt for a time and on 15 December was on hand to help in an emergency concerning repairs to the engines of the *Berenice* which had broken down:

> The "Berenice" steamer arrived at Suez on the 18th December, having left Bombay at 6 pm 30th November, being 17½ days; during 10 of which she had worked with only one engine, the other having the piston and cylinder-cover broken. In this dilemma the officers of the ship saw no resource than to transmit to England models of the damaged portion of the machinery, in order to have duplicates sent immediately to Egypt; and in the meantime expected the "Berenice" would be useless for three months. Mr. Waghorn, however, with that promptness of decision and energy which so remarkably distinguish him, immediately applied to the Pasha; and although the application was made at midnight, such is the influence which Mr. Waghorn possesses with Mahomed Ali, that he obtained an order to employ the resources of the arsenal day and night until the engine of the "Berenice" was sufficiently repaired to enable her to run to Mocha, (which she did on the 30th December) to meet the "Atlanta" with the dispatches of the 25th or 30th December from Bombay. This would enable the latter vessel to return immediately, and the "Berenice" would probably again arrive at Suez on or before the 15th January with that dispatch. The "Berenice" is thus, through Mr. Waghorn's intelligent activity, rendered useful of the Red Sea, instead of lying at Suez, waiting the arrival of machinery from England, for a considerable period.[138]

Waghorn's altercation with Campbell had not gone un-noticed and the same journal reported it:

> Mr. Waghorn's letter to Colonel Campbell, agent to the East India Company, of October 16th, on the latter's refusal of a gift of a depôt from Mahomet Ali Pacha, was published in the *Englishman*, December 7. The subject matter of this letter has already appeared

138 *Parbury's Oriental Herald and Colonial Intelligencer*, vol. I, 252-3.

> in England, by Medium of the *Morning Chronicle.* It is known that Colonel Campbell refused the offer of the depot in furtherance of the steam object, on political grounds. Mr. Waghorn is indignant with the Colonel for allowing his prejudices to blind him to the merits of the Steam Communication Question; which, whether politically, or as respected commerce, was a point on which there could be but one opinion, and that entirely in favour of its advancement.
>
> The Bombay Courier of the 25th of January, has the following:- "We have heard from authority, on which we think considerable reliance may be placed, that Mr. Waghorn is likely to be superseded in his post of agent in Egypt. The Court of Directors, which has been appealed to, (in respect to the difference between Mr. Waghorn and Col. Campbell), appears to have taken an opposite view of the case to that which Mr. Waghorn anticipated, and we fear that the supercession of this gentleman will be the result."[139]

So Waghorn's employment as Deputy Consul was brief. Throughout his life he treated officialdom with disdain and the conflict with Campbell was just one of many altercations. As a senior civil servant representing England, no doubt Campbell preserved diplomatic niceties when dealing with Mehemet Ali and his officials, but many of his countrymen passing through the country did not view the ordinary Egyptians as equals, but as underlings to be ordered about and treated as inferiors. On the other hand Waghorn, in running his agency, was dependent on the good will of his workforce and he took great pains to treat them well, as the instances noted earlier show. They trusted him and treated him as a friend.

Having resigned from the Pilot Service of the East India Company in 1831 and removed from the position of Deputy Consul which they had given him, where was Waghorn to turn now? It is clear that Campbell and the East India Company had been uneasy about Waghorn's arrangements for carrying mail as a private venture while also working for them, but he now had the opportunity to develop his service as he wished.

---

139 *Ibid.,* 315-16 and 437-8.

6

RIVALS FOR THE OVERLAND ROUTE

It is clear that Waghorn's primary interest was to speed the communication of mails between England and India. Passengers were always a secondary concern to him, although he often seems to have gone out of his way to help them. Those in India, however, made passengers a priority and in this the lead seems to have been taken by the Bombay Steam Committee, which had been formed in 1833. On 15 March 1838 they received a report from a Colonel Barr, who had travelled to Egypt to set up the means for travellers to cross Egypt, both via Cosseir, Thebes and the Nile and by the Suez-Alexandria route.

Those choosing the former route landed at Cosseir, crossed the desert for a hundred miles or so to either Qena or Luxor, and thence sailed by boat on the Nile to Cairo. One advantage of travelling via Cosseir was to avoid the seasonal contrary winds in the Red Sea, which hindered sailing ships and which even the early steam ships had trouble overcoming. It also allowed the opportunity to view the many Egyptian antiquities on the river bank.

> Sailing vessels are constantly three weeks, and even longer, performing the last five hundred miles of the run to Suez, which makes it advisable for all who can do so to disembark at Cosseir, thereby having an opportunity of visiting the ruins of Thebes, and being at Cairo long before their vessel reaches Suez.[140]

A notice of 'A Recent Overland Passage' summarizes a journey by this route in 1838:

> The *Ernaad* arrived at Cosseir on the 24th February, making the passage in fifty days from Calcutta; ... The party crossed the

140 George Parbury, *Handbook for India and Egypt*, 225.

> Desert in five days, stopped at Zuecla six days, were fifteen days in descending the Nile to Cairo, where they arrived on the 22nd of March, and sailed on the 24th in the steamer for Alexandria, thence to prosecute various routes home.[141]

George Parbury's *Handbook* goes on to detail several reports by individual travellers, the first 'by a gentleman who left Calcutta in the early part of the year 1840':

> If the additional expense is not an object, by far the most advisable plan is to request Hill & Co., at Cairo, by the mail two months previous to that by which you start, to send a boat up for you from Cairo to await you at Luxor, and an Arab servant at Cosseir. The voyage ought not to exceed three weeks, it is frequently done in less—I adopted this plan in 1840, and had no reason to regret having done so, as, in consequence of a large party landing at Cosseir, those who had not taken this precaution had great difficulty in finding boats, and were eventually obliged to put up with very uncomfortable and dirty ones. Particular instructions should be given to Hill & Co. what to send up in the way of supplies, cabin furniture, &c.
>
> In 1840, not having specified my wishes in this respect, Waghorn & Co. (then a separate concern) sent up a supply of the needful articles, nothing superfluous; but having provided myself with all I required in Calcutta, they took every thing back at a very moderate reduction, and I was perfectly satisfied with W. & Co.'s agency and charges.
>
> The hire of boats varies, of course, according to the demand. I paid W. & Co. £17 per month; another party at the same time paid £20 for a somewhat larger boat.
>
> The hire of servants is generally from 12 to 15 dollars per month; that of camels from Cosseir to the Nile ¾ to 1 dollar. The journey across is about 110 miles, or, at camel's pace of 2½ per hour, 42 to 44 hours riding.
>
> There are two or three routes, the choice of the camel-drivers

141 [George] *Parbury's Oriental Herald and Colonial Intelligencer*, Vol. II July-December, 1838, 285

> being guided by the more or less abundant supply of water at the wells.[142]

Problems could arise, however. The gentleman having hired a Nile boat from Waghorn while still in Calcutta, found that 'owing to the uncertainty of a sailing voyage up the Red Sea, the boat was waiting for us much longer than would be otherwise necessary. ... Waghorn dispatched our boat on the 20th January, and we did not reach the Nile till the 26th March!' So 'Hire of boat 2 months and 20 days', at £17 [per month] cost £45 and 'Use of Waghorn's tent, crockery. &c., and sundry items' was a further £12.[143]

John Blackburn, quoted from a pamphlet published in Calcutta, confirms the 'gentleman's' advice:

> The adoption by many travellers of the route by Cossier having rendered it worth the while of Mr. Waghorn, Mr. Hill and other residents in Cairo, to arrange for the convenient transit of the traveller, for a reasonable consideration, it is deemed advisable to write from India beforehand to one of these persons, intimating the extent of party, the probable date of arrival at Cossier, &c., in order, on landing, that servants, Arabs to pitch tents &c., may be found in readiness. Mr. Waghorn provides likewise *tukt-i-rowans*, donkeys furnished with side-saddles; also, a Janissary, a good cook and interpreters. The former will take charge of the tents, water, supplies, &c. &c. The same agents will provide boats at Luxor or Khenneh, according to your previously expressed desire, and it may be taken as a certain fact that, without this precaution, the voyage from those places down the Nile to Cairo will be attended with very serious annoyance and inconvenience.
>
> Immediately on landing at Cossier, the traveller should proceed to the house of the Company's agent, and, with his assistance, engage camels and donkeys for the trip to Luxor or Kenneh, if not already engaged for him.[144]

---

142 George Parbury, *Handbook* ... , 467-8

143 *Ibid.*

144 *Ibid.*, 479-80.

All informants tell of the necessity of prior ordering of boats for the Nile journey from Waghorn or Hill at Cairo, failing which any available river craft would be full of vermin. Mr D. Carmichael Smyth writes as follows:

> If you do not mind the expense, I should recommend your sending money and an order to Mr. Waghorn or to Mr. Hill, at Cairo, to send up boats for you to Luxor. Excellent clean boats are procurable at Cairo, with good boat-people; and by writing from Calcutta beforehand, and stating the time you expect to be at Luxor, they will be able to have the boats all ready waiting your arrival. The size and number, of the boats must depend on your party: but this (if the number of persons is stated) may be safely left to them. A separate cook-boat is, however, at all events necessary, and should be indented for. If you do not choose to go to the expense of having boats up from Cairo; then, directly you land at Cossier, lose no time in sending an express to the Company's agent at Kenneh, requesting him to send up boats for you to Luxor. These boats are country boats, and sometimes are very dirty indeed; they must always be well cleaned and purified before you can use them, to get rid of the vermin—rats, bugs, and fleas. The boats should be sunk in the river for twenty-four hours, and then well scoured and washed; you should take three or four bottles of chloride of lime with you, and have the cabins washed out with the mixture every day, not omitting to have some sprinkled over your cot and bedding. The front part of the boat, extending from the cabin to the mainmast, should be covered over with canvas, and if well done, it will make a very good place to sleep in: for in the cabins of a country boat I would not recommend any one to place his cot. … Our party left Luxor the 7th March, and arrived at Cairo on the 26th.[145]

On behalf of the Bombay Steam Committee Colonel Barr acquired 'small tents, sedan chairs, covered chairs for ladies and children; tables, small table chairs and cooking utensils', some being left at Cosseir for use between there and Thebes, and the rest for passengers between Suez and Cairo. An approach was made to the Pasha for buildings to be erected between Suez and Cairo and 'arrangements were entered into with Messrs. Hill and

145 *Ibid.*, 491-2.

Raven of Cairo, to provide the necessary establishment of Carriages and baggage wagons, &c., for conveying passengers across the desert.'[146] For the sum of £1000 Hill and Raven agreed to procure and hold on account of the Steam Committee

> 4 Light Vans with Canvas or Woollen Awnings and Stuffed Seats
> 2 Luggage Waggons
> 40 Mules
> 5 Sets of Harness for Light Vans of 4 Mules each
> 3 Sets of Harness for Luggage Waggons of 6 Mules each.—
> and to keep up the following establishment,
> 6 Carriage drivers
> 15 Assistants at Station Houses
> 1 Harness mender and
> 2 Shoeing Smiths; one at Suez and one at the Centre Station House.—
> The whole to be kept in a thorough and efficient state of repair for the space of five years, commencing from five months after the 20th April, at which time the £1000 was paid to the contractors.

Barr's report goes on to regulate times of starting and rate of travelling for passengers and sets the fares between Cairo and Suez or vice versa at £6 for ladies or gentlemen and £3 for children under ten years of age and for servants, including

> the carriage of one cwt. of luggage for each lady or gentlemen, and ½ cwt. for each child or servant, with provisions, attendance, &c.; but not including wines, spirits, beer. Extra luggage to go by the luggage wagons, and be charged at the rate of five shillings per cwt.
>
> With regard to the buildings between Suez and Cairo, plans have been prepared of a centre station, and four intermediate ones in the Desert, which are now before the Committee, all of which Messrs. Hill and Raven offer to contract to build, for the sum of 5,117 dollars, or about 12,000 rupees. The centre station to contain one room of 24 feet by 18, and five sleeping apartments of 14 by 12, and 15 feet high, with stabling and other requisite buildings: the whole protected and

146 Barr's report is in *Parbury's Oriental Herald* ..., II, 1838, 160-3.

enclosed by a wall 15 feet high to be built of stone … A water tank also to be added sufficiently large for the use of the mules.

The intermediate Bungalows to be built with walls 12 feet high, and to have stabling attached, together with water tanks; the whole to be built in the same substantial manner as the centre station. […]

The Committee have every reason to believe that the Pacha will himself undertake the erection of these buildings, but in the event of his declining to do so, it will be necessary to place at the disposal of Col. Campbell the requisite funds for carrying on the work on his obtaining His Highness's sanction to do so. In the meantime, however, a sufficient number of Tents have been provided as substitutes for the buildings; and as the contract with Messrs. Hill and Raven comes into operation on the 1st of October, passengers on landing at Suez, from and after that date, will find there a branch of the Cairo Hotel where they can remain comfortably, free of all expense, (except for wines, &c.) for as many hours as they please. From thence a ten hours drive in a comfortable open or close carriage over an excellent road, will take them to the half-way house whence an additional drive of nine or thirteen hours will bring them to Cairo, where they will find comfortable accommodations in the English Hotel.

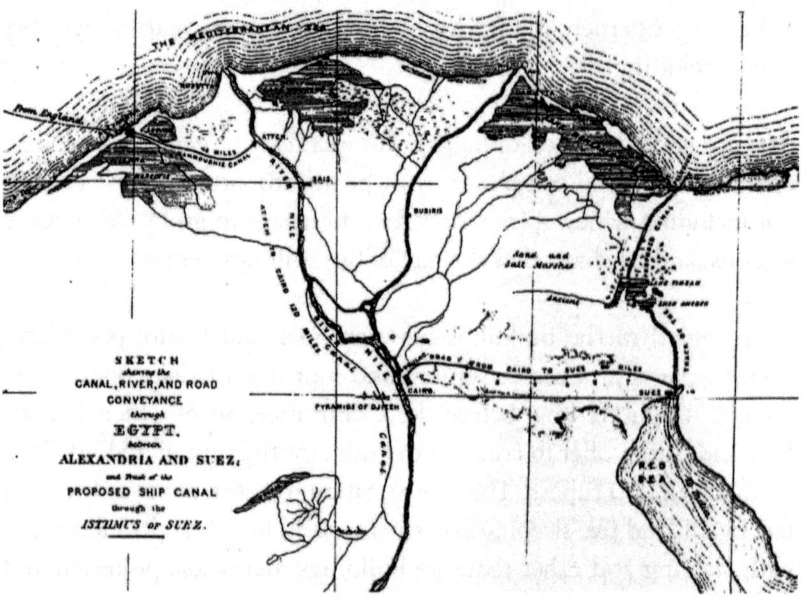

Map showing the desert halting places
(A. Anderson, *Communications with India, China &c, via Egypt*)

A similar scheme was proposed for the other route, with a building at Luxor, another at Cosseir, and four intermediate ones in the desert, all built and supervised by a Mr. Prisse, a civil engineer formerly employed by the Pasha and who lived at Luxor. It is not apparent that these were built and the camel-drivers used the regular wells and watering places for stops. The Pasha promised to build a number of boats for the Nile journeys which would be controlled by the consuls. A further requirement was for 'an accommodation building at Mocha or Aden, if the latter should be selected as the coal depôt, … for the comfort of passengers as all complain of the discomfort of having to remain on board the Steamer, while the coals are being taken in.' In another account George Parbury emphasizes this and a further hazard:

> It is impossible to give an idea of the nuisance of the coal-dust, which literally pervades everything; and, whether below or above, to be clear of it for a single hour, is totally out of the question. … The plague of flies is still prevalent in Egypt: on approaching the coast from the sea, they congregated on board the steamer in vast quantities.[147]

Hill and Raven built the rest-houses in the desert, but at least one was still unfinished when Emma Roberts reached it in October 1839; she comments that the funds of the Steam Committee were 'lamentably mismanaged' in the construction and design of the buildings.[148] Waghorn's mail service used donkeys and camels in a direct journey between Alexandria and Suez, so he had no need of the route from Cairo to Suez until forced by increasing numbers of passengers to adopt it. In 1839-40 he recorded 255 travellers eastwards to India and 234 westwards.[149] Hill and Raven had the advantage that they already controlled the rest-houses and owned hotels in Cairo and Suez; Waghorn's clients were not welcomed at their stations, nor could they obtain water there. Given Waghorn's capacity for argument, it is not surprising that matters eventually came to litigation. Hill and Raven insisted the houses were private property, while Waghorn retaliated

---

147 George Parbury, *Handbook for India and Egypt*, 1842, 229.

148 See below, p. 141

149 Sarah Searight, 'A Waghorn Letter Book for 1840', *Journal of the Royal Asiatic Society*, 3rd series, vol. 7, part 2, July 1997, 236.

that they were really public inns. The British consul in Cairo found in favour of Hill, but his superior the consul-general soon reversed the decision. In the meantime Waghorn had taken control of all the animals, so depriving Hill and Raven of all transport on the route. He also planned to erect his own tents across the desert—salvaged from a mock-mediaeval tournament at Eglintoun Castle—but Samuel Bevan records them in the custom-house at Alexandria in such a state that they surely were never used. Nor did Waghorn's belief that 'a large Central Station will be built for me at the Pasha's expense' come to fruition.[150]

Following his stint as deputy-consul in Egypt, by 17 February 1838 Waghorn was back at his desk at 71 Cornhill, London, from where he submitted to the East India Company his Plan for the Overland Route. It bears a striking resemblance to that of Colonel Barr, but evidently was formed rather earlier.

The Plan

It is proposed during the summer months of the year viz from April to December that a small Iron Steam Boat 80 feet long by 20 feet broad,[151*] to draw within 30 inches water, should be built and always in waiting at Alexandria for the arrival of the Mail from England, that she should receive it and the passengers on board and proceed as speedily as possible via the Rosetta branch of the Nile to Cairo. This can be done with certainty during these months within 28 hours –

It is further proposed that Mails and passengers should remain in Cairo 20 hours for rest and refreshment and for the purpose of preparing carriages to convey them to Suez -

Five [*Two*] carriages of roomy dimensions should be built to convey the mails and 8 passengers each besides servants and light luggage on the roof to be drawn by Mules to go at the rate of 5 or 6 miles p hour (of which only four of these carriages will be required at one time.) These mules to be changed every 16 miles

150 *Ibid.*, pp. 238-9; see Bevan's description, below, p. 184.

151 * Note during the winter months from 1st December to 1st April the Iron Steamer will ply from the end of the Canal at Atfeh to Cairo, (for certain local reasons, occasioning no loss of time) having a Track boat on the canal for the conveyance of mails and passengers to Atfeh to join the steamer there.

where halting places or stables will be erected at the expence of His Highness the Viceroy.[152§] This can easily be done on an excellent road of 82 miles.

At 34 miles from Cairo it is proposed to erect the principal halting place C ... on a large scale for refreshments and repose if necessary for 6 hours each way [containing Iron Bedsteads, Tables, &c. &c.]. The whole of this part of the journey including the above stoppage of 6 hours may be accomplished with the greatest ease within 24 hours.

For this system which is intended to convey mails and passengers from Alexandria to Suez and vice versa in 3 days certain at all seasons of the year, an establishment will be required in addition to the Boat and carriages before mentioned, as stated in G annexed.[153]"

T. Waghorn
G
Abstract
First outlay
Total cost of steamer, Flat &c for carrying mails passengers &c to & from Alexandria and Cairo as p statement A annexed £7,400.
Total cost of carriages, Carts, Mules, Harness &c for conveying mails, passengers & Coals to and from Cairo to Suez as p statement C annexed £5,942. 10.
Total first outlay[154] £13,342. 10.

152 § Note 1st Halting place at A two miles from Cairo at the Caliphs Tombs
2nd Do at B 18 Do
3rd Do at C 34 Do
4th Do at D 50 Do
5th Do at E 66 Do
Suez F 82 Do
By this arrangement it will require 30 mules for each carriage or 120 mules for the four carriages in use, which leaves 30 available for loss by death or for being disabled and also for drawing heavy luggage across in 3 or 4 Carts.

153 Marginal note added by Waghorn: 'The whole of the establishment to be employed Coaling when mails are not in transit.'

154 A more detailed costing of each item appears among the papers of Lord William Bentinck.

Although this manuscript copy of 'The Plan' is filed among the papers of Sir John Cam Hobhouse, President of the Board of Control, it was addressed by Waghorn to the Secretary of the East India Company, H. Melvile. Not all the papers are present among the Hobhouse collection:

> Sir,
>
> My Letter (No. 1) of this day's date and the papers A.B.C.D.E.F. & G. which accompany this, give the expence & returns to be expected from such an Establishment as is therein detailed on the part of the Honorable Court of Directors.

Waghorn goes on to offer his services to the East India Company

> to contract for the conveyance of Mails & Coals between Alexandria, Suez & vice versa in three days (each month) for a period of 3 or 5 years as may be determined by the Honorable Court for the purpose of keeping up a monthly communication between England & India.

He asks that the items described in the 'First Outlay' should be placed under his control, to which

> I should require a salary of £500 p annum (and £150 for a Clerk) a ... packet agent in Egypt and an annual payment of £3500 for the conveyance of 2000 tons of Coal thro Egypt at 35/- p ton the charge now incurred by the Honorable Court & any greater or lesser quantity at the same rate for the ... Steamer at Suez.
>
> In return for the outlay & annual expenditure, The Honorable Court will be relieved from all other payments as now incurred under the present system (except the salaries of the packet agents), will have the advantage of a more rapid communication by three days each way for the despatches ... providing the means of a safe & Expeditious & at the same time comfortable & economical conveyance for those of their servants who are constantly passing to and from India and thus perfect their line of Steam Communication with India – in Egypt -
>
> I solicit most earnestly that the Honorable Court will be pleased to honor me with as early a reply to these five communications as

may suit their perfect convenience, as I am anxious to leave London on my return to Egypt on the 9th proximo unless the Honorable Court are desirous of prolonging my stay in furtherance of the object in which case it will give me great pleasure to receive their comments – […]

Annual Returns to be derived from conveyance of Passengers, Mails, &c.
For conveying 50 Passengers p. month to & from Alexandria & Suez @ £10 each: £6,000
Saving in conveying Mails as p. present by steam: £1,000
Saving caused by Mules in conveying 3000 Tons of Coal continually across the Desert at present carried by Camels & which cost about 35/- p. Ton: £5,250
For conveyance of Sundry small Parcels, Passengers &c. up the Nile during the idle part of the month, say about £1,000
£13,250

Given his altercation with Campbell and the associated reprimand by the 'Honourable Company', this submission for a contract to oversee the Company's interests in transporting mails, coal and passengers through Egypt is the action of a thick-skinned man!

The *Times* was on Waghorn's side, to judge by comments in the issue of 10 July. Having expressed satisfaction that news from India was reaching England more speedily:

There was an arrival yesterday by the Egyptian route of steam communication with India, and being now the third of the kind, at regular intervals of a month each, with dates from India of two months back, little more or less, the best proof is afforded that the system is working well. … (48 days only) from Bombay.

The paper went on to castigate the authorities for their treatment of Waghorn:

It may be collected from some of the letters by this arrival, that a despicable sort of intrigue is carrying on for the removal of Mr. WAGHORN from his station at Cairo, where he has taken up his residence as agent and superintendent of the steam communications with India. Now, if ever any man was entitled to derive a permanent reward and occupation from the completion of a great measure in which he has personally borne an active part, it is Mr. WAGHORN in relation to the communications with India through Egypt, which are wholly indebted to his extraordinary energy and perseverance for the state of perfection which they have now reached, as evinced in the arrival of this day and those which have preceded it. Colonel CAMPBELL, the Consul-General of Egypt, is said to have put himself prominently forward in this matter, and to have attempted to damage Mr. WAGHORN with the Government at home by decrying his arrangements, and attempting to substitute others which would appear to be very far from efficient. Whether inferior or not to those of Mr. WAGHORN, the services of the latter have been so clear and indisputable, that he was entitled to the opportunity of curing any defects, assuming them to exist, in his arrangements, by having them pointed out to him. In India, where the sense of Mr. WAGHORN'S services is more deeply felt than in England, the strongest desire is manifested to keep up the agency in Egypt through his means rather than any man of less experience and less power of exertion. This is a feeling which the Ministry at home and the India Company would do well to attend to, for Mr. WAGHORN can have no influence there which is not derived from his absolute fitness for the trust. He contrived, long before the matter was thought of by the Government and the Post-office at home, a series of most excellent arrangements for a speedy communication between Alexandria and Suez or Cosseir, which formed the only real difficulty in the route; and when the matter was taken up by the Post-office, with all the superior advantages of an official character, which Mr. WAGHORN then had not "all communications despatched by him" (to adopt the words of the Bombay Gazette) "had the advantage of the speediest mode of conveyance, and his packets were not unfrequently half way across the Mediterranean while the Government mails was lazily awaiting the arrival of the regular steamer. In fact, it may be said that it is principally owing to his exertions that the communication between India and England has been so greatly accelerated, and that the two countries have been brought, as it were, many thousand miles

> nearer to each other." This is literally true, and it is to be hoped public sympathy may be extended to a man who has no family influence, no patronage to back him, and whose claims on that account and under these circumstances ought to be enhanced in the minds of all men who can feel properly and judge rightly.[155]

That summer Waghorn received an official reply to one of his own from his successor, Captain John Lyons, which confirms that he was still actively pursuing the scheme:

> To T. Waghorn Esq^{r,} Cairo, July the 18th [1838]
> Sir, I have had the honor to receive y^{r} letter from Suez dated 11th Inst., acquainting me with your offer to convey the Mails from Suez to Alexandria. I have reported the circumstances to Col. Campbell in conformity with your order.

In October *The Times* returned to the theme that the English Government and Post-Office 'were unwilling agents' in efforts to improve communications with India, and the paper examined the regulations implemented for sending parcels via the Peninsular Steam Navigation Company between England and Gibraltar and the Navy packets to ports in the Mediterranean. It surmised:

> As this is a new order, and the range of the Mediterranean packets includes Egypt, whither few persons would desire to send anything except as the "half-way house" to India, the interpretation put upon it generally was that of an aid to the communications with that part of the world. Its operation is a limited one, since it prohibits "letters, bills, or money", but still, to the extent permitted, there was a practical good held out to those who have connexions in India, and might wish to avail themselves of the agencies established in Egypt to send light and valuable articles thither with greater speed than could otherwise be done. [...]
>
> Mr. WAGHORN, on behalf of his agency in Egypt, adopts implicitly the belief that this order is intended as an accommodation to the trade and intercourse with India, and he puts forward a

155 *The Times*, 10 July 1838, 5.

circular on the occasion, of which we give all that is material to the object in view:-

"Mr. Waghorn observes with much satisfaction the circular issued by the Peninsular Steam Navigation Company, under sanction of the Lords Commissioners of the Admiralty, for the conveyance of parcels by their Falmouth line of steamers between London and Alexandria, and, ever desirous to co-operate in giving the public all the facility in his power through Egypt, begs to state that his agent in Alexandria will, immediately on the arrival there of each steamer, receive all parcels for India, &c., addressed to his care, provided they have been first registered and paid for at his London office, which will guarantee their safe and rapid delivery (dangers of the sea excepted) at Bombay; and at Calcutta and Madras, when steam communication is fully established." [...]

The Times was dismissive of the exclusion of 'letters, bills and money' from the scheme:

Why should such articles be excluded which naturally constitute the chief value and utility of such a medium of communication? The answer may be readily anticipated, which is this—that the Post-office revenue would suffer, and thus it is that an administration which, if conducted on wise and liberal principles, must become a blessing to a commercial community, is turned into its bane and destruction, whenever it is made to appear that a particular object cannot be carried through without pecuniary loss, and every man of common sense must indignantly ask how long this "dog-in-the-manger" system is to govern us.

The paper had also met another problem with the official route:

We are assured by a correspondent, on whose veracity we can rely, that not only are parcels for India refused when presented, but also those which are suspected to contain parcels for India, though under cover and addressed to parties in Egypt. Thus, so far from any facility being given to the transmission, the most jealous care is exercised to prevent any advantage from the arrangement for India purposes, the only circumstance that could give it any

> value whatever. If this really arises, as our correspondent declares his suspicion to be, from a desire to embarrass and break up the new agencies struggling into existence in Egypt, a more disgraceful proceeding is not to be found in the annals of any government.[156]

For his part Waghorn soldiered on and soon announced the establishment of 'Waghorn and Co.' in a printed paper:[157]

> Cairo 26th Decr 1838
>
> In consequence of the much extended, and still expanding intercourse, between Europe and India by way of Egypt, I have found it necessary to form an Establishment to conduct the Agency business therewith connected; which, with the aid of powerful friends in England and India, commences on the 1st January next, under the firm of WAGHORN and C.°
>
> The primary objects of this Concern may be enumerated as follows:- the most expeditious transmission of Letters, Parcels, and Packages, between Great Britain, the Continent of Europe, India, and China – the transit of Merchandise, Bullion and Specie – the forwarding of Passengers by the best means, and in the most economical manner; at the same time affording them all necessary information and facilities – the Factorage business of the Red Sea – the sale of India and China commodities, as well as the purchase of the same in those Countries – and whatever other transactions may be connected with a Branch of Commerce, which the Steam Communication seems about to revive.
>
> To compass these objects, the House of WAGHORN and C.° will have Agencies in the principal Ports of the Red Sea, as well as at every eligible point throughout Egypt; while at Alexandria, a Mercantile House will be especially charged with the superintendence of its interests.
>
> The devotion of many years of my life, and all my energies, to the creation and development of the mighty enterprise still only in partial operation, affords an earnest of the promptitude, and

156 *The Times*, 26 October 1838, 4.

157 University of Nottingham, Portland Collection, Pw Jg 373.

> fidelity, with which any business will be conducted, that you may be pleased to confide to the Concern, which I have the honor now to recommend to your notice and support.
>
> Craving reference to the signatures at foot, I remain, with much respect, / Your Ob.^{dt} H.^{ble} Servt / THO.^{s} WAGHORN
>
> Signatures of THO.^{s} WAGHORN and GEORGE ROBBINS GLIDDON pp. Waghorn & Co.

George Robbins Gliddon was the American Vice-Consul in Egypt and, following the difficulties which subsequently overtook the enterprise, himself prepared a plan for establishing the Overland Route. In 1841 he visited London and distributed this to the British government. Lord Palmerston approved it and it was actually adopted by the Peninsular and Oriental Company as the basis for their scheme. However, through jealousy and intrigues Gliddon was excluded from it.[158] It appears that he soon fell out with Waghorn and had separated from him by July 1839. Writing to Benjamin Brown, Gliddon revealed:

> After your departure from this, Waghorn arrived from England, and in a few days behaved like a fool and a scamp, and we parted company. I brought action against him [for paying what was due for a year's contract], and got my claims settled.[159]

There were other American connections around this time. One was James Ewing Cooley, who thinly disguised references to Waghorn as 'Mr. Firkins'. According to Gliddon, Cooley 'accepted and received all kinds of civilities and attentions from this Mr. Firkins, although in the most ungrateful manner.' Gliddon went further in vilifying Waghorn after the break with him:

> By his impostures, his deceptions, his vile propensities, his utter disregard to principle, and his infamous notoriety, Mr. Firkins,

158 Obituary of George Gliddon, Academy of Natural Sciences, 128 ANSP ms 239, no date; author unknown.

159 Gliddon in Cairo to Brown in the Upper Country, 23 September 1839; J. Clements Library, University of Michigan, Benjamin Brown Collection.

> since the summer of 1839, had sifted himself down so low in the estimation of respectable residents in Egypt, that he was 'blackballed' from all intercourse with them, and reduced to the most ludicrous artifices to inveigle into his snare unfortunate strangers … Mr. Firkins is Author of an Annual, styled 'Egypt in 1837' – 'in 1838' – 'in 1839', as well as of a correspondence, finally rejected by the *Morning Chronicle* in 1838. … In the Autumn of 1840, wherein he was publically bastinadoed for insulting the Commandant of the National Guard. …[160]

This last remark seems to concern an altercation at Alexandria reported in *The Times* of 9 October 1840, but it was not Waghorn himself who was punished:

> 'As Mr Waghorn was returning from taking a drive with his lady, he was informed that one of his domestics, a soldier of the redif (militia), had received the bastlaade, and was under arrest for having absented himself during seven days from parade. He immediately drove off to the residence of General Garbi Bey, and, leaving his lady in the carriage, jumped out, ran to the prison door, and used every effort to break it open. The disturbance attracting the General's attention, he sent out word to Mr. Waghorn, inviting him in, that he might learn what had occurred. To this Mr. Waghorn, who was greatly exasperated, answered in English, and was therefore only intelligible by his gestures. Meanwhile Mrs. Waghorn drove off, and the General's clerk arrived, between whom and Mr. Waghorn a violent altercation arose, which ended in the clerk's receiving a blow from Mr. Waghorn. The storm increased, and the General was threatened. He had sent a message to acquaint the English Consulate of the affray, but no one returned. In these circumstances he directed his servants to remove Mr. Waghorn, at the same time strictly enjoining them to do him no injury, but to carry him off with all precaution. The first man who approached Mr. Waghorn

160 James Ewing Cooley, *The American in Egypt, with rambles through Arabia, Petraea and the Holy Land during the years 1839 and 1840*, [with appendix by George Robbins Gliddon], Philadelphia, 1842. The 1837 and 1838 publications confirm Waghorn as 'Mr. Firkins', but no 1839 issue is known. (But Wheatley, *op. cit.* also mentions an 1839 edition.)

> received a blow from his fist; he was however got out of the room, on which he seized hold of a Moor by the hair of his head. Every effort was made to induce Mr. Waghorn to release the unfortunate captive, but in vain. At last a bystander drawing his sabre cut off the Moor's hair, and thus released him from Mr. Waghorn's iron grasp. Mr. Waghorn was then carried off in procession and conducted without the yard-gate, which, out of precaution, was closed behind him. When the Viceroy heard of this affray he seemed highly amused, saying, with a hearty laugh, 'Waghorn is my friend, and if he [the General] comes to me for satisfaction, he shall not have it.' When Garbi Bey applied to Mehemet Ali [the ruler] for satisfaction, he was put to silence. This affair, it seems, originated in the following facts:-"Mr. Waghorn's servant had married a young Arab, without the consent of her brother, an officer of the redif, who, applying to his colonel, prevailed on him to call his sister's husband before him, and urge him to divorce her, holding out as an inducement that he should keep the dowry, which he would otherwise have to give up in the case of a divorce. The young man refused to comply. It then occurred to them that he had been enlisted in the redif previously to the order obtained by Mr. Waghorn in favour of his domestics. Profiting by the fact that the subsequent order did not destroy the previous enrolment, they ordered his daily attendance on parade. He had been absent seven days when he was apprehended.

During his time in Egypt Waghorn wrote a pamphlet extolling the country's merits and the desirability of improving relations between England and Egypt for the benefit of trade and of communications with India and beyond: *Egypt as it is in 1837.* His hope that his advocacy would be taken up by Parliament was evidently in vain, for a second edition was printed, *Egypt as it is in 1838*, dedicated to 'General the Right Honourable Lord William Bentinck, M.P. late Governor General of British India':

> My Lord,
> "Egypt in 1838" is most respectfully dedicated to your Lordship; and its object is to impose upon you the onerous task of convincing Parliament that times and circumstances, as well as foreign intrigues, call upon England to will the independence of Egypt,

as a powerful ally in promoting the stability of British interests, particularly in the East.

The Times published another strongly worded condemnation of the Post-office as an official body which sought to crush Waghorn's enterprise. Full of praise for his efforts, it noted that on 20 April 1839:

> A subscription is raising in the city to which the names of many of the first mercantile firms are already attached, for the purpose of assisting Mr. Waghorn to defray the extraordinary expenses to which he has been subjected by the Post-office, in transmitting letters from Egypt to London and back. Such are the services rendered to commerce and the country generally by the exertions of this gentleman in improving the communications with India, that there probably never occurred any case of the kind in which so strong a case for protection and support was established. Our acquaintance with Mr. Waghorn is now of above 12 years' standing, when his great projects were still in embryo, and we were led to afford him our cordial aid by the powerful recommendations he brought with him from India and the Cape of Good Hope, and by marking in him an ardent, intelligent, and disinterested mind, which led him to overlook or to disregard the immense difficulties which lay in his way. We came early to the conclusion that all which it was possible for a single individual to accomplish would be achieved by Mr. Waghorn. In that long interval we have kept him in view, moving as he did from India to England and back again, once or twice in every year; at one time urging the merchants of the Indian presidencies to second him, as they did most cordially, in the cause to which he has devoted himself; at another fixing himself for months together in Egypt, contriving means to secure the friendship of the Pasha, and for lessening the difficulties of the route through the desert; then, on his return to England, engaged in making converts of the merchants in London and the outports to the practicability as well as the great importance of his undertaking, encountering some personal but more official hostility, yet making way in spite of all opposition. So great was his activity and perseverance, that an impression was gradually made upon the Board of Trade, the Board of Control, and that

other almost unapproachable board (by any private effort), the East India Direction. The power that sustained him in these immense and long-continued efforts is almost beyond comprehension, but the fact is quite undeniable, that whatever has been done for the improvement of the communications with India, and we hold it to be one of the greatest and most substantial benefits ever conferred upon the country, is entirely and exclusively owing to the exertions of Mr. Waghorn. All that has been done by others has been done by following in the path he was the first to traverse and point out. Even now, though the realization of his plans is ostensibly confided to the Post-office and the East India Company, with all the knowledge he has collected and all the facilities he has provided, after driving him from any participation in arrangements which, but for him, would never have existed, we find Mr. Waghorn, with energy scarcely slackened by the years which have since rolled over him, establishing a private agency of his own for the communications with India, and repeatedly getting the start in point of time over both his powerful rivals.

Opposition, therefore, in this stage of his career, is, in appearance, quite exhausted. But there is yet one more danger to be surmounted. Mr. Waghorn himself can undertake conveyance only for a portion of the route, though he can superintend the whole; he must be indebted for the rest to the assistance of the Post-office arrangements of this country, and is at their mercy for the terms on which they think fit to render him this service—that is, he is at the mercy of a power which he has repeatedly humbled and mortified, and offended consequently past all forgiveness. The terms therefore are such as to stifle his undertaking, to crush him utterly, unless some friendly hand is stretched out for his support. This then is the object of the subscription now raising in the city, and wherever the circumstances out of which it arose have become known, the sympathy with Mr. Waghorn has been unequivocally manifested. When they are more generally diffused and reach the outports and manufacturing districts, where his services are still better understood and more highly valued than in London, a large and liberal subscription may safely be anticipated.

The Post-office tax, here referred to, is recently imposed and amounts to 2s. per ounce upon letters from Malta to Alexandria

> alone, besides other charges. If not expressly got up to crush Mr. Waghorn, we should say that there is the strongest prima facie evidence of it, and if so, it discovers a meanness and baseness of spirit which should be held up to universal execration.
>
> The subscriptions raised in the city for this purpose, in the course of the last three days, amount to nearly 500l.[161]

In Alexandria on 12 May 1839 the Scottish artist David Roberts (1796-1864)

> received from Colonel Campbell an invitation to breakfast and afterwards to accompany him to an interview with the Pasha, which had been arranged for that day. Our party started for the Arsenal, where Mehemet Ali was ready to receive us. After passing through numerous guards we were ushered into the presence-chamber, which, from the window, commanded a magnificent view of the harbour. The fleet, consisting of about twenty sail of the line fully equipped, the Arsenal, the dockyards, and numerous batteries – displaying a power created by his own forethought and energies – lay before us, a glorious scene. The room was spacious and lofty, and crowded with officers in rich uniforms, many of them wearing the decorations. The Pasha was in simple costume, without any mark of distinction upon him which Nature had not stamped, and which was acknowledged by the respect paid to him by all present. His reception of Colonel Campbell seemed to be most cordial, and as unpretending as the reception of an old friend. Having received us and taken his seat on the divan, he beckoned his visitors to be seated. Coffee was then served to us by attendants in rich costumes. The Pasha alone smoked. Only officers of the very highest rank are invited to this enjoyment in his presence.

161 *The Times*, 22 April 1839, 4.

Roberts painted the scene representing

> the Pasha seated, whilst Colonel (now General) Patrick Campbell explained to him the proposed route across the Desert. Artem Bey interpreted to His Highness in Turkish the conversation, which was carried on in Italian. There were present, Bogos Bey, his oldest friend and first minister; the Pasha's grandson, Abbas Pasha, the present Viceroy of Egypt; Linant Bey, the French engineer, and others. Among those with Colonel Campbell were Lieutenant Waghorn, the projector of the Overland route to India, and who has since been so indefatigable in its accomplishment; Mr. Tatum, the distinguished Coptic scholar; Mr. Roberts; Mr. Pell, and other English gentlemen. The interview was partly to congratulate His Highness on his recent safe return from upper Egypt, and partly in connection with the projected plans for improving the transit of passengers and merchandise across the Isthmus of Suez.[162]

---

162 David Roberts, *The Holy Land*, London, 1855. Margery Sankey, *op. cit.*, 89, notes that Waghorn was not entitled to the lieutenant's uniform when Roberts painted him in 1839, although he had acquired it by 1855 when the lithograph was made.

In 1839 much diplomatic and military activity was concerned with the likely expansion of Mehemet Ali's empire, following the battle of Nisib, in which Turkey was defeated. Five European nations gathered at a Congress in Vienna to thrash out a solution which they intended to impose on Ali. Waghorn was sent by Mehemet Ali and English merchants in Egypt as a confidential messenger to Koshru Pasha, Grand Vizier to the Sultan at Constantinople, as well as to Lord Ponsonby, who was at the time also there as Ambassador from England. Waghorn also alerted the mercantile firms to possible disruption to their activities, as reported in the *Times* of 29 October:

> The private letters received today from Alexandria, which are dated on the 7th inst., are important in a commercial point of view, since they refer to the stoppage of the communications with India through Egypt as a probable event, should the allied Powers proceed to a blockade of the port of Alexandria. In fact, Mr. Waghorn, who had recently returned to Egypt from a visit to Constantinople, which he had made at the instance of some of the English merchants resident in Egypt, has issued circulars to the merchants both of England and of India, to give them warning that such a turn of affairs was likely to take place, and to enable them to guard against the consequences. According to the private letters, the policy of the Pasha of Egypt continued to be of the same wavering character. He was apparently firm in his declarations that he would neither abandon any of his territorial acquisitions nor surrender the Turkish fleet, but it was believed at the same time that he relied mainly on the want of sufficient unison among the allied Powers to take any decisive measures against him; and that, were he once persuaded of the contrary, a different tone would be adopted. … The following is a copy of the circular of Mr. Waghorn above referred to:—
>
> ALEXANDRIA, Oct. 7, 1839
>
> TO THE CHAMBERS OF COMMERCE OF CALCUTTA, MADRAS, BOMBAY, AND CEYLON, AND CANTON, ALSO OF LONDON, LIVERPOOL, BRISTOL, GLASGOW, BIRMINGHAM, MANCHESTER, AND SHEFFIELD.

Gentlemen—The present critical state of affairs is a political point of view between Egypt and Turkey in which the representatives of the five great Powers of Europe are now assembled in Congress at Vienna to arrange and settle, may not be so easy a matter, if Egypt is to be shorne of the ascendancy she has had ceded to her by the late Sultan in Syria, Arabia and Candia. Ever anxious, ever watchful, as I have been to improve the mercantile interests of my country, by opening and establishing a rapid channel of intercourse through Egypt for the purposes of trade, I must confirm that I am now obliged to write them that there is a chance of its being speedily shut up by the blockade of the port of Alexandria by England or France on the behalf of the above five Powers in order to carry out by force what they may term 'a settlement of the Eastern question'.

To my mind England and India have more to lose than other countries on the score of this communication, already become so valuable, not only to the interests of the merchants, but to all other interests of our country, in every point of view, without any exception.

Under the idea that politicians, in looking to the interests of the Porte, may overlook those of Egypt, and undertake by force to compel her to obedience, my candid opinion is that Egypt will not yield one inch without that right being guaranteed which she has gained, and had ceded to her, and which countries she is now already improving in all things.

Without more comment I warn you all, the Chambers of Commerce (I now write to each), to begin and calculate upon such stoppage to the communications of your mercantile arrangements and business, thinking that you are not at present prepared to have your letters and business conducted in nine months instead of three by its stoppage, even partially, for a few months.

I do not say that such stoppage is certain, that is out of my power to foresee; but I feel it my bounden duty to ask your Chambers to look forward that it may happen speedily.

With respective compliments,
I have the honour to remain, gentlemen,
Your faithful servant,
THOMAS WAGHORN.

The same month Waghorn wrote

> when the news arrived at Alexandria from Bombay, of Sir John (late Lord) Keane's success at Ghuznee, he [Waghorn], one day after her Majesty's steamer had left Alexandria, obtained the use of the Pasha of Egypt's own steamer, *Generoso*, and personally commanded that vessel, and conveyed that mail to Malta, which was immediately sent on by the admiral there to England.[163]

In the event it seems the mails continued in spite of hostilities. One quite farcical story bears this out:

> In 1840, during the attack on the castle of Gabriel, the Admiral in charge of the British squadron perceived a white flag flying from the castle of the Pasha, hostile proceedings were immediately suspended, and a boat from the Admiral's ship sent to the fort; upon reaching the landing place the officer in charge was surprised by having the overland mail, which had just arrived, presented to him with the Pasha's compliments. The British Admiral acknowledged the compliment, and the firing again commenced.[164]

On 22 November 1839 'Mr. Waghorn had presented to his Highness a portrait of Queen Victoria in her state robes. It was received very graciously, and ordered to be placed in the Harem.'[165] She had been crowned just eighteen months before. 'Mr. Waghorn at the same time presented his own portrait to the Pasha, which was ordered to be sent to the Hall of the Dragomans.' This was probably the lithograph of the portrait by Charles Baxter (1809-1879) which shows Waghorn with *Egypt as it is in 1837* on his desk.[166] Typically, Waghorn insisted

---

163 *The Working Man's Friend, and Family Instructor*, London, 1850, p. 116. The *Generosa* reached Malta from Alexandria on 19 October 1839. *Manchester Courier …*, 9 November 1839.

164 *The Illustrated Australian Magazine*, vol. I (1850-1), p. 225.

165 *The Times*, 11 December 1839; *Royal Cornwall Gazette*, 20 December 1839.

166 The original painting, which had been handed down in Waghorn's sister Sarah's family in Australia, was sold at Sotheby's on 21 November 1979 [misattributed in the catalogue to Sir George Hayter]; the lithograph version is National Portrait Gallery D37969.

on having his own say in the conflict, his friendship with the Pasha colouring his argument and showing the forthcoming congress on whose side he was placed. In 1840 he published a 23 page pamphlet, *Truths concerning Mahomet Ali, Egypt, Arabia, and Syria: addressed to the five powers, or to their representatives in the contemplated congress.* He also wrote numerous letters to the press; those of May, June and July were 'still neglected' on 14 September when he wrote to Lord Palmerston that the English reaction to a 'partial insurrection' 'in the vicinity of Mount Lebanus' was unjustified and un-necessary.[167]

The antiquarian Charles Roach Smith felt Mehemet Ali had acted nobly in keeping the mails and Overland Route open in spite of England being one of the powers fighting against him in successfully restoring Syria to Turkey. Smith decided to commission a medal for the Pasha and was advised to consult Waghorn about it. This he did, the two men became friends and the medal was produced and presented.[168] Smith and Waghorn were the two secretaries acting for the committee set up to administer the funding and creation of the medal, using Waghorn's office at 34 Cornhill to receive subscriptions and as a place where the medal could be inspected. For one guinea each subscriber received a bronze copy of the medal and their name 'attached to an address in vellum and gold.'

167 *John Bull*, 17 October 1840; see also 24 and 31 May 1840.

168 Details are in Charles Roach Smith, *Retrospections, Social and Archaeological*, vol. I, London, 1883, 132-6; also 'Medal to Mehemet Ali, struck in England', *The Numismatic Chronicle and Journal of the Numismatic Society*, Vol. 5, 1842-3, 146-150.

MEHEMET ALI PACHA
FROM THE COMMITTEE
THE FRIEND
OF SCIENCE COMMERCE
& ORDER WHO PROTECTED
THE SUBJECTS AND PROPERTY
OF ADVERSE POWERS
AND KEPT OPEN
THE OVERLAND ROUTE
TO INDIA
1840

7

TWO TRAVELLERS TRY THE OVERLAND ROUTE

By 1840 the Overland Route was increasingly used and we are fortunate that a number of accounts survive illustrating the pleasures and perils of the journey between Alexandria and Suez as it became established.

Emma Roberts

'The unsettled state of affairs between Mehemet Ali and the European powers' were a cause for concern of the writer Emma Roberts (1791-1840) as she prepared to experience the Overland Route in September and October 1839. Her journey was undertaken in fulfilment of a literary project, in which she had promised to write of her experiences for the *Asiatic Journal*. The whole appeared as *Notes of an Overland Journey through France and Egypt to Bombay*, published posthumously (with a memoir) in 1841.[169] She has no axe to grind, but offers an honest opinion of the pleasures and rigours of the journey, which was still being developed. The following extracts summarize her experiences of the Egyptian section, which was not yet under control of the Transit Company established by the Pasha. It would appear from her comments that Waghorn's principal concern remained the speedy transit of the mails, but he also had in place an operation which could offer a good service to passengers under his agency. Nevertheless it is interesting to note that competition between Hill & Co. and Waghorn continued to this time. Having reached Malta, Emma 'thought it advisable to make the best of my way to the Red Sea, and defer the pleasure, which a more protracted residence promised, until my return in the ensuing

169 The ensuing quotations come from Chapters 3: Marseilles to Alexandria; 4: Alexandria to Boulak; 5: Cairo; 6: The Desert.

year.' Rather than wait for a merchant vessel she embarked on the government steamer *Volcano*, but found

> We were now to be taught a new lesson—the extreme nonchalance with which the officers of a Government steamer treat the passengers who have the misfortune to choose these boats instead of making the voyage on board merchant vessels. Some minutes elapsed before any notice was taken of us, or any assistance afforded in getting up our baggage; our own people being obliged to look on and do nothing, since, had they touched the ship, they would have been obliged to perform eighteen days of quarantine.

Having left Malta on 25th September, they arrived at Alexandria on the 30th and took up residence in Rey's Hotel, 'in which we found every comfort we could desire.' However,

> As I had not intended to reach Alexandria so soon, neither Miss E. nor myself had given notice of our approach; consequently, there was nothing in readiness. … In this emergency, we applied to Mr. Waghorn, who, in the expectation that I might wish to remain at Alexandria, had most kindly prepared an apartment for my reception at his own house. The aspect of [political] affairs, however, did not admit of my running any risks, and I therefore determined to proceed to Suez without delay. Under these circumstances, he did the best that the nature of the case permitted; assured me that I should have his own boat, which, though small, was perfectly clean, when we got to the Nile, and provided me with all that I required for the passage. Mrs. Waghorn also recommended a servant, whose appearance we liked, and whom we instantly engaged for the trip to Suez.

Alexandria[170]

> I had brought letters to the consul-general, and to several residents in Alexandria, who immediately paid me visits at our hotel. Colonel Campbell was most particularly kind and attentive, offering one of the government janissaries as an escort to Cairo; an offer which we most readily accepted, and which proved of infinite service to us.

Emma learned that Waghorn's little Nile vessel would soon have more competitors:

> a large handsome boat, with ladies' cabin detached, and capable of carrying forty passengers, had been built by the merchants of Alexandria, and when completed—and it only wanted painting and fitting up—would convey travellers up the canal to Atfee, a distance which, towed by horses, it would perform in twelve hours. Small iron steamers were expected from England, to ply upon the Nile, and with these accommodations, nothing would be more easy and pleasant than a journey which sometimes takes many days to accomplish, and which is frequently attended with inconvenience and difficulty.

170 Pictures in this chapter are taken from *The Illustrated London News*, May 1845.

She continues:

> We found that Mrs. Waghorn had provided Miss E. and myself with beds, consisting each of a good mattress stuffed with cotton, a pillow of the same, and a quilted coverlet, also stuffed with cotton. She lent us a very handsome canteen … As there may be a danger of not meeting with a canteen exactly suited to the wants of the traveller, for sale at Alexandria, it is advisable to procure one previously to leaving Europe; those fitted up with tin saucepans are necessary, for it is not easy to carry cooking apparatus in any other form. We did not encumber ourselves with either chair or table, but would afterwards have been glad of a couple of camp-stools. Our supplies consisted of tea, coffee, wine, wax-candles (employing a good glass lanthorn for a candlestick), fowls, bread, fruit, milk, eggs, and butter; a pair of fowls and a piece of beef being ready-roasted for the first meal. We also carried with us some bottles of filtered water. The baggage of the party was conveyed upon three camels and a donkey, and we formed a curious-looking cavalcade as we left the hotel.

Unfortunately, the boat to take the party to Atfee was 'forlorn and uncomfortable … dirt was now the predominant feature, while the holes and crannies on every side promised free egress to the vermin, apparently long tenants of the place.' After 'a long and dismal night' they eventually reached Atfee around noon.

> The place was in great confusion, in consequence of the actual presence of the Pasha, who, for himself and suite, we were told, had engaged every boat excepting the one belonging to Mr. Waghorn, in which the mails, entrusted to him, had been put. … [Once on board this vessel] we … found that, in the narrow limits to which we were confined, we must only retain our carpet-bags and dressing-cases. The small cabin which occupies the stern was surrounded on three sides with lockers, which formed seats, but which were too narrow to hold our beds; moveable planks, of different dimensions, to suite the shape of the boat, fitted in, making the whole flush when requisite, and forming a space amply wide enough for our mattresses, but in which we could not stand upright. To our great

> joy, we found the whole extremely clean, and in perfect repair, so that we could easily submit to the minor evils that presented themselves. … A clerk of Mr. Waghorn's, an European, who had the charge of the mails, went up in the boat with us.

THE NILE-BOAT.

(from James Barber, Overland Guide Book)

By noon the next day they were half-way to Cairo.

> Arriving at a village, Mr. Waghorn's agent determined upon going on shore, and carrying the mails on the backs of donkeys, in order to ensure their arrival at Suez time enough to meet the steamer. He had been assured that we had passed the Government mails in the night, but had not been able to ascertain the fact himself. I think it necessary to mention this, as a proof of the indefatigable endeavours made by Mr. Waghorn to ensure the speediest method of transit.

After three nights on board, the party reached Boulak on the evening of 4 October, but had some difficulty in gaining entrance to Cairo due to the lateness of the hour. Two days were spent sightseeing and shopping, during which news of the *Berenice* having reached Suez arrived, together with the homeward bound mails. Spurning the offer of a carriage across the desert, Emma declared

I wished particularly to proceed leisurely to Suez, and in the manner in which travellers had hitherto been conveyed. The mighty changes which are now effecting in Egypt, should nothing occur to check their progress, will soon render the track to India so completely beaten, and so deeply worn by wheels, that I felt anxious to take advantage of the opportunity now offered to traverse the desert in a more primitive way. [...]

We found the equipages in which we were to cross the desert waiting for us at the City of Tombs. They consisted of donkey-chairs, one being provided for each of the females of the party, while my friend Miss E. had also an extra donkey, with a saddle, to ride upon occasionally. Nothing could be more comfortable than these vehicles; a common arm-chair was fastened into a sort of wooden tray, which projected in front about a foot, thereby enabling the passenger to carry a small basket or other package; the chairs were then slung by the arms to long bamboos, one upon either side, and these, by means of ropes or straps placed across, were fastened upon the backs on donkeys, one in front, the other behind. Five long and narrow vehicles of this kind, running across the desert, made a sufficiently droll and singular appearance, and we did nothing but admire each other as we went along. The movement was delightfully easy, and the donkeys, though not travelling at a quick pace, got on very well. Our cavalcade consisted besides of two stout donkeys, which carried the beds and carpet-bags of the whole party, thus enabling us to send the camels a-head: the three men-servants were also mounted upon donkeys, and there were three or four spare ones, in case any of the others should knock up upon the road. [But] the extra animals were so weak and inefficient, that they could not have supplied the places of any of those in use. There were eight or ten donkey-men, and a boy. ...

A halting place

Our first stage was the shortest of the whole, and we came to the rest-house, or travellers' bungalow, just as night closed in … The bungalow was not yet completed, which we found rather an advantage, since it seems to be exceedingly questionable whether the buildings erected for the accommodation of travellers on the track to Suez will be habitable even for a few hours in the course of another year. The funds of the Steam-committee have been lamentably mismanaged in this instance. However, there being no windows, we were enabled to enjoy the fresh air, and the room we occupied, not having been long whitewashed, was perfectly clean.

Nothing can have been worse planned than the construction of these houses. The only entrance is in front, down a narrow passage, open at the top, and having apartments on either side, the two in front being sleeping-rooms for travellers, with a kitchen and other offices beyond, and at the back of all a stable, which occupies the whole width of the building. The consequence is, that all the animals, biped and quadruped, inhabiting the stable, must pass the traveller's door, who is regaled with the smell proceeding from the said stable, cook-rooms, &c.; all the insects they collect, and all the feathers from the fowls slaughtered upon the spot; the plan being, when parties arrive, to drive the unhappy creatures into the house, kill and pluck them immediately.

The persons in care of these bungalows are usually a mongrel sort of Franks [i.e. Europeans], who have no idea of cleanliness, and are regardless of the most unsavoury odours. The furniture of the rooms consisted of a deal table and a moveable divan of wicker-work, while another, formed of the same solid materials as the house, spread in the Egyptian fashion along one side. …

Occasionally we saw a small party of Bedouins, easily distinguished by the fierce countenances glaring from beneath the large rolls of cloth twisted over their turbans, and round their throats, leaving nothing besides flashing eyes, a strongly developed nose, and a bushy beard, to be seen. One or two, superior to the rest, were handsomely dressed, armed to the teeth, and rode camels well-groomed and richly caparisoned; wild-looking warriors, whom it would not have been agreeable to meet were the country in a less tranquil state.

To the present ruler of Egypt we certainly owe the security now enjoyed in passing the desert; a party of ladies, having only three servants and a few donkey-drivers, required no other protection, though our beds, dressing-cases, and carpet-bags, to say nothing of the camels laden with trunks and portmanteaus a-head, must have been rather tempting to robbers by profession. The Pasha is the only person who has hitherto been able to oblige the Sheikhs to respect the property of those travellers not strong enough to protect themselves from outrage. It is said that occasionally these Bedouins, when desirous of obtaining water, make no scruple of helping themselves to the supplies at the bungalows; the will, therefore, is not wanting to commit more serious depredations. Consequently, in maintaining a good understanding with Egypt, we must likewise endeavour to render its sovereign strong enough to keep the neighbouring tribes in awe.

Having made a slight refection on the road, of hard-boiled eggs, bread, grapes, and apples, we came up at mid-day to a rest-house, where it was determined we should remain for an hour or two, to water the donkeys, and afford them needful repose, while we enjoyed a more substantial luncheon. …

Our five vehicles sometimes trotted abreast, … but more frequently they would spread themselves all over the plain, the guides allowing their beasts to take their own way, provided they moved straight forward. … Once or twice, the ropes slipped, and my chair came to the ground; fortunately it had not to fall far; or a donkey would stumble and fall, but no serious accident occurred; and though one of the party, being behind, and unable to procure assistance in righting the carriage, was obliged to walk a mile or two, we were all speedily in proper trim again. Towards evening, the easy motion of the chair, and the inclination I felt to close my eyes, after staring about all day, caused me to fall asleep; and again, much sooner than I had expected, I found myself at the place of our destination. …

We were, as usual, rather late the following morning; our dear little play-thing, the baby, bore the journey wonderfully; but it seemed very requisite that she should have good and unbroken sleep at night, and we found so little inconvenience in travelling in the day-time, that we could make no objection to an arrangement which contributed so much to her health and comfort. … I mention her often, not only for the delight she afforded us, but also to show how very easily infants at her tender age—she was not more than seven months old—could be transported across the desert.

During this day's journey, we met several parties, passengers of the steamer, coming from Suez. … The monotony usually complained of in desert travelling cannot be very strongly felt between Cairo and Suez, for though there is little else but sand to be seen, yet it is so much broken and undulated, that there is always some diversity of objects. … We made a short rest, in the middle of the day, at a travellers' bungalow; and just as we were leaving it, one of Mr. Hill's caravans arrived—a tilted cart upon springs, and drawn by a pair of horses; it contained a family, passengers by the *Berenice*, consisting of a gentleman and his wife, two children and a servant. We conversed with them for a few minutes, and learned that they had not found the road very rough, and that where it was heavy they added a camel as a leader.

At this place we found some difficulty in purchasing water for the donkeys; competition in the desert is not, as in other places, beneficial to the traveller. By some understanding with the Steam Committee, Mr. Hill has put his people into the bungalows; and they, it appears, have orders not to sell water to persons who travel under Mr. Waghorn's agency. If the original purpose of these houses was to afford general accommodation, the shelter which cannot be refused is rendered nugatory by withholding the supplies necessary for the subsistence of men and cattle. We procured water at last; but every thing attainable at these places is dear and bad.

We arrived, at rather an early hour, at our halting place for the night; and as we considered it to be desirable to get into Suez as speedily as possible, we agreed to start by three o'clock on the following morning. … We made no stay at the rest-house, which we reached about nine o'clock in the morning. …

This was now our fourth day upon the desert, and we had not sustained the smallest inconvenience; the heat, even at noon, being very bearable, and the sand not in the least degree troublesome. Doubtless, at a less favourable period of the year, both would prove difficult to bear. The wind, we were told, frequently raised the sand in clouds; and though the danger of being buried beneath the tombs thus made, we had reason to believe, was greatly exaggerated, yet the plague of sand is certainly an evil to be dreaded, and travellers will do well to avoid the season in which it prevails. The speed of my donkeys increasing, rather than diminishing, after we left the well, for they seemed to know that Suez would terminate their journey, I crossed the intervening three miles very quickly, and was soon at the walls of the town.

Distance lends no enchantment to the view of Suez. It is difficult to fancy that the few miserable buildings, appearing upon the margin of the sea, actually constitute a town; and the heart sinks at the approach to a place so barren and desolate. My donkeys carried me through a gap in the wall, which answered all the purposes of a gateway, and we passed along broken ground and among wretched habitations, more fit for the abode of savage beasts than men. Even the superior description of houses bore so forlorn and dilapidated an appearance, that I actually trembled as I approached them, fearing that my guide would stop, and tell me that, my journey was at an end.

Before I had time to make any observations upon the place to which I was conducted, I found myself at the foot of a flight of steps, and reaching a landing place, saw another above, and Mohammed[171] descending to meet me. I followed him to the top, and crossing a

171 The servant recommended by Mrs Waghorn.

large apartment, which served as dining and drawing room, entered a passage which led to a light and certainly airy bed-chamber; for half the front wall, and a portion of one of the sides, were entirely formed of wooden trellice, which admitted, with the utmost freedom, all the winds of heaven, the sun, and also the dust. There was a mat upon the floor, and the apartment was whitewashed to the rafters, which were in good condition; and upon Mohammed's declaration that it was free from rats, I felt an assurance of a share of comfort which I had dared not expect before. There were two neat beds, with musquito-curtains, two tables, and washing apparatus, but no looking-glass; an omission which I could supply, though we had dispensed with such a piece of luxury altogether in the desert. Well supplied with hot and cold water, I had enjoyed the refreshment of plenteous ablutions, and nearly completed my toilet, before the arrival of the friends I had so completely distanced. I made an attempt to sit down to my desk, but was unable to write a line, and throwing myself on my bed full dressed, I fell asleep in a moment, and enjoyed the deepest repose for an hour, or perhaps longer.

Waghorn's Hotel at Suez

We arrived at Suez on Wednesday, the 9th of October, and were told to hold ourselves in readiness to embark on Friday at noon. We were not sorry for this respite, especially as we found our hotel, which was kept by a person in the employment of Mr. Waghorn, more comfortable than could have been hoped for from its exterior. The greatest annoyance we sustained was from the dust, which was brought in by a very strong wind through the lattices. I endeavoured to remedy this evil, in some degree, by directing the servants of the house to nail a sheet across the upper portion of the perforated wood-work. The windows of our chamber commanded as good a view of Suez as the place afforded; one at the side overlooked an irregular open space, which stretched between the house and the sea. At some distance opposite, there were one or two mansions of much better appearance than the rest, and having an air of comfort imparted to them by outside shutters, of new and neat construction. These we understood to be the abodes of officers in the Pasha's service. Mehemet Ali is said to be extremely unwilling to allow English people to build houses for themselves at Suez; while he freely grants permission to their residence at Alexandria and Cairo, he seems averse to their settling upon the shores of the Red Sea. Mr. Waghorn and Mr. Hill are, therefore, compelled to be content to fit up the only residences at their disposal in the best manner that circumstances will admit. I had no opportunity of forming any opinion respecting Mr. Hill's establishment, but am able to speak very well of the accommodation afforded by the hotel at which we sojourned. …

There was nothing in Suez that could make a longer stay desirable, and we quitted it without regret. My journey through Egypt had been much too rapid for me to presume to give any decided opinion concerning the strongly agitated question respecting the merits of the Pasha's government. It is very evident that he has not learned the most instructive lesson of political economy, nor has yet understood that the way to render himself powerful is to make his subjects rich; nevertheless, though his exactions and monopolies may be felt at present as very serious evils, yet, in establishing manufactories, and in embodying a national force, there can be no doubt that he has sown the seeds of much that is good; and should his government, after his death, fall

> into the hands of people equally free from religious prejudices, we may reasonably hope that they will entertain more enlarged and liberal views, and thus render measures, now difficult to bear, of incalculable advantage to the future prosperity of the country.
>
> The British Consul politely offered to conduct myself and my female friends on board the steamer; he accordingly called for us, and I bade, as I hoped, a last adieu to Suez, it being my wish and intention to return home by way of Cosseir. Previous to our embarkation, a series of regulations had been placed in our hands for the engagement of passages in the Honourable Company's armed steamers, with instructions to passengers, &c.
>
> Upon repairing to our cabin, Miss E. and myself were surprised and disappointed at the miserable accommodation it afforded. The three cabins allotted to the use of the ladies had been appropriated, in two instances, to married couples, and we were obliged to put up with one of smaller size, which had the additional inconvenience of opening into the public saloon. There were no Venetian blinds to the door, consequently, the only means of obtaining a free circulation of air was to have it open. A locker with a hinged shelf, which opened like a shutter, and thus afforded space for one mattress to be placed upon it, ran along one side of the cabin, under the port-hole, but the floor was the only visible means of accommodation for the second person crammed by Government regulation into this den. There was not a place in which a wash-hand basin could be put, so awkwardly were the doors arranged, to one of which there was no fastening whatsoever. Altogether, the case seemed hopeless, and as cock-roaches were walking about the vessel by dozens, the prospect of sleeping on the ground was anything but agreeable, especially with the feeling that we were paying at the rate of four pounds a day for our accommodation.

Some months earlier another lady had written of her experience in crossing the desert from Suez to Cairo, which was printed in the *Liverpool Mercury* of 13 September 1839:

> Cairo: 19th March: Nothing could be easier, nor more comfortable, than our passage across the desert; we made it in four days on the donkies, by stages of twenty miles, and four three or four small tents at

each stage. The weather was intensely cold during the whole of the first three days, and we were glad of cloaks, blankets, &c. Mr. Waghorn's agent accompanied us, supplied us with everything, and was very civil and attentive. It seemed like a pic-nic the first three days, and I found it more agreeable to cross the desert, than I ever found travelling in India. As to any difficulties, it is quite a farce to think of them. There is nothing, it appears, like competition, whether in the city or the desert; it excites invention, insures zeal, attention, and civility; and however it may set upon the parties, is always beneficial to the public. The rival concerns of Hill and Co. and Waghorn and Co. bid fair to make the passage across the desert, so long the great bugbear of the overland route, as light an affair as a trip from London to Southampton. We trust there is ample employment for both at present, for both are deserving of support; but however this may be, they may confidently rely that, before another twelvemonth elapses, neither will have any cause to complain of their exertions being unrewarded. By those in a hurry, Mr. Hill's conveyances will probably be preferred; others, differently, will patronise Mr. Waghorn, of whose system the foregoing letter gives a very agreeable picture.[172]

Georgiana Damer

Two months after Emma Roberts had made her journey from Alexandria to Suez, another English gentlewoman, Georgiana Damer[173], travelled the Overland Route, but in the opposite direction. Her detailed diary paints a vivid picture of the hardships that such wealthy passengers encountered on their travels, as well as of the sights and scenes they encountered along the way. It also provides glimpses of Waghorn and the services that he offered.

She had begun her trek on 26th December 1839, when her group set off for what seemed to be a short journey to Suez:

In spite of somewhat damp tents, and not very dry sand, we all met at breakfast, in the best possible health and spirits, which the

172 Quoted from the *Bombay Courier* of April 16th.

173 Damer, Mary Georgiana Emma Seymour Dawson, *Diary of A Tour in Greece, Turkey, Egypt, and the Holy Land*, London, 1841, 121-158, 165.

> pure air of the Desert certainly inspires. We felt great satisfaction in looking forward to a short day's journey to Suez, which appeared five or six miles off, within a short ride, but here, as on many other occasions, we were deceived by the clearness of the atmosphere. It took us five hours to reach Suez, the journey being somewhat prolonged by the extended tour we were compelled to make to avoid the quicksands and estuaries, which extend for many miles from Suez. At half-past three we arrived, and found ourselves, as we entered the town, in an atmosphere of dirt, insects, and offensive smells, and from the effect produced by the half-ruined miserable appearance of the exterior of what is distinguished as "the British Hotel," we were agreeably surprised at finding very clean, comfortable-looking bed-rooms. The entrance of this oriental dwelling being hung with advertisements, of—"Guinness Porter" and "India Pale Ale," seemed vastly incongruous, and put whatever poetical ideas we might have indulged in, most strangely to flight; and we met with the disappointing reality of hearing that our steam-boat had started the day before for Cosseir, anticipating by a week its usual departure, on the first of the month.

The diary reminds us that the Overland Route was not exclusively for travellers to India and the East, but was also used by Muslims making the pilgrimage to Mecca—a religious duty required to be undertaken at least once in their lifetime. The time of the Hadj varies from year to year because the Islamic calendar is lunar, but clearly was active when Georgiana Damer encountered it.

> The place did not possess any sort of beauty; but it borrowed a temporary interest from the circumstance of its being the season at which Hadjis of every country had assembled to embark for their pilgrimage to Mecca, and the varied form and colour of their encampments (chiefly made on the sea-shore) produced the most picturesque effect it was possible to imagine. This pilgrimage included specimens of every variety of national and oriental costume. To these Hadjis we (perhaps uncharitably) attributed the *extraneous* population of every *un*-nameable insect; for Greece, Turkey, and Syria, were clean and sweet, in comparison with this our first introduction to Egyptian plagues and customs. [...]

> Our dinner was exactly what we might meet with at Canterbury, rather better than it would have been at Dover, and on a most liberal scale; but mulligatawny soup, round of beef, and heavy plum-pudding, were too substantial substitutes for our good and wholesome Desert fare. Before it was quite ended, the sound of drum and tabret attracted us to the door of the hotel, and we found that an Arab marriage was taking place, by the light of coloured lamps and torches, the former hung on poles, and the cry of—"the bridegroom is coming," was another instance of the constant recurrence of familiar images used in Scripture; and he was thus announced, as going forward to meet the bride at the mosque, where both processions were to join. The bridegroom was conducted between the other Arabs, dressed like himself, in scarlet *caftans* and white turbans, but he looked the very image of grief, and appeared more like a criminal pinioned for execution, than a *nouveau marié.* [...] The scene had been by far the most picturesque and characteristic I could have conceived, and it was continued for three hours.

It is brought home to us how isolated travellers were at times. At Suez fresh water had to be imported from Cairo, while a stack of old newspapers were eagerly devoured by passengers anxious to catch up on events at home. The death of the Duke of Wellington proved a false alarm, since he did not actually die until 1852, but at least news now was less stale than hitherto, thanks to the Overland Route developed by Waghorn and his contemporaries.

> We found that we could not set out at the early hour we proposed, for as every drop of fresh water comes from Cairo, and its sale is only twice a day, at the hours of our nine and three, ten o'clock is the earliest hour at which we can start. The Consular agent, a very obliging Mr. Levecke, came to see us, and very kindly promised to expedite matters, by making over some of his provision of water to Hadji Barak. Mr. L. brought a large file of English papers and magazines, destined for Indian readers. This was a most unexpected treat, although after thirty days had passed without a communication of any kind from Europe, the dread of one's eye glancing to bad news connected with those at home,

preponderated over every other feeling. An account of the Duke of Wellington's severe illness was the first article that struck us in the newspaper of the latest date, and a subsequent report of his death written on the cover of the packet, was of most dispiriting effect; but Mr. Levecke was able to tell us that he had heard that morning from Cairo a verbal contradiction as to the full extent of such a calamity. A further search into the older newspapers brought us to the important subject of the Queen's intended marriage with Prince Albert, her cousin; the very same good-looking prince we had remarked at St. Peter's a few months before, as presenting, in expression of countenance, such a contrast to his companion, Don Miguel, notwithstanding the share of good looks possessed by the latter. Although our host was in our bad books, George called on him to furnish supper and claret, that we might loyally drink our young Queen's health. The wine was so dreadfully sour, that our visitor, Mr. Levecke, was obliged to decline doing more than appear to go through the form of drinking our patriotic toast.

DECEMBER 27TH. —We had time to make another little stroll by the sea-side, where several vessels were preparing to embark their pilgrim passengers. The town of Suez seems fast tumbling to decay. [...] We are told, however, that Europeans are much encouraged to improve the place, as the station of the steam-boat makes it so general and advantageous a position, and that almost everything may be found at Suez, from the increasing facility of communication with Cairo, from whence every necessary of life is brought, while Suez itself is completely unproductive.

Suez

Our caravan *got under weigh* at twelve. In spite of the temptations offered us, in the way of station-houses, vans, and donkey litters, provided for the travellers to and from India, we preferred keeping to our tents, notwithstanding a little patriotic remorse at not adding our mite of encouragement to Mr. Hill's Desert arrangements. The road from Suez was enlivened by our meeting numerous caravans of Hadjis, some included the harems in their suite; and several camels were actually piled with female slaves who, muffled in their yashmacks, were elevated on the baggage to a height perfectly alarming, while the wives travelled in tartahuans, which I suppose they manage better than we could contrive to do, as they really appeared to *repose* on their mattresses, an object we never could achieve.

After one hour's progress we made a halt at a fountain, but of such brackish water that the camels drank but little, though allowed to do so *à discretion*. It was a regular watering establishment, not like the wild spots in our former desert; and the scene of contention for the foremost places, by the caravans that met, was very stirring and amusing: some of the conductors fell into the water, from their eagerness to fill the skins.

We only made a five hours' journey on an uninteresting, broad, beaten track; in short this is the *Hounslow road* to Cairo, and quite of a different character to our late unfrequented Desert.

DECEMBER 28TH. —Set off early, determining upon a thoroughly long day's journey, to enable us to reach Cairo the next day. We found our nine hours' journey most unusually tedious, from the monotony caused by the straightness and uniformity of the road, which must have certainly been the sixth of a mile broad, and consisted of about twenty distinct camel paths, presenting no variety, or any object but camel bones.

We found Denino encamped near an excavation, which had been made by Mehemet Ali in hopes of obtaining water, which (unfortunately for us) turns out to be only the half-way spot from Cairo. This excavation is at least two hundred feet deep and one hundred wide. It was next to impossible to look down it, it was so trying to one's steadiness of head! It was a sort of waking nightmare. We were obliged to take additional precautions in tethering the camels and horses, who, in their midnight peregrinations might fall into what appeared so bottomless a pit.

One regrets much that this very laborious and desirable undertaking should have failed, as no trace of water was discovered. It is believed that the Arabs of this district are acquainted with the positions of springs in this part of the Desert, but carefully conceal their knowledge from others. The number of wild beasts that frequent this part of the country almost prove the existence of springs. We were quite disturbed at night by the howling and contention of the hyenas for the bones that had remained strewn around our kitchen establishment.

DECEMBER 29TH. —Alas! still too far from Cairo, for exertions like those of yesterday to compensate for the fatigue we underwent; for although we determined upon a moderate day's journey, and terminating our Desert expedition at leisure, yet owing to the hard road and the illness and fatigue of two of our camels, we were nine hours reaching our encampment.

Poor Kalid seemed quite knocked up with his fourteenth consecutive day's journey, and the pony could really hardly drag one leg after another: the hard soil seemed more fatiguing to the animal than the previous sand. Our tents were pitched considerably out of the road, for security against Hadji travellers, (or robbers,) and we could only discover it by the intervention of fire-arms, for the evening closed in so suddenly with rain, that we only traced Denino by his firing off his pistols, and then his gun, to attract our attention. He had contrived, in giving us this notice, to shoot into a covey of partridges, which added a very dry and tasteless dish to our bill of fare. Our supplies from Suez had been limited, as we were told, that at the station-house we should meet with *all the delicacies of the season*, but one turkey and a gigantic cauliflower was all that could be found, as it seems that a Christian party, as they described it, had arrived from Cairo, to make their *beiram* in the Desert, and had eaten up everything. I suppose the want of change of scene and customs must be greatly felt at Cairo, when Europeans could find it a party of pleasure to come a long day's journey into the Desert, in such bad weather too, to eat their Christmas dinner.

At this station Mr. Hill, proprietor of an hotel at Cairo, has built a considerable inn. There are four other station-houses, beside the principal one, on the Desert, and Mr. Hill's public spirit may be conceived from the fact, that he had to carry all his materials, even the water with which to make the mortar, either from Suez or the Nile. In this inn there are a dozen good bed-rooms, and at the other stations, sufficient accommodation for a moderate party. Cairo is so contradictory, that one does not know whom to believe. It is, however, a consolation to feel that we are in reality approaching the end of our journey, as the distance cannot now be above thirty miles. We read the Evening Service, and I think Divine worship in a tent, in the Desert, must a good deal approach to the impressiveness of what I have so often heard described at sea.

We met, during this day's journey, many Hadjis, chiefly from Morocco, wearing immense broad-brimmed straw hats, resembling umbrellas. Some of these poor pilgrims were so anxious to obtain a drop of water, that they came up to us, and endeavoured to ascertain, by thrusting their spears into our baggage, whether we had any. George and the Cavasse drew up, pointed their guns, and prevented further aggression.

DECEMBER 30TH. —We arrived at the last station about two, and then found donkey-chairs, chairs, horses, and luncheon, sent out by Mr. Waghorn, to meet us. It was a great relief to find shelter, after a long ride, against cutting wind and dust, which I think must have been of the sharp quality, engendering ophthalmia.

The donkey-chairs are perfectly charming, consisting of an easy arm-chair, fixed on a board like a dinner-tray, with poles slung on two donkeys, one before, and the other behind, in short, occupying the place of sedan-chairmen, but with infinitely more steadiness and activity. Their action is a sort of amble, and the smoothest manner of progress I ever experienced. A boy is in attendance on each equipage, who runs by the side of the chair, which will proceed, without apparent fatigue to boy or beast, at least six miles an hour.

The city of Cairo, which is said to contain 350,000 souls, appears perfectly immense at the first view, which it presents at the abrupt termination of the Desert, and the effect of the extreme verdure of the borders of the Nile appeared almost dazzling, before it became refreshing, so bright is the character of the vegetation, (at least at this season) independently of the contrast it afforded, after fifteen days passed in a sandy region, including Suez, where not a trace of vegetation could be seen. The Caliphs' tombs were our first architectural objects. We were very much disappointed at the pyramids not rising in gigantic grandeur before us, as we had so completely anticipated. They were not, in fact, to be seen from this approach. [...]

How our humble donkeys and ourselves escaped annihilation from the highly loaded and gigantic race of camels, which passed us in all directions, I cannot imagine, particularly as the general din of the camel conductors removed any single or distinct order of precedence. Our attention was so attracted towards our means of escape, through the activities of our attendant *imps*, that it quite secured us against alarm. Not so an elderly English lady, whom we met riding with, we supposed, her two daughters. [...] She was seated on a very tiny donkey, *en grande toilette*, her bonnet and cloak of enormous dimensions; the latter was of very glaring colours, and so completely covering the donkey, that only his head and tail could be distinguished. The old lady looked as if she were swimming, attended by a tall turbaned Turk, who held his arm tight round her waist to support her, and who, in consequence of this exertion, leaned himself against the nearly invisible donkey.

The whole progress seemed to be achieved by machinery, and the effect was so ludicrous, that, in spite of my attempt to be decorous, I actually laughed in my countrywoman's face; but her fears occupied her too much for us to dread her resentment. [...] Apropos to ignorance—on leaving our last encampment, we

> found strewed on the road several pieces of what appeared to be logs of wood, and we regretted not having been able to appropriate them for our kitchen fire, where fuel had proved so scarce. On closer examination, however, we found them to be all petrifactions, and of so perfect a character, that even the splinters were solidly *attached and detached*, and these *bûches* (for they appeared exactly like those prepared for a good French fire) had so completely the appearance of light and dry wood, that only on lifting them (which was a matter of difficulty) could one be convinced of the fact of their being solid stone, and of greater weight than the size justified, as if partly of metal. We are quite anxious to have our dark minds illuminated on the subject.

We have seen that Emma Roberts was grateful for the help she received from Mrs Waghorn. Another family member, Robert Munday, husband of Waghorn's sister Ann, had been requisitioned to run the Cairo hotel. He is named as a plumber and glazier in Rochester directories of 1826-8, but by 1835 had become an innkeeper and in 1838 was the licensed victualler at the City Coffee House, High Street, Rochester. It could have been no more than a year or so since he had moved to Cairo, but he remained there even after Waghorn had given up his agency, as the Snodland Poll Book for 1847 still lists both men's residence as 'Cairo'.

> We found in the Frank quarter very tolerably comfortable rooms, at the hotel kept by Mr. Waghorn's brother-in-law. Mr. Waghorn himself had just arrived from Alexandria, but did not bring any news later than what we had read at Suez. He seemed to engage heart and soul in forwarding rapidity of conveyance to India. He deserves great credit for what he has already achieved. The voyage from England to Bombay can now be performed in thirty-seven days. Mr. W. asserts, that it was Mr. Pitt's opinion, that when England could communicate with India and receive a reply in the course of eight months, then, and not till then, might she think of changing her system of government, and that what he (Mr. W.) was considered as a visionary for attempting but a few years before, is now more than realized.
>
> Mehemet Ali has greatly imbued him with his own opinion, both of his resources and stupendous influence, and of his power

> of raising a million of Arab soldiers, to fight his battles. This at least is in strong contradiction to what we heard in Turkey and Syria, but I believe there is no doubt of the degree of national pride the Egyptian Arabs entertain, with regard to the splendour and consequence of Cairo. The improvements Mehemet Ali is conducting may tell more than is suspected on the general mass of the people.
>
> The comfort of arriving at this end of our journey is greatly diminished, from finding none of the letters we were most anxious to receive.

The next two days were occupied in sight-seeing, apparently not of the usual antiquities, but rather of the city's mosques and gardens.

> We set off on our donkeys, after a most noisy struggle among the donkey-boys, candidates for our selection. The little by-street in which our hotel stood was, unluckily for us, one of the chief stations, and we had the *too* great choice of at least fifty of these little animals and their conductors, screaming in Italian and particularly good English, their individual recommendations,—"My good donkey, my lady! he go ten miles hour!"—"My donkey little race-horse!" &c. &c. Some of the boys' dresses were so picturesque, from their wearing tunics of deep blue linen; the loose sleeves, and sometimes the drapery was confined by a scarlet cord: the combination produced so much the effect of Raphael's and Correggio's colouring. I never before experienced the perfection of smooth progressive motion. The fleetness of the Egyptian asses' amble is not to be described: one glides on, and, as on a rail-road, you only can judge of the rapidity of your progress by seeing how fast you lose sight of succeeding objects. I am longing to take some to England. What charming shooting ponies they would make! [...] The Egyptian mules are beautiful animals, and seem to be as much in use among the officers and richer classes as horses. A handsome one cannot be had for less than 50*l*.

On 1st January Georgiana provides another illustration of Waghorn's kindness to those who served him:

> An hour's theatrical attendance satisfied my curiosity, and I came home to find in our court a very merry and noisy party of camel-drivers and donkey-boys, to whom Mr. Waghorn had given a New Year's feast. Their dancing and singing resembled those of the most savage tribe, at least so an American traveller told us, who had been a good deal with the North American Indians. One, however, danced very gracefully, with a scarf he formed by unrolling his turban, and in a manner reminding one so much of the Spanish dancing, and probably of this its Moorish origin. [...]

It was not until January 19th that the party reached Alexandria:

> Our arrival having been early reported, Mr. Waghorn sent some of the valuable donkey race to take us into Alexandria. We were quite surprised at the cheerful and European aspect of the town, and were soon comfortably lodged in an excellent French hotel, superior to any at Marseilles, although the *Aubergistes*, and nearly everything else, are imported from that city. We held *salon* all day, so numerous were our visitors among the Consular authorities. The kind attentions of Ex-Consul-General Campbell and regnant Colonel Hodges, made up a good deal for our numerous *contretems* at Cairo, in the letter and boat line.

Because of the increasing use of the Overland Route, Waghorn took steps to ameliorate the hardships of desert travel and in 1840 he commissioned 'an iron express coach' which was described and illustrated in *The Mechanics' Magazine* ... of that year.[174]

174 *The Mechanics' Magazine, Museum Resister, Journal and Gazette*, London, 1840, 233-4.

MR. WAGHORN'S IRON EXPRESS COACH FOR THE DESERT.

The floor is composed of a trellis work of thin hoop iron, with intervals of about two inches between, to allow the freest circulation of air; the seats are made in the same way, covered with comfortable hair cushions. There are two shafts in the centre formed of iron tubes, with swing bars on either side for the attachment of three "Arab steeds" running abreast, and driven by a postillion. The whole is placed upon two well-tempered springs, and the wheels are cylindrical, of wrought iron, upon the suspension principle. The front, roof, and the sides, little more than breast high, are covered in with the best storm stay-sail canvass, with curtains above of the same. ... Among its other excellencies may be mentioned lightness, strength, free ventilation, and its entire indestructibility by atmospheric influences. It seems calculated when brought fully into operation, to be a safe and comfortable conveyance for travellers, despatches, and the lighter articles of commerce.

It is clear from Samuel Bevan's account of the Overland Route (in the next chapter) that he thought this carriage far superior to that provided by the nascent P&O Company. He also shows that some time in the early 1840s Richard Hill of Hill and Raven had died. This may have been the catalyst to cause the union of Waghorn and Co. with Hill, Raven and Co., which was announced in the *Times* of 13 September 1841 'for the express purpose of giving increased facilities and comforts to passengers by that route to India'. One obvious advantage was that all passengers could now avail themselves of accommodation in the desert station houses without fear of refusal.

8

WORKING FOR WAGHORN IN EGYPT

During the 1840s traffic on the Overland Route grew sufficiently for it to become necessary for agents to provide practical information for passengers. Their texts are typical of travel agents' brochures with quotations from a few postcards thrown in for good measure.[1] *Waghorn and Co's* 1842 brochure reports that 'We have lately added as assistants in our Egyptian Establishment, Messrs. Turner and Bevan, in order to pass with travellers to and from India between Suez and Alexandria, and vice versa, and thus give a further security to all parties and their baggage through our agency.

A less formal appraisal of the desert crossing can be gleaned not only from Emma Roberts's account summarized earlier, but also from Samuel Bevan's *Sand and Canvas.* Bevan's is a colourful account, no doubt dressed up somewhat for publication, but it gives many insights into the workings of the Overland Route. He begins by describing the extraordinary way he was appointed to the post:

> On a sunny morning in the spring of 184-, I sat lingering over the remains of a late breakfast, at my lodgings in Regent Street. My deed of partnership with Messrs. – having been cancelled but a few days before, I found myself left without any ostensible means of disposing advantageously of my time, which began to hang somewhat heavily on my hands, for although, in London more especially, there are a thousand ways of killing time, it is by no means so easy to hit upon the right method of making the best use of it. Whilst musing on this subject, my eyes wandered over the columns of the "Times" newspaper, which lay on the table before me, and having glanced over sundry announcements of "eligible opportunities," and notices of various seductive offers of "Partnership," my attention was suddenly arrested by the following: "Wanted immediately, for service in a foreign country, a gentleman

of business-habits and good address. Salary £250. per annum. All expenses paid. Apply personally to Messrs. * * * *, Solicitors, Tokenhouse Yard."

Whether it was that this particular advertisement seemed to me to possess a greater claim to good faith than others in the same column, or that the words "foreign country" had some particular charm about them, I know not; all I can say is, that in a quarter of an hour after the third or fourth reading of it, I was on my way to Tokenhouse Yard, having paid a rather more than ordinary attention to the appearance of my outer man.

Arrived at the office of the solicitors, I found upon the staircase, some ten or more persons of various degrees of respectability, each of whom seemed to be regarding a scrap of paper which he held in his hand. With a similar document, I, in my turn, was duly served, and found it inscribed, "* * * * of the Overland, 34, Cornhill, destination Egypt." I followed the rest of my fellow candidates, for such they doubtless were, into Cornhill, although by the time we got there, I remarked that the number of them was sensibly diminished, but not daring to enter the lists with so many individuals, who, if not exactly "gentlemen", might possibly, in the terms of the advertisement, be more accustomed to "business habits" than myself, I took the precaution of waiting in ambush near the street door, until, one by one, I counted them all out. As I watched their faces to mark what success they might have met with, I was not very greatly surprised to hear some such expressions as "No go," "Walker", &c., and gathered considerable encouragement therefrom. Having seen the last of them out, I presented myself and paper, and was ushered through an outer office, into the presence of the great "Overland" himself, who, receiving me with a bow, inquired if I came from his solicitors.

"I do."

"Then go, Sir, and get your hair cut, and return here in a quarter of an hour."

This cool reception might have damped the courage of any applicant not quite so hard up as myself, and probably if used, had its weight with many of those who had preceded me. I stood my ground however, and removing my wig (rather an exuberant one, by Truefit,) I rammed it into my hat.

"Pray, Sir, be seated," said the "Overland."

I took a chair and screwed up my courage for a cross-examination.

"Can you drive an engine?"

"I can."

"Can you speak French?" "Yes."

"German and Italian?" I nodded affirmatively.

"Arabic?" I was about to assent to this query also, but suddenly recollecting that my interrogator might himself be an adept at that tongue, I seasoned my denial with the assurance that I could make myself master of it in a fortnight.

"Do you understand book-keeping by doubly entry?"

Here was a poser. I have since wondered how I ever got over it. I winked at the Overland, and replied, "I ought to."

"I think you'll do, Sir", was his rejoinder; "come and breakfast with me tomorrow morning."

I bowed and withdrew, and whilst adjusting my wig in the outer office, I heard an order given to the head clerk to admit no more applicants. This I regarded as a sure earnest of an engagement and began to feel myself a man of business again. I fancied myself a full head taller than before, and stooped very low as I threaded some narrow archways near the Bank. How I got home, I cannot distinctly remember, but I packed my portmanteau in readiness for an immediate departure, in spite of the remonstrances of my worthy landlady, who looked on a journey to Egypt in the light of a wanton sacrifice of my life, assuring me that I should die of the plague in less than a week after I got there, and making me promise that I would send her off a mummy immediately on my arrival.

I was punctual to my appointment next morning, and it was fortunate that I was so, for * * * * was never known to be a minute behind time in any thing, and was in the act of pouring out my cup of tea when I entered his apartment. Had I been four minutes later, I might have whistled for my new engagement. Our breakfast over, and some preliminary matters discussed, we hastened to the office.

"Is that letter ready, Mr. Wateley? [Wheatley] Very good. Now, Sir, here are your credentials; deliver that document on your arrival in Alexandria, to which you are booked through, via Marseilles; call here tomorrow morning at eight for your despatches, take this cheque, and don't bother me any more. Good morning !"

And the "Overland" vanished into the inner office—the door was shut, and I never saw him afterwards!

Bevan duly travelled via Southampton to Le Havre, then coach to Paris and on to Chalons sur Saone, where he transferred to a steamer down the Rhone to Marseilles. He discovered a passage had been booked for him to Alexandria on the *Minos*, leaving in the evening of 21 June. The *Minos* was

> one of a fine class of armed French steamers, which serve the Mediterranean, running from Marseilles to Malta, Syra and Alexandria, calling at most of the larger ports on the southern coast of Italy. The accommodation on board these vessels is perfect, and the discipline of the first order, and they are withal so strongly built, that they defy the ugliest weather, and are very rarely overdue.

Marseilles

At Malta he met Waghorn's agent stationed there, and Mr. Portenier, the Alexandria agent, then journeying to England. Alexandria was reached on 2 July, where Bevan was greeted by Mr Furner, Portenier's deputy. A donkey ride brought them to the doors of "Waghorn's India agency" in the great square.

> I ... had the satisfaction of learning from Furner that I was appointed to as good a post as any one, and equal in point of emolument to that of any English employè in Egypt.
>
> We had scarcely finished our meal, when a loud thumping at the out-door announced a visitor. This proved to be Mr. Raven, the resident partner, fresh from Cairo, to whom I was forthwith

introduced. This gentleman was, in the first instance connected with a Mr. Hill, who is since deceased, and has done a great deal towards establishing and improving the communication between Cairo and Suez, having been indeed, in conjunction with his late associate, one, if not the projector of the original Transit Company. It needed however the enterprizing spirit and untiring perseverance of Mr. Waghorn, before the undertaking could be brought to assume any thing like a flourishing appearance; and now that the energies of both are united in one common object, the Egyptian portion of the Overland journey is as perfect as individuals[175*] can make it.

Bevan began his duties on 18 July, when about two dozen passengers for the Overland disembarked from the mail steamer *Tagus* from Southampton.

The mail consisted of a number of square tin-boxes, which, when hauled on deck, it was my duty to see shifted into a barge alongside, destined to convey them to the mouth of the Mahmoudieh Canal, observing at the same time, that each individual case was duly ticked off upon the bill of lading ... Whilst the mail barge was making its slow way round to the Mahmoudieh, I had time to reach the shore, and join the passengers at Rey's Hotel, as they were starting for Moharrem Bey, which is the point of departure of the passage-boats. The pushing and scrambling for donkeys, on such occasions, is sometimes highly amusing, and it is long ere the cavalcade is in motion. ...

Half a mile's ride brought us to the avenue of trees upon the banks of the Canal, where the covered passenger-boats were waiting to receive us, that containing the mails and luggage, having already gone on ahead. The choice of seats, for berths there were none, was of course given to the ladies, the rest accommodating themselves where best they might. Four strong horses, mounted by as many Arab riders, were attached to the one long iron boat, which contained us all, and the word having been given to cast loose, we bid a hasty adieu to our friends on shore, and by a little after midnight, found

175 [Footnotes marked * are Bevan's own.] * Since leaving Egypt, I have learnt that the whole concern has passed into other and more powerful hands [the P&O], who by the employment of considerable capital, have succeeded in facilitating the passage of travellers across the Isthmus.

ourselves in motion. Our crew consisted of a fat Maltese pilot, two or three Arabs, and a cook, named Antonio, and it was gratifying to remark, that the latter had not forgotten several well-stored cafasses, or provision baskets, with apparatus for making tea and coffee, and a large brazier of ignited charcoal for heating his kettles.

The dew was falling like rain, soaking every thing that was exposed to it, but this did not deter some of our party from throwing themselves at full length upon the roof, where, snugly shrouded in their cloaks, they ran a much better chance of getting a little rest, than when squeezed into a sitting posture below. Having given a look round to see that all was as it should be, I retired into my little cabin in the bows, where, after a cold chicken and a bottle of Bass's ale, I was soon deep in my first packet of letters from England. Sleep however, overcame me before I had finished, and I was dreaming most agreeably of far-off persons and scenes, when a sudden shock and instantaneous stoppage of the boat, upset my candle and empty beer-bottle, and caused a dire commotion among the cups and Spode-ware in Antonio's pantry. I ran on deck immediately, and found, as soon as I could collect my scattered senses, that our precious Maltese captain had run us into the bank, having quietly followed the example of those around him, by dropping to sleep at his tiller. Fortunately for the horses, the rope had parted with the sudden check, or they would have been pulled into the Canal, which I afterwards found was not an uncommon occurrence. After a little delay, we were soon making way again at an average pace of seven or eight miles an hour, and met with no farther mishap before day-break. We were amused in the morning by the uncouth gambols of the buffaloes, who were taking their early bath in the shallow water at the sides of the Canal. Some of them seemed so accustomed to the passing of our rope, which often gives them an unpleasant rap over the horns, and sometimes completely upsets them, that they would duck under water at the approach of the horses, and rise again as soon as we had shot past. At mid-day we reached Atfeh, a considerable village on the Nile, at the southern extremity of the Mahmoudieh Canal.

The water in the Mahmoudieh Canal being at this season of the year very low, and the steep muddy banks extremely slippery, it was no easy matter to disembark all the heavy luggage belonging to our passengers. The Arabs, however, are excellent porters, and will carry enormous loads; so much so, that I was surprised at the apparent facility with which the shifting of so great a quantity of material was accomplished. One of Mr. Waghorn's agents, who is located at Atfeh, sends off a lot of camels to the landing place, which transport the heavier baggage to the river side, where it is immediately stored on board the Nile steamer. This agent, who is an intelligent Italian, must lead a weary life in Atfeh, for of all places it has been my lot to visit, I never saw one so truly forbidding. It is a town of considerable trade, and the quays are covered with timber and bales of merchandize. Pigs by the thousand run about in all directions, whilst the path from the canal-boat to the steamer is through a perfect Slough of Despond. With the exception of the Pasha's corn-store, there is but one decent-looking building in the place: this is, of course, the hotel, where, on extraordinary occasions they can make up three or four beds, though woe befall the unhappy wight who trusts himself to the tender mercies of its host. On the ground-floor is a sort of wine and spirit-store, where the traveller can be accommodated with all the various growths of the Levant, and this is perhaps the only redeeming quality in the character of the "Grand Hotel de France."

Atfeh

In the course of two hours, we had everything removed on board a little steamer, which lay fizzing at the quay side, capable of carrying, at a pinch, fifty passengers with their effects. On this occasion, we did not muster much more than half that number, and therefore found ample accommodation. [After a sleep] I beat a retreat towards the caboose, and made friends with the head engineer, who was in the act of sitting down to a steaming mess of savoury stew, laid out upon the head of a cask, with a garnish of sparkling pale ale. On the paddle-box above us, sat the old Reis or pilot, gazing at us with extreme complacency, whilst waiting for his turn at the dish. This individual is the most important in the ship, as, without his knowledge of the river, we should be continually running aground on one or other of the numerous shoals, which at "low Nile" render the navigation somewhat intricate and dangerous. There he sits by day and by night, always at his post, and ever wakeful, giving an occasional sign to the Arab at the helm.[176*]

We had now progressed a long way up the river. … As night came on, our little deck was gradually deserted, very few of the passengers choosing to encounter a wetting from the dew which was now descending almost as heavily as rain. I gave one look below to see if there was a chance of making my bed on or under some table or other, but every available place was occupied, and I was forced to throw myself upon the deck, rolled up in a thick Bernous cloak, which defended me from both dew and mosquitoes, and had it not been for one of the boatmen; who very unceremoniously walked on my leg, I should have slept undisturbed until daybreak.

About ten o'clock on the day following, we were just able to see the Pyramids of Ghizeh, pointing faintly upwards in the distance, and at noon reached Boulac,[177*] the port of Cairo, where we disembarked, and rode a mile and-a-half into the city, some on donkeys, and others in a sort of donkey chair. Consigning the mail boxes to the care of an agent, who was in waiting to receive them, I cantered on into Cairo, under the guidance of the lad, who ran behind me; and passing through the outer gate of the city, found

176 * Our little vessel when originally sent out to Egypt by the Oriental Company, was fitted with a rudder-wheel, but as the native boatmen could never be induced to work it, a long tiller was substituted in its stead.

177 * The distance from Atfeh to Boulac, by the Nile, is about 120 English miles.

myself on the Esbikier, or "great square," a vast area of dry, cracked mud, surrounded by deep canals, devoid of water, and bordered by a double row of dusty-looking trees.

Leaving the Esbikier, we entered a very narrow street, in the which, about half way down, an overhanging board directs the traveller to the "Grand Eastern Hotel," and turning down a still narrower alley, rendered almost dark by the extreme contiguity of the upper parts of the houses, we passed under an arched gateway, and entered the courtyard. A grim-looking Maltese waiter ushered me into the presence of Mr. Raven, who was busy writing in his office, a little sort of sanctum on the first-floor, which I shall describe at length hereafter. This gentleman welcomed me very kindly, inquiring how many passengers I had, and if they had all found conveyances to the city, &c., but before he would permit me to answer him, he pointed to a goolah of water and brandy bottle which stood by, and would hear nothing until I had taken a draught.

I then gave him a detailed account of our journey so far, and handed him a parcel of letters and a passenger list, which I had brought with me from Alexandria. I had made up my mind to something like a day's rest in Cairo, and was therefore somewhat surprised, though by no means disappointed, when told that I had better accompany the caravan to Suez, and make preparation for an immediate departure—"And," added Raven, "if you want anything "to eat, find your way to the kitchen, and lay hands on "anything you most fancy, for if you wait till dinner-time and sit down with the rest, ten to one but you are called away before you can swallow a mouthful!" This advice was no sooner given than acted upon. [...]

On my return to Mr. Raven's office, I found him busy with a list of the passengers, arranging their various places in the carriages which were to convey us to Suez. ... One or two of the passengers who had escaped from the dinner-table, were changing English money into nine-piastre pieces, and asking innumerable questions. Motioning me to a seat at a desk alongside him, ... Raven supplied me with a cheroot and a bottle of pale ale, and handed me a rough list of the transit accounts to be put into proper form, before collecting the monies. "When," said he, "you have "receipted all these, and returned them to me, you may get "away as soon as you like." I found each little bill to consist of a printed form; so much for transit from Cairo to Suez, so much for camel-hire for baggage, and a third item for hotel expenses, the whole very simple and easily comprehended. The taking of the money was not so readily accomplished, as I had some little difficulty in making people understand how the charge for luggage was regulated. The hire of a camel to cross the desert is about twelve shillings, and his load seldom or never more than two packages; one on each side. A lady, therefore, with a heavy portmanteau and two large paper bandboxes, might be called upon to pay a camel and a half, whilst her husband, with two enormous and weighty bullock trunks, would probably pay but for one camel. A hat-box and writing-desk have been assessed at half a camel, for the Bedouins have but little idea of properly balancing a load; and I have frequently seen a heavy iron-bound trunk, counterpoised by a huge, but light, paper bonnet-box, or a colossal carpet-bag and a bird-cage, in ludicrous contraposition.

The loading takes place in a spacious court-yard at the back of the hotel, the camels kneeling to receive their burdens, which are secured in rude net-work bags, and the noise and confusion at such times is almost distracting. The animals are very touchy, and manifest their displeasure by a child-like groan, which it is almost distressing to hear. The motion of their heads too requires constant watching, as they turn round to bite and snap at the slightest provocation, and seem to have a peculiar dislike to the Frank [European] dress, which attracts them more than the blue smocks of the Bedouin. The distribution of the loads is superintended by different servants of the company from every quarter of the globe; and as each tries to make himself heard amid the general din, there is a perfect Babel of tongues.

With all this, just under the open window of the little room in which we were sitting, I found my labour in the way of accounts to progress but slowly; and it was no little relief to me, when the hubbub was exchanged for a state of comparative quiet, produced by the departure of the camels with the baggage, which generally precedes the rest of the caravan.

By five in the afternoon, everything was reported in readiness for a start, but as I had occasion to wait for some papers entrusted to me by Raven, I was almost the last who reached the place of departure. In a wide part of an adjacent street, I found five or six covered carts with two wheels, and four stout horses attached to each; these are capable of holding four persons comfortably, and as they are well balanced, and run on enormously large wheels, their motion is both easy and agreeable. Each passenger has his particular seat assigned him before starting, so that there is no confusion or scrambling for places, care being also taken not to separate the members of one family more than can be avoided; children and ladies are generally confided to the care of the most experienced English drivers, while the gentlemen are handed over to the tender mercies of some Maltese, or native knight of the whip, if the caravan be so large as to put all the carriages in requisition.

On looking over the list, I found myself booked with two missionaries and a reverend divine; a fact which manifested a kindly interest in my welfare on the part of Mr. Raven, who pushed in after me a couple of black bottles, and gave the order to go forward. Whisking round the Esbikier, we passed the outer gate and suburbs, and then after a jolting drive of near a mile through narrow lanes, bordered by hedge-rows of prickly pear and luxuriant aloes, emerged on to the smooth sand of the desert; half a mile on, are two curious looking erections of brick, called the Tombs of the Sheiks, and these once out of sight, there is nought to greet the eye but a vast expanse of sand, enclosed at the horizon on either side within a low range of sand hills, which extend almost without interruption the entire way to Suez. [...]

For the convenience of passengers to and from India, places of refuge or Stations, have been erected at uniform distances, where man and beast may find refreshment, and shelter from the scorching sun. Those travelling through the agency of Messrs. Waghorn, [in 1842-3] are entitled to avail themselves to any extent of the accommodation afforded, saving to wines, &c., which are charged extra; but should a party making the journey, independent altogether of such agency, neglect to provide himself with a ticket of admission to these Stations, he will find himself condemned to abstinence from food and water for the entire eighty-four miles, unless he carry with him a sufficient supply. Wells there are none, saving one of dirty brackish water near Suez, and this is more often dry than not. At the Stations, however, there is always an abundant supply of good water, kept cool under ground in iron tanks, and brought from the Nile in skins at a great expense; and should this by any untoward chance be wanting, the traveller may slake his thirst with the best of ale or beer at a shilling the bottle. If too fastidious to descend to vulgar malt, he will find a modest looking "carte des vins" in the dining-rooms of three out of seven of the Stations, from which he may make his selection, without risk of being compelled to complain either of quality or price.

I am aware that there are many who have found fault with the apparently high charge made for the transit between Cairo and Suez; but these may not have sufficiently considered the great trouble and expense necessarily incurred in providing due accommodation. They have scarcely any idea of the number of skins of water required to fill one tank, nor, perhaps, do they reflect, while filling out or polishing their own skins, and using as much of the precious fluid as they can desire, that the poor camel or donkey which brought it forty weary miles from the Nile, returns all the way back again, without having wetted its lips more than once, if even so much as that. Then again, should a goat-skin spring a leak, or burst while on the road, which not infrequently happens, what is to recompense the poor Bedouin, who has tramped the whole way on foot, and whose donkey, on which he solely relies for a livelihood, is the bearer of but one skin of water at a time.[178*]

But to return to our caravan, which we left on the margin of the desert. Our rate of travelling was about five miles in the hour, for the track, which in some places, lay over smooth and tolerably hard gravel, was at others exchanged for a loose sand, in which our wheels became buried to the depth of a foot or more, causing a deal of labour to our horses. At such times, our Seis, or running-footman, one of whom accompanies each carriage, would apply his shoulder to the wheel and help us over the soft spot, whilst on occasions we found it necessary altogether to alight, and unite our

178 * A young officer, on his way *out* to India, having upon one occasion ordered Champagne, really was, or appeared to be, extremely annoyed that it was sent up un-iced! I never found any one *returning*, make any unreasonable objections of this kind.

efforts. We changed horses at No.1 Station, which is nine miles from Cairo, and a mere stable, reaching No.2, at about ten o'clock. This is a building containing a large saloon, with divans and a long table, three sleeping rooms, kitchen, &c., and here we found a good supper laid out, consisting of smoking dishes of Irish stew, cold turkeys and fowls, and eggs *á discretion*. During the meal, I was. beckoned out of the room by the head driver, Mr. Hill,[179*] to debate as to the length of time we should allow for resting. As there was a full change of horses for each carriage, I considered it would be as well to make the most of the cool night air, and secure a long halt the next day at the centre Station, and our passengers concurring in this idea, we were soon again en route.

No. 3 Station is a repetition of No.1, being only a stable, tenanted by one old, melancholy Arab, who, on our arrival, was found squatted over his little fire of camel's dung, upon which he was baking his evening cake of Indian corn. This, with his pipe, and a drink of water, forms his only food. In the morning, in his scriptural little mill of two flat stones, he grinds sufficient flour to last him through the day, tasting nought else until his return to the city, which takes place when the transit season is over. Such, at least is the old fellow's own account of himself; but as very few who cross the desert, pass by a Station without a call, it is more than probable, that he picks up something, more palatable than maise-bread, in return for the sundry half-pints of water and handsful of corn, which he distributes, sub-rosé, among his Bedouin friends.

Early on the following morning, we came in sight of No. 4, the centre Station, forty-one miles from Cairo, which, with the one solitary tree that stands near it, is visible nearly six miles before it is made. This is a resting-place of much more pretensions than the others, having an upper-story, with a rickety flight of stone-steps, and a tolerably spacious court-yard below, where, at the time of our arrival, a queer-looking sheep, and some lean shrivelled fowls were sniffing and pecking about, and scraping up their last earthly meal, whilst a turkey-cock, perched on an empty cafass or hamper, was dismally sounding his death-rattle. The live stock, and eatables of all sorts are brought from Cairo in sufficient quantity to supply

179 * A brother of the late Mr. Hill, before alluded to.

the larders of all the Stations for several weeks, but occasionally, when the number of passengers to and fro is very large, a sort of famine takes place, and we have been compelled to subsist for a time upon dates and other dried fruits, of which there is always a good store; the change of diet proving rather agreeable than otherwise. Chickens, very lean and tough, and roasted to dryness, are a standing dish in Egypt, and these with the larger sorts of fowl, and plenty of curries and Irish-stew, form the principal fare of the desert.[180*] A second course generally makes its appearance at dinner in the shape of huge rice-puddings, or a sort of sweetmeat called mish-mish, a favourite dish of the Arabs.

The central station in the desert
(© P&O Heritage Collection www.poheritage.com)

On arriving at No. 4, we found that the cool night air had given us considerable appetite, and our ablutions performed, there was a general rush to the long table in the common room, where sundry tea-pots and coffee-biggins were soon in rapid circulation, and boiled eggs disappeared by the score; bread there was none, as that becomes too much dried up by the heat when carried across the

180 * I once met with a "loin of camel," at No. 4 Station, a *pièce de resistance,* I am not ambitious of tasting a second time.

desert, but hard biscuits we found to be an excellent substitute, and the Egyptian butter is delicious. Breakfast over, I spread my carpet on the top of a long wooden sideboard, and soon fell fast asleep-my example being followed by the others who disposed themselves to rest, some in the bed-rooms, and others on the divans which extend round three sides of the room. In the middle of the day the heat was excessive—the thermometer standing at 100° of Fahrenheit—and the slight breath of air which was stirring outside was so very far preferable to the confined heat of the rooms, that I left my hard couch for a little patch of shade under one of the carts, where I was soon joined by one of my fellow-travellers, with whom I whiled away the hours in chat, until summoned by Ibraham the cook to another trial of his culinary art.

At the approach of evening, the horses were again attached to their respective carts or vans, and after some little jibbing on the part of the poor animals, who were evidently averse to moving, we were again upon the desert. The road near the centre Station is hard and gravelly, and affords most easy travelling for the first mile or two. We passed within a stone's throw of the solitary tree before alluded to, with its sun-burnt branches all festooned with rags; the followers of the prophet who pass this object on their pilgrimages to Mecca, hang thereon an old shoe or some portion of a garment by way of peace-offering. If the wind is stirring, it is quite as well to take the weather-side of this hanging mass of old clothes, for as there are few devotees who care to part with anything really serviceable, the breezes which come athwart the tree are by no means of the most balmy.

About a quarter of a mile to the southward of this pestilential landmark, is a pit in the sand, of enormous dimensions, excavated by the French in the vain hope of obtaining water. Two or three of us went so far just to gratify our curiosity, but were obliged to use extreme caution in approaching the edge of the pit. Its diameter is so great that the well, although one hundred and fifty feet deep, appears rather shallow than otherwise, and the section of the ground exhibits a succession of layers of fine sand and gravel, but without the least appearance of water. Two or three dead animals, for which the well had served as a pitfall, lay at the bottom.

The road to No.5 Station is scarcely to be distinguished, as the ground is so hard as to take no impress of wheels, and there would be great difficulty in making it out at all, were it not for the dead and dying camels and blanched skeletons, which strew the path and serve as finger-posts. Should a camel drop through exhaustion, and there be no means at hand of relieving it, the Bedouin removes its load, which is distributed among the others, and the poor beast is left to die, for to shorten its miseries by a coup de grace, would be at variance with the law of Mahomet. This is the more to be regretted as these animals are peculiarly tenacious of life, and when left in this manner, are sure to fall a prey to the jackal and vulture, who feast upon the body before life is extinct. A sly bullet from my carbine has often terminated the agonies of such as I have found thus abandoned in my frequent journeys, when I could use it without fear of detection, for the Arabs will not lightly pass over an infringement of their law in this particular; and as they have, if so inclined, the power of causing us much trouble, I have invariably sought to be on the best terms with them.

Passing the next Station, a mere stable, and still keeping between the two lines of hills, which increase in height as you approach Suez, we came suddenly upon No.6, where, as it was now ten o'clock, we had to arouse the inmates. This Station is the counterpart of No.2, and was tenanted by an agreeable and pretty Englishwoman, who, having in haste, united herself to an Arab, was now in the solitude of the desert, repenting at her leisure. Under her good care we remained several hours, doing ample justice to a plentiful supper, and refreshing ourselves with a comfortable nap. It was therefore broad daylight when we reached the well of brackish water, and came in sight of the walls of Suez, a desolate and miserable town, where there is no water, save that of the Red Sea, and such as is afforded by a casual shower, and not the most remote appearance of vegetation in any shape. The inhabitants, who appear to live exclusively upon fish, and dried fruits from the interior, consist principally of Jewish merchants and small Arab traders; for there is considerable traffic between Suez and the shores of the Red Sea, especially with Aden and Missouah, which latter, is the chief port of Abyssinia. The Indian steamers come up to within three or four miles of the town, and obtain a tolerably safe anchorage outside a perilous bar, which entirely prevents any nearer approach for vessels drawing more than five feet of water. Communication is effected, and merchandize shipped, by means of small lateen-rigged boats, which, if the wind be contrary, are also managed by oars; but in a high sea, I have sometimes been as long as six hours in getting out to the steamer.

Suez
(© P&O Heritage Collection www.poheritage.com)

Waghorn's hotel is a quaint-looking low building close to the water's edge, containing accommodation for thirty or forty people, and is managed by a clean bustling Englishwoman and her nephew. Two hundred yards or so nearer the gate, stands the old hotel, used only on extraordinary occasions, or when the steamer, not true to her time, causes a meeting at Suez between the India-bound passengers and those returning homewards. The little square before the door was filled as we drove up, with the baggage camels, which having disposed of their burdens in various heaps upon the ground, were now quietly chewing the cud, and resting themselves after their weary march, while their drivers were lolling near, either shrouded in their bernons cloaks and fast asleep, or lazily getting their morning meal. Portmanteaus, bullock-trunks, sword-cases, and three-cornered hat-boxes, with all the innumerable etceteras in the way of baggage, comprising an Indian outfit, lay scattered about in wild confusion, and it required no little skill on the part of our drivers to manage a four-in-hand through such a sea of valuables. Fortunately for myself, the boxes containing the mails lay all in one heap close to the door of the hotel, so that my task of counting and checking them was more easily accomplished than I had anticipated. Consigning them, therefore, into the hands of Mr. Manson, the agent at Suez, and obtaining from him a suitable receipt, I was left to discuss an excellent "dejeuner a-la-fourchette," [light meal] provided for me by the good-natured landlady, of whom I had contrived to get the blind side, by the opportune present of a few English needles which I happened to have in my valise.

I learned, on inquiry of the agent, that the "Berenice" Bombay steamer, which had the day before landed two or three homeward-bound passengers, and was now lying smoking at her anchorage, was to start at five in the afternoon; and as the shipment of the mails and luggage is a work of time and labour, the sooner they were got off the better. I found this by no means an unpleasant part of my duty, for as there was a delightful breeze blowing, and the weather of the finest, the sail down the arm of the gulf into the open water, was extremely pleasant.

By six o'clock every one was on board, and the "Berenice" under weigh; and at midnight, I had turned my back upon Suez, with the now nearly empty carriages, for there were only three passengers, and as it so happened that neither of these contemplated reaching Alexandria in time for the English steamer, there was no occasion for any extraordinary dispatch. We therefore jogged along quietly enough, and for the first few stages, I found an amusing companion in my driver, a countryman of my own, who, having been long resident in Egypt, was able to afford me a good deal of information. He was, however, no follower of Father Mathew[181], and falling into the popular error that brandy is the best and safest restorative in a hot climate, he indulged in such repeated pulls at the black bottle, that on leaving No. 4 Station, he was compelled to resign the reins to the attendant Seis, and sleep away the effect of his potations at the bottom of the cart.

181 Theobald Mathew (1790-1856) an Irish Catholic teetotal reformer.

Resting during the hottest part of the day, we reached Cairo at the close of the second afternoon, where having consigned my travelling companions to the attentions of the head waiter, I paid my respects to Mr. Raven, whom I found entertaining a large party of his English friends, resident in Egypt. [...]

At the end of the month I accompanied Mr. Raven to Alexandria in one of his Nile sailing-boats, which are light and commodious little vessels, drawing but two or three feet of water, and especially adapted for the voyage into upper Egypt, to which purpose indeed they are principally applied. Having sunk it under water for a day or two, and cleansed it as much as possible of fleas and cockroaches, we shipped a goodly cafass of provisions, and taking with us an Arab cook, embarked at nightfall. The wind was unfortunately against us, obliging our crew to use their oars, and very much retarding our progress. Our boat, which was somewhat of a hobby of Raven's, was very completely fitted with every possible convenience, and had two compact little cabins under the poop-deck, just long enough for a person to lie down in, one being furnished with bed-places. In the middle of the forward cabin, was a sort of tuck-up table, on which our supper was now laid out by our swarthy factotum, who had for some little time been tickling our appetites with the grateful odours of certain savoury ragoûts, concocted over a charcoal fire 'midships. Over our heads, suspended from the roof, swung a monstrous stable-lantern,. shedding a dim yellow light, just sufficient to show us the way to our mouths, for to read or talk were equally impossible, owing to the unceasing song of the Arab boatmen, who accompany themselves as they row, with a rude melody, by no means grateful to English ears. All we could do, was to recline at our ease, and puff away at our chibouques[182], until the heavy dew, which wetted everything, as effectually as if we had been exposed to a drizzling rain, drove us to our couches.

I awoke several times during the night, and emerging from the cabin, found every one but myself fast asleep, the vessel gliding noiselessly down the stream. Even the head of the old Reis, who was perched upon the roof of the cabin, had dropped down upon his chest, and saving the ripple of the water under our bows, and

182 A long Turkish pipe for smoking tobacco.

the measured snore of some of our party, no sound was to be heard, and we moved imperceptibly onwards in perfect stillness. I had no heart to arouse any of the poor tired Arabs from their stolen slumbers, the more especially, as I knew the danger of running aground to be but slight; so once more seeking my hard bed, and covering myself completely in my cloak, I bid defiance to mosquitoes and cockroaches, and was soon deep in pleasant dreams of home.

The two next days were passed in our boat, the monotony of the voyage being varied by occasional runs on shore, when we moored at some village or other, to take in a fresh supply of milk or vegetables. At other times, where the high banks afforded good walking, we indulged in a little shooting, for doves and small birds were very plentiful, and afforded excellent eating. As the third night closed in, a light breeze sprung up, which aided us considerably in our progress, and inspired our tired crew with fresh energy.

As we made our preparations for turning in, I remarked that Raven drew from his pocket a huge knife, which, after a careful inspection, he deposited with great gravity under his pillow, though whether as a precaution against intrusion, or any act of foul play on the part of our boatmen, I did not inquire, merely viewing such unwonted preparation with considerable curiosity.

I had not been long asleep, when I found myself suddenly rolled from my sofa on to the floor, our stable-lantern and dining-table bearing me company; and on opening my eyes, I could just catch a glimpse of Raven escaping from the door-way with his big knife, whilst the violent vociferations of the Arabs on deck, mingled with a confused rushing sound of both wind and water, and the alarming lurch of the vessel, left me in some doubt as to whether I was murdered or drowning. A moment more and tranquillity was restored; the boat righted, and I found my legs. Emerging from the cabin, I learnt that a sudden puff of wind had caught our huge lateen sail, which, in true Arab fashion, had been made fast to a ring in the deck, whilst the lazy sailor, who ought to have held it, was enjoying a comfortable nap. Had it not been for the promptitude displayed by Raven, who had severed the rope with the trusty knife from under his pillow, it is more than probable that he would have got a sound ducking, and I have served as a bonne bouche for some stray crocodile; for the Nile boatmen, who are. amphibious, and look upon an unexpected dip rather as a treat than otherwise, have the unpleasant habit of extending assistance only to those in supreme authority. Thus, while they would have rescued Mr. Raven, I might have bubbled away my last breath in the cabin, or have floated down the stream, entirely unheeded and uncared for.

Providentially, however, we were saved from capsizing, and having bestowed two or three hearty kicks on the man who had caused the sudden alarm, we retired again to our couches, and reached Atfeh about daybreak, without farther mishap.

Half-an-hour was passed here in preparing one of the iron track-boats to convey us down the Canal to Alexandria, where we arrived about three in the afternoon, and just in time for me to put off in a little boat to meet one of the French steamers, which was visible in the offing. Furner and I had a sharp race with a rival boat from Colomb's Hotel, and as the French captain suffered their agent to come on board, whilst he politely saluted us with a copious sprinkling of warm water, it was some satisfaction to remark that there was not even one solitary passenger for either of us. There is considerable jealousy between the proprietors of the "Rey" and "Colomb," by which names the two principal hotels are distinguished, and we hear that the opposing party is about to start some canal-boats, and a couple of desert carriages, at a lower rate of transit. This is doubtless all very fair, and as competition generally benefits the public, we shall watch with interest the progress of our rivals.

Mr. Raven quitted us again the next day to return to Cairo, taking with him Mrs. Hill and her little daughter, the widow and child of his late partner, who had been sojourning some time in Alexandria. We drove down to Moharrem Bey in one of Rey's carriages, and the evening being very dark, we had much difficulty in picking our way through the ruins which mark the site of the ancient city, and ran many chances of an upset in one or other of the deep holes which skirt the track. Raven gave me instructions, upon this occasion, to look after and see to the safe conduct of the Marquis of —[Tweedale], the newly appointed Governor of Madras, who is expected by the next steamer from England, and enjoined me to pay particular attention to the comfort of his lordship during the voyage to Cairo, and to place at his disposal the whole of one of our track-boats, that he may be delayed as little as possible. Having received my orders, I returned to the Okella with the agreeable prospect before me of a few days quiet, prior to the arrival of the next mail.

[…] On the 18th of the month, the "Great Liverpool" arrived at Alexandria, bringing the expected Marquis of [Tweedale], and about forty other passengers. We got away about three in the afternoon, reaching Atfeh at midnight, but the quantity of luggage was so enormous, that it took us upwards of three hours to shift it on board the "Cairo" steamer, and two hours more would very likely have been occupied, but for the assistance of a French gentleman named Cler, connected in some way with the Company, who had accompanied us thus far. We did at last turn our backs upon Atfeh, and after a brief stoppage at Cairo, arrived at Suez just in time to catch the "Berenice" steamer, although some of our party, who stuck fast in the sand, between Nos. 2 and 3 Station, had a hard push for it: these were the Governor of Goa and his suite, four gentlemen in one carriage, who were compelled to vary the monotony of their journey by a ride of sixteen miles on the bare backs of the horses, which brought them on to No. 4 in a deplorable condition. It was some consolation to them to find a good meal in readiness, for having seen their mishap, I had ridden quickly forward, in order to dispatch an empty carriage to bring them on, a procedure, now rendered useless by their appearance. So anxious were they about catching the steamer, that I could with difficulty persuade them to sit down while they swallowed their hot stew.

On reaching Suez, I went on board the "Berenice," with Mr. Hill, who, having personally driven the Marquis of [Tweedale] across the desert, obtained a flattering testimonial as to care and attention during the journey, which had in fact been made in little more than twelve hours, by those in the first three carriages. At the hotel, I met with a Captain J—, an officer on sick leave, from India, who bore me company on my return to Cairo; and as time was no particular object to either of us, we spent two days and nights on the way, changing horses only once. Our "Seis," or running footman, kept up with us the whole weary eighty-four miles, relieving himself only by occasionally hanging on behind, and refusing our offer of a seat inside with stoical indifference. He, poor fellow, like the rest of his class, was a mere skeleton, his flesh being wasted away by undue perspirations, and a lack of such food as is essential to keep up the stamina during such continued exercise. Each set of horses, or team, has its attendant "Seis," who, whilst the animals are resting, snatches a brief sleep, and swallows his unpretending meal of bread and water, with perhaps a relish in the shape of an onion, or a pull at the nargileh of the old bawaub, or doorkeeper. As it sometimes happens that the same team of horses has to perform two or three stages, the poor "Seis" comes in for a double duty, which is, nevertheless, unhesitatingly accomplished, and even entered upon with joyful alacrity, should the prospect be seasoned with the promise of a trifle of bucksheesh on the part of any of the travellers. I have known them to convey a letter or message from Cairo to Suez with incredible speed, running all the way, and carrying with them in the bosom of their blue cotton shirt, just as much bread as would serve to sustain them on the journey.

[Cairo was reached.] As Captain J— was anxious to be off to Alexandria, I ordered a cafass of provisions to be sent down to Boulac, and one of our best boats to be got in readiness. We set sail with a fair wind, and a tolerably high Nile, at seven in the evening, and were one day and two nights in reaching Atfeh. I much regretted the loss of my travelling companion, whose society had proved most agreeable, although his health was so impaired, that he appeared to move with difficulty. I lost sight of him on reaching Alexandria, and imagine that he joined some one in an extended tour into Upper Egypt.

On making my appearance in the morning at the "Agency Office," I was introduced by Furner to a Captain Proudfoot, who had just arrived in a small steam-vessel called the "Little Nile," recently purchased by Mr. Waghorn, for the service between Cairo and Atfeh. I was astonished, when I went on board, that so frail a cockle-shell could ever have lived in a rolling sea, like that of the Bay of Biscay. She is of iron, flat-bottomed, and used to ply on the Thames, above bridge, and it could scarcely have been any common inducement that tempted Captain Proudfoot and his little crew, to undertake so perilous a voyage. Off Cape Finisterre they encountered a severe storm, which lifted the very boilers from their fastenings, and drove her on shore almost a wreck, but they managed to repair her in such a way, that they reached Malta in safety, and there patched her more effectually. Mr. Raven has now put her into the hands of one of the Pasha's engineers, who is altering her to suit the nature of the Nile service, and when complete, she will be the fastest and most jaunty of the river steamers.[183]

In the beginning of September, Mr. Raven paid us a visit, in order to see what progress had been made, and to carry out some ideas of his own, with respect to the interior arrangements of the new vessel. ... I got Captain Proudfoot to explain to me the arrangement of the magnets, with which a sea-going iron boat is always furnished, so that I might be able to replace them, in the event of their being wanted.

Some person having mentioned to the Pasha, that some curious tents. belonging to Mr. Waghorn, were lying in the custom-house, we have received intimation of a vice-royal wish to see some of them erected. It seems that the tents in question, formed part of those put up at Eglintoun Castle, on the occasion of the famed tournament, and that they were afterwards purchased by Mr. Waghorn, to serve as sheltering-places on the desert, between the Stations. Mr. Raven accordingly gave directions that the cases should be transported to the far end of the square, where a fit spot, near the Greek Consulate, was selected, Furner and I being deputed to unpack and overhaul them. [...]

We could not induce the Pasha to cross the threshold and inspect our handiwork, although some of his suite had the curiosity to take a peep at the interior. His Highness seemed fully satisfied with this one visit, as he never again honoured us with a call, and the tent was soon after taken down, and re-consigned with its fellows to the custom-house, where I think it not unlikely that they still remain. [...]

As it is not my intention to weary the reader with a description of each of my several journeyings across the Isthmus, I shall allude

183 Here is another instance of Waghorn's recklessness in trusting a small boat to make such a journey.

> only to two more at the close of the year 184-, when my engagement with Messrs. Waghorn came to an end.

Evidently even river journeys were not free of risk and the weather as much as human error could cause problems:

> I had the pleasure of conducting the late lamented Baboo, (Dwarkanauth Tagore,)[184] who was returning to India with a large retinue of friends and dependants, after a rather protracted stay in England. On our way up the Mahmoudieh, the boat of which I was in charge, encountered a very severe storm or tornado, the wind setting with extraordinary violence right in our teeth, and bringing us to a complete stand still. We lay-to whilst it lasted, for the space of half-an-hour or so, and as we had no sail, or other impediment, to offer any resistance, it passed over us without doing any injury; but its effects, on resuming our course, were very apparent. A mile farther up the Canal, we found a fine boat turned completely upside down, and floating in a sea of sesamen and grain; hen-coops and dead poultry, with half-emptied baskets of provisions, covered the surface of the now still water, whilst the banks were strewed with fragments of earthenware, and such valuables, as had been rescued from the wreck. Two little children had perished, and the distracted mother was wringing her hands and tearing her hair, in the intensity of her sorrow. Farther on, a second boat lay swamped, with a portion of the mast only out of water. A half-resuscitated English gentleman lay gasping on the bank, having been rescued by one of the boatmen, who had dived under to his assistance. A little brandy served completely to restore him, and I then recognised a Mr. L—, who had been staying for some time in Alexandria, having retired from India on a pension. We took him a mile or two with us, and then transferred him to another boat, deeply bewailing the loss of some valuable property, which the ducking would render useless.
>
> This trip seemed destined to be replete with accident. A young

184 Dwarkanath Tagore (1794-1846) spent some time working for the East India Company, but then became a leading Indian industrialist in banking, insurance and shipping. He had strong ties with England, where he died and is buried.

cadet, who had vainly sought below for some place wherein to stow himself for the night, rolled himself up in two or three pea-jackets, and lay down to sleep on the roof. A sudden lurch pitched him over into sixteen feet of water, and had not some one who lay near him, heard the splash, and raised an alarm, it would have been all over with him, for the night was dark, and we were shooting rapidly a-head. The boat was instantly stopped, and I then bade one of our Arabs to jump in and rescue the unfortunate lad, promising him a liberal bucksheesk. No, he would not go—if it had been in the day time, a dip would have been of no consequence, but at night he was afraid. His companion was equally inexorable, so, seeing that farther delay must prove fatal to the cadet, I pushed the first in, when the other, fearing to lose a share of the buckskeesk, followed of his own accord. Then succeeded a few moments of very painful suspense, for they had a long way to swim before reaching the spot where the accident occurred, and it was probable that the cadet, encumbered as he was with three coats, had sunk at once to the bottom. Great was our relief, therefore, when the exclamations of the Arabs assured us that they had succeeded in landing him, although it was not very easily that animation was restored. As the young gentleman himself had little or nothing to offer in the shape of reward, to those who had been the means of saving him, and seemed indeed to regard his return to mother earth with perfect nonchalance, a subscription was got up among the passengers, and one of the dripping Arabs went round to collect the offerings, which were liberally showered into his greasy tarboosh. About three or four pounds were thus netted, which certainly ought, in equity, to have been divided between the two boatmen, but the glitter of the precious metals proved too strong a temptation for our worthy collector, who, as he emerged from the cabin, cast one glance towards the poop, where his companion was seated at the tiller, and then securing the cap with its contents, between his teeth, glided noiselessly over the side of the boat, and dived clear off with his booty. I afterwards learned, that he ran back to Alexandria, and invested his treasure in the purchase of a snuff and tobacco shop.

As Dwarkanauth travelled with many retainers, and there was also the usual average of Overland passengers, our party for Suez was rather a large one, and the murrain having robbed us of upwards of a score of horses during the last few weeks, there was but little accommodation in the way of carriages. The invalids, and most of the ladies, got seats, but the rest were obliged to have recourse to the donkey-chair or saddle, whilst I selected a light dromedary, and trotted along with the hindermost. We found it very difficult to keep together, and as the darkness increased, were guided only by the harsh cries of the drivers, as they urged on their unwilling animals. Every now and then some chair would come down with a run, from the unequal motion of the two donkeys attached to it, spilling the frightened occupant on to the hard sand, or, what was still worse, a portion of the wretched harness would give way, and cause the dropping of one corner of the sedan, which, if not speedily rectified, is sufficient to tire the patience of the most stoical. If the donkeys are well trained, no locomotion could be more agreeable than that of these machines, but should the foremost animal indulge in a canter, whilst his follower is not to be coaxed out of a trot, the effect is perfectly indescribable.

Our mishaps and delays were so frequent, that I at length grew weary of perpetually dismounting from my lofty perch to render assistance, and having fallen in with an interesting companion in the person of T—, of Anti-slavery celebrity, we made up our minds to push on together, the more especially as the Calcutta steamer was waiting for the Baboo and his party. At No. 5 Station, we exchanged our tired montures, for two of our van horses, which had been left by one of the foremost of the carriages, and thus, with halters of twisted straw, and without saddles, we galloped away through the darkness, very much to the amusement and satisfaction of my fellow-traveller, who declared he had seldom experienced anything so pleasurable in the way of a ride. It was certainly a glorious night, and the road, saving where an occasional stone or piece of rock, threatened to bring down our stumbling hacks, safe and pleasant. I could not, however, enter very fully into the feelings of my companion, for I was fearful that the steamer might have put to sea before we could reach Suez, and I had yet a good deal to receive from several of the passengers, who had quitted Cairo before I had collected their monies. There was nothing either to be got at the Stations in the way of provision, for the parties who preceded us, had demolished everything eatable, saving a few potatoes and onions, which we sliced up and made into soup.

By the time we reached the hotel, every one was gone to the ship, to which I also made the best of my way in a light skiff. They were raising the anchor as I gained the deck, and I had but little time to parley with such of the passengers as were on my books. With the Baboo I had no trouble, as he immediately handed me a cheque on his bankers, but with some of the others I was not so fortunate for finding themselves in security, and the vessel almost under weigh, they would fain have taxed their bill. In this emergency, I pencilled a hasty note to our agent at Bombay which I dropped into the letter-box on board, and having taken this precaution, quitted the ship.

I was driven back alone to Cairo in two days, staying the intervening night at No. 4 Station. As we approached No. 2, which is some twenty miles from the city, we came upon Messrs. F— and D—, of the Peninsular and Oriental Company, making a trial of one of the new iron carriages, constructed for desert use, by the eminent builder, Andrews of Southampton. In respect of comfort and appearance, they are all that can be desired, but the account which I received of their go-a-head capabilities, was certainly not much in their favour. My two friends had quitted Cairo two days before I fell in with them, with four horses and a plentiful larder, and after countless stoppages, had at last come to a complete standstill, in the middle of a vast field of loose sand, in which the narrow iron wheels were effectually embedded, more than half way up to the axle, and still deeper they would have gone, but for the body of the carriage, which was resting on the sand. I found the two travellers and their driver lolling at great ease, over a fine ham and sundry chickens, and as they robbed my driver of two of his horses, we levied a counter contribution on them, and made free with their knives and forks. Soon after quitting them, they made another advance of half-a-mile, and then, finding the loose sand too powerful an opponent to their progress, turned their horses heads round, and returned to Cairo. These new carriages do not appear (to me at least,) adapted to the peculiarities of the desert, inasmuch as the wheels are too small, and the tyres not nearly broad enough, whilst the cranked axles are directly opposed to easy draught. I am not aware with whom the design originated, but it would have been wiser in my opinion, to have fairly established a fault in those already so long in use, than to have risked the expense of building half-a-dozen new ones, on a principle, which any one moderately experienced in Egyptian travelling, would have immediately condemned. The carriages used by Mr. Waghorn, in appearance, a cross between a bathing-machine and. an errand-cart, are really constructed on good sound principles, and cost Raven a great amount of trouble and expense in their perfection. The wheels are six feet in diameter, and will clear a tolerably large lump of rock or stone, without breaking a spring; they are also so skilfully balanced, that when loaded, there is but little weight thrown on the shaft horse, and their motion is both easy and agreeable.

Two or three days after my return to Cairo, and during some conversation with Raven, I learnt that the affairs of the Company by whom I was employed, were likely to undergo a change, and that arrangements were about to be entered into, to dispose advantageously, of the whole concern. I should scarcely have received this information so soon, but for the kindness of Raven, who was anxious that I should be on the look out for some other mode of employing myself, as in the course of another month or two, the management would probably pass into other hands, and I should then be at loose ends in a foreign land. In the event of my wishing to remain in Egypt, he promised his best influence in my behalf with his successors, though it was not likely they would retain many English in their employ.

Thanking him very cordially, I promised to think the matter over, and proceeded once more to Alexandria, to meet the "Great Liverpool," and make my last official trip across the desert. She arrived on the 29th of the month, and brought some thirty or more passengers, among whom were the Imaum of Muscat, and to my great satisfaction, my friend P—, with his amiable and accomplished wife, whom he was transplanting from the bogs of Ireland, to cheer his solitude in Egypt.

We reached Cairo without let or hindrance, but scarcely had we passed the tombs of the Sheiks, on the verge of the desert, than our horses began to gib, and I foresaw that a night of trouble was before us. The van in which I rode, contained rather a mixed party, in the persons of the Rev. Dr. T., a Frenchman, a Portuguese nobleman, and myself, together with two or three bottles of orgeat and eau sucrèe, and a heavy carpet bag, the property of the Hidalgo.

With considerable difficulty we got past No. 2 Station, between which and No. 3, we came to a complete standstill, and no efforts on the part of either the driver, Seis, or myself, could induce our poor horses to move: they were completely done up, and as ours was the last van of the six, there was no chance of assistance from any of our own people. After waiting for about an hour, the doctor and the French gentleman decided upon attempting to reach No. 4 Station on foot, which they might easily accomplish; though being late at night, and quite dark, it required some presence of mind. Fearful, however, that they might wander from the track and get into difficulty, I dispatched the Seis with them as a guide.

The Portuguese declared he would stick by his carpet-bag which contained all his valuable property, and we two, therefore, made what service we could of the two seats of the van; and rolled up in our cloaks, slept till near day-break; the Arab driver curling himself up as close as possible to one of the horses which lay on the sand, almost incapable of motion. At dawn we awoke and tried anew to get the horses on, but with no better success than before, and at this fresh disappointment, my companion's slender stock of patience entirely forsook him, and he showered upon me a volley of abuse in such curiously broken English, that despite our unpleasant predicament, I could not refrain from laughter.

[...] By degrees I managed to convince him, that instead of blubbering like a child, it would be more expedient to aid me in devising some means of locomotion, by which we might reach the next Station. Making a bundle of all the cloaks which had been left in the van, I slung them and the carpet-bag across one of the leaders, flinging my prayer-carpet over the whole by way of a saddle. My ferocious Portuguese was thus tolerably mounted, and sending with him the Arab driver, on a second horse, to show him the way, I bade him "good speed," and particularly enjoined him not to omit sending me some assistance on arriving at the Centre Station. This he promised faithfully to do, although I afterwards found, he had abused me like a pickpocket, on finding himself once more in safety.

I was now left to the quiet enjoyment of the empty carriage; and a bottle of the eau sucrèe, left behind by the Frenchman. Upon a portion of the latter, and one or two limes which I had in my pocket, I made a sort of breakfast, and was thinking of composing myself to sleep, by way of shortening the weary hours which must elapse before assistance could reach me, when I was startled by the sound of voices. Looking out, I saw two Bedouins approaching, on dromedaries, to whom, when they came up, I at once explained my unpleasant position, soliciting their aid to set me once more a-going. There was, fortunately at this time, a very good feeling existing between our people and such of the

Bedouin tribes as frequented this portion of the desert, as it was to them we looked for the supply of camels to convey the mails and baggage between Cairo and Suez, paying them according to an established tariff, varying with the price of provision. I had, therefore, no sooner explained to them who and what I was, than the good fellows dismounted, and drawing from their saddle-bags a feed of chopped straw, which they saturated with water, I very soon had the satisfaction of seeing my two jaded horses on their legs again. To myself they administered a few hearty whiffs of a chibouque which wonderfully animated me, and then, putting our shoulders to the wheel, we succeeded in moving a turn or two ahead. Having fairly started me,—my two friends, stoutly refusing any offer of remuneration,—gave me a parting blessing, and sent me on my way rejoicing.

I did not reach No.4 Station until near two in the afternoon, when I found the Seis coming to the rescue with a pair of fresh horses. Dr. T. and the Frenchman had arrived safely on foot, and had been taken on in another van, whilst the Portuguese was sleeping off the fatigues of his ride in one of the bedrooms above. I called him down to partake of some refreshment, and at three o'clock, we again pursued our journey, reaching Suez at midnight, and becoming on the way, the best friends imaginable.

Having some business of importance to transact for Mr. Raven, I had no time to take any rest in Suez, and therefore, set off almost immediately on my return to Cairo. It was Christmas eve, and the night proved unusually cold, whilst I found it impossible to keep off the wind, which blew steadily through the open cart, piercing the ample folds of my bernous. On we jogged through the dark, the weary Arab fast asleep on his driving seat, bobbing his head to the measured creak of the springs; that, and the jingle of the harness, being the only sounds which disturbed the silence of the desert. Warming my inner man with a spoonful of brandy, I threw myself into the bottom of the cart, and giving my slumbering Jehu an apparently accidental poke in the ribs to recall him to his duty, courted some short repose.

We had, however, reached a portion of the desert, which one would think ought more properly to have belonged to Arabia Petrea, so covered is it with large round stones. Every now and then a wheel would come in contact with one of these, giving us a shock sufficient to drive the breath out of us, and recalling me from pleasant dreams of roaring fires and Christmas cheer, to a chilly sense of my uncomfortable position at the bottom of the cart, with the wind whistling through every crevice. Being however considerably fatigued, I again relapsed into an unquiet slumber, which gradually subsided into a complete state of repose, as we exchanged the stoney track for the fine hard sand. I slept long and uninterruptedly, until I was suddenly aroused by a shock which had well nigh thrown me out of the vehicle. Raising myself, I looked out and missed my only companion, the driver. The shaft horse had fallen over the body of a dead camel, and had brought the other down with him, whilst poor Hassan had been pitched clean off his perch, and was picking himself up with many lamentations. I scrambled out in front as well as I could, to assist him in getting under weigh again, for our contiguity to the carcass was anything but agreeable. Fortunately nothing had been broken, and after a delay of ten minutes or so, we were jogging on as before, although both. of us were now thoroughly awake. A good supper awaited us at No.6 Station, and as I had to perform half the journey with the same horses, I turned for a few hours into bed. …

I reached Cairo the following morning, and thus ended my engagement with Messrs. Waghorn and Co. On resigning my office, I was gratified with a flattering testimonial from Mr. Raven, and an invitation to consider the hotel as my home, so long as I might incline to remain in Egypt. Being as yet quite undetermined what to do, I accepted his very kind offer, occasionally resuming my accustomed seat in the little office, and rendering what assistance I could, in expediting the mails and passengers. There was a good deal of business also, consequent upon the almost daily arrival of parties bound on a visit to Upper Egypt; and not only were all our own boats put in requisition, but many more were hired for the excursion from Boulac and other places.

Boulac

9

THE PASHA ASSUMES CONTROL OF THE OVERLAND ROUTE

Bevan's account shows that by the early 1840s Waghorn had in place in Egypt an effective and efficient administration, with agents at Alexandria, Atfeh, Cairo, and Suez to see to the transfer of mails and passengers, with Bevan and Turner acting as couriers for the parties crossing the desert. Traffic had increased to such an extent that, as noted earlier, firms began issuing guidance and travel brochures for passengers. *Messrs W[aghorn]. & Co's Overland guide to India, by three routes to Egypt*, London, was published in 1842, 1844 and 1846, while Grindlay and Co. provided *Hints for Travellers to India detailing the several routes* in 1847. All these brochures gave information on alternative routes, the regulations issued by the various companies or countries, prices for each part of the journey and for specific baggage. Emma Roberts gave her own advice in a series of articles for *Parbury's Oriental Herald*, but surely she must have assumed that large items of furniture would not be hauled across the overland route, but would travel via the Cape?

> Ladies carrying out pianos should, unless they engage very large cabins, be content to have them packed up and deposited in the hold; they take up a very inconvenient quantity of space, are liable to be damaged in heavy seas, and are, moreover, in nine cases out of ten, dreadful nuisances to the rest of the passengers. Musical instruments on board ship form the annoyance in fine weather; half a dozen performers, instead of playing in concert, will vex the ears of all on board by executing at the same times as many different pieces of music, which altogether create the most horrid discord imaginable.[185]

185 *Parbury's Oriental Herald and Intelligencer*, Emma Roberts, 'The East India Voyager: Ten minutes' advice to the outward-bound', 5

Grindlay was brave enough to publish letters received from passengers who had crossed the desert. 'T. M.' (1843) complained that charges for both small and large parcels were the same. 'If you remonstrate with Messrs. Hill and Co., at Cairo, their answer is, 'You are at perfect liberty to convey your luggage any other way, IF YOU CAN.' 'C. H.' (1843) advised on wearing light clothing, reporting that 'Everything here at native shops is cheap and bad, at European shops dear, double English price, and of ordinary quality,' and he also complained of extra charges. In another letter 'C.H.' (the same?) noted:

> As regards crossing the Desert, the journey would be much better if about £5 were outlayed in picking the large stones out of the road, the stations being kept cleaner, and the horses better fed and treated. But I cannot but omit to mention the creditable, civil, clean manner in which No. 4 station is kept, (would that all were like it!) by a William Clerk and his wife (English). The treatment was really quite luxurious, although in the middle of the Desert; pray recommend all to try and sleep there if they can, instead of rolling over and over in No, 2, as we did, literally eaten up; it can generally be contrived. At Suez—dirty place, filthy inn; but a new one is building, so we must not complain.[186]

These complaints would appear to have substance: the cost of carrying packages, the stones on the desert road (mentioned in Bevan's account), the uncomfortable journey in the track-boats between Alexandria and Atfeh, the unwelcoming nature of Suez, and the variety of accommodation at the various Stations in the desert. As a private agency Waghorn had to fund the enterprise himself, so it is not surprising that in true entrepreneurial style he looked to purchase items he needed as cheaply as possible. The river boat and the tents were two examples and another was also seen by Bevan in Alexandria on the night before his departure from Egypt:

> There [at the back of the Okella, close to the sea-shore], in its cobwebbed solitude, stood the old Enfield stage, umwhile the pride of Glover, who little thought, as he rumbled along to and from the

186 *Hints for Travellers to India detailing the several routes*, 36-40.

> Bank twice a-day, with his six insides, that his rickety old machine was ever destined to run from Enfield Wash to the Red Sea. Such had nevertheless been the intention of Mr. Waghorn in purchasing it, and sending it out to Egypt, though if it ever get there now, it must certainly be through the intervention of miracle.

Passengers on the Overland Route were booked into various hotels: Rey's at Alexandria, the Grand Hotel de France at Atfeh, the Great Eastern Hotel at Cairo, while Waghorn's hotel was available at Suez. In the early days, from 1835 and before Bevan's arrival, Waghorn found himself in competition with 'Mr. Hill', but the two joined up around the end of 1837. Commander Wilson again is sour on the subject and tries to show that neither party was first in the field:

> [The Bombay steam committee] took the opportunity of Colonel Barr's going to Egypt in 1837, to avail themselves of his services to negotiate with Mahommed Ali for permission to build station-houses in the desert; which he did successfully, and arranged a contract with parties for building them, and also providing vans and mules for the transport of passengers. Thus it was that the first four station-houses, with vans and mules for the transport of passengers, were provided by the Bombay Steam Committee, and did not, as is the popular belief, start into existence through the instrumentality of Mr. Waghorn. It was no fault of the Bombay Committee, who had then dissolved, that soon after their construction Messrs. Hill and Co., to whom they had been confided, did not keep them in so comfortable a state as they should have been.[187]

From 1840 onwards the P&O Company also had its own agents, with whom it seems Bevan was on friendly terms. But, as Grindlay showed, this service was supported by the British government and thus in direct competition with the Waghorn/Hill enterprise—disregarding all the effort that they had expended in setting up the scheme. Bevan's comments on the suitability of the donkey-carts whose design was developed in Egypt by Raven, compared with those unsuccessfully tried by P&O from a design by Andrews of Southampton, shows the

187 Wilson, *op. cit.*, 68.

value of being on the spot. Equally he gives due acknowledgement to Raven and Hill as being the instigators of the Overland Route, but 'it needed however the enterprizing spirit and untiring perseverance of Mr. Waghorn, before the undertaking could be brought to assume any thing like a flourishing appearance.'

Waghorn was aware that his efforts were not being duly acknowledged by the British Government and wrote from 34 Cornhill on 20 November 1841 soliciting an 'interview' with Sir Robert Peel in order to explain his 'fifteen years of gratuitous toil' and to request some kind of reward for his services.[188] No meeting was arranged, so on 4th January 1842 Waghorn set down his request in a letter:

> Honorable Sir, My object last November [was] in seeking […an interview…] to explain my just claims on H. M. Govt and the Country at large, for having unaided and alone and with powerful opposition, first established the present Overland Route to India whereby we now communicate on the 4th of every month with that Country in from 31 to 35 days.
>
> In effecting this great object I have toild gratuitously and unceasingly for fifteen years, sacrificing my health, my prospects, my private property, I have nothing in return for this, on the other hand am involved in debt to private Relations and Friends who assisted me with means years ago when I urged them to do so, hoping that in due course of time my Country would not fail to reward me, and thus enable me to repay them.
>
> Under these circumstances my <u>own heart</u> tells me that I am fully entitled to a Reward from Govt. and the Country at large who are deriving the exclusive benefit of my toils, not myself. Many friends have urged me to make my appeal to you in your official capacity as the first minister of the Kingdom and I trust that it will not be made in vain.
>
> From the year 1829 till 1839, <u>ten years</u>, the communication with India was in my own hands and oftentimes the Govt. and the Country were out in possession of all the important intelligence from the East through <u>my means</u> by my unceasing toils and usefulness. I could detail the almost incredible despatch that followed one

188 British Library, Add. MS 40495, f.187.

> after the other achieved by me, but my name and usefulness in this matter is too generally known to need recapitulation.
>
> One point beyond another may not be out of place to mention. I remained in Egypt during the War in 1840 against Mehemet Ali, after all the Officials of the Govt. were ordered to leave it or cease their functions, and I hesitate not to say that it was principally owing to myself that the Communication was not disturbed, for I was continually urging the Pasha to protect it as before and to his honor he did so although our then Govt. was the main party against him.
>
> I therefore most respectfully solicit that my claim may be taken into your most favourable consideration, and if you consider my better course would be to lay them before the House of Commons in the shape of a Petition, I will do so, or any other course you deem fit.
>
> Honourable Sir, The public feeling in England, India and China, &c., is in my favour, and that I ought to be remunerated by Govt. for my toils: from the good they have done to the Country at large. I have hastened by many years and successfully brought about the establishment of this great object so fraught with benefits to all the Foreign, Commercial and domestic Relations which now unite our Eastern Empire more closely than ever to Great Britain.
>
> It may be urged the present diminution in the public Revenue will not allow of my claims meeting due compensation. Surely Great Britain has yet enough at disposal left to reward Individuals like myself who have toiled so many years for her benefit at all personal risks and sacrifices. I therefore trust that this appeal to you will not suffer my name and Services to be neglected and in this hope I have the honour to subscribe myself / Your most humble / and very obedient servant / Thomas Waghorn.[189]

Again no response seems to have been forthcoming, so March 1842 finds Waghorn endeavouring to persuade the Government to accept a scheme he proposed for moving troops through Egypt to India. Identical letters were sent to the Earl of Aberdeen at the Foreign Office and to Thomas Duke, Sir Robert Peel, Lords Haddington and

189 British Library, Add. MS 40499, f.67.

Fitzgerald and Sir Henry Hardinge. To the Earl of Aberdeen he wrote on 18 March:

> With reference to my conversation with your lordship last Saturday I have now the honour to send on the other side the Plan (by quickest rapidity) for Troops to Bombay through Egypt.
>
> The Plan of Mr Waghorn
>
> 1st. The Troops through Egypt at 1000 men a month for the months of May, June, July, August and September by steamers from Southampton touching at Gibraltar and Malta to Alexandria.
>
> 2nd. If thought proper the first 1000 men might be taken up at Malta for Egypt.
>
> 3rd. The salt, provisions, wines, or spirits for the troops can also be taken from Malta with the first 1000 men. Biscuits, flour, water and other rations can be got in Egypt.
>
> Another 1000 men might be sent the month after from Gibraltar and replaced at both Malta and Gibraltar afterwards. These men would arrive in Bombay in 25 days from Malta, in 30 from Gibraltar. The other troops could go 1000 a month by steam from England to Alexandria and rapidly through Egypt to Bombay. The Pasha will allow troops to go through when it is explained to him that they will go unarmed. The Pasha does not consider it political to permit any armed soldiers in Egypt except his own. Mr W is ready to go at once to arrange the whole through Egypt to the satisfaction of all. By the above plan these 2000 men can be got through Egypt before France knows anything about it in Paris.[190]

Although he was often previously referred to as 'Lieutenant' Waghorn, it was only now that he finally received the full rank, having qualified eleven years earlier. He used the occasion to emphasise to Lord Aberdeen that he would be a fit person to oversee any arrangements for troop movements through Egypt:

> 34 Cornhill, 31 March 1842
>
> I am most happy to affix to this as gratifying proof of H. M. present Government towards my Overland labours [a newspaper cutting]:

190 British Library, Add. MS 43239, ff. 91-2.

> 'On Thursday last the Lords of the Admiralty promoted Mr Waghorn to the rank of Lieutenant in the Royal Navy—a step that had been refused to him by successive Governments during the last ten years. This act of Lord Haddington's administration, evidently intended as an official acknowledgment of Mr. Waghorn's exertions in establishing the overland route to India, will be received by the public as a new proof of the Conservative Ministry to recognise and reward the meritorious services of individuals forwarding the commercial and general interests of the country.'
>
> The next Express from India will arrive on or about the 2nd prox. – then we shall better know of Affairs in India; and if emergent, I shall be ready to go at a minute's notice to Egypt for the purpose of doing and carrying out the matter of Troops through that country if required.[191]

By letter of 5 April the Earl informed him, not surprisingly, that his services were not required. Never one to let matters rest, Waghorn continued to press his claim and in a letter to Aberdeen's confidential secretary, Clinton G. Dawkins, he emphasised his close association with the Pasha:

> 20 April 1842. I beg leave to offer the following to you for Lord Aberdeen's information. The Pasha of Egypt, Mehemet Ali, is under a great personal obligation to me and one that he never can forget, and I believe that I have more interest with him than the Consuls General of England, France, Russia and Austria, and this (without egotism) I can prove to Lord Aberdeen should he require to know the nature of this extraordinary obligation.

He also recorded that 'the whole of the Egyptian route is under my control' and suggested, to maintain secrecy, that if ordered to suddenly depart for Egypt, it could be announced in *The Times* and elsewhere

> that I was obliged to go to Egypt on account of one of my partners (Mr Hill) having unexpectedly arrived in England in bad health

191 British Library, Add. MS 43,239, f. 100.

> which caused my going there to look after my private establishments in that country.[192]

On 23 April Dawkins replied that there was 'no intention at present' of moving troops according to Waghorn's scheme.[193]

Two months later, on 29 June, Waghorn again wrote to Lord Aberdeen, this time concerning the transmission of mail to and from India. Through C. J. Dawkins he requested an appointment with the Foreign Secretary to discuss it, enclosing a second letter to Aberdeen himself:

> I have the honour and satisfaction to hand you on the other side a New Plan for the Overland Route independent of France, having been induced to direct my attention thereto, for reasons which have too often ~~suspiciously~~ interfered with, and delayed, letters &c from India, at Marseilles, Paris or Boulogne.
>
> I shall send in this Plan to Lords Haddington and Fitzgerald, and when the Government and the East India Company wish to carry it out, I shall be ready for such service, with all that energy which marked my humble labours at the onset of the "Overland Route".
>
> I beg to assure your Lordship, that I am in possession of all the necessary detail for successfully carrying out the same to its utmost extent.
>
> A quicker Route to Egypt without going through any part of France
> London to Antwerp by steam: 20 hours
> Antwerp to Liege by Railway: 5 hours
> Liege to Aix la Chapelle by Land: 4 hours
> Aix la Chapelle to Cologne by Railway: 2 hours
> Cologne to Mannheim: 19 hours
> Mannheim to Insbruck by Kempten: 45 hours
> Insbruck to Venice: 35 hours
> [Total] 135 hours
> As above: London to Venice: 5 days 10 hours
> A first rate steamer at 10 miles an hour, can go from Venice to Alexandria and vice versa, distance 1204 miles, in 5 days 10 hours

192 *Ibid.*, f. 127.
193 *Ibid.*, f. 129

> [Time between London and Egypt: 10 days 10 hours]
> Government Dispatches from London to Alexandria, can thus be conveyed within Eleven Days.
> The Austrian Government will grant our Couriers all the privileges enjoyed by their own Diplomatic ones. The most perfect secrecy would be secured, together with a shorter conveyance than at present, free altogether of France by a Treaty with Germany &c for that purpose.[194]

Perhaps with relief a reply was scribbled on the verso of Waghorn's letter to Dawkins: 'all arrangements connected with the transmission of the India Mail from and to the Country are under the direction of the Lords of the Treasury.' One feels that Waghorn was overstepping the mark with his proposal and clearly the Government felt the same: the tiresome man would have to pester someone else!

Wilson states that 'some time about 1842, a company was formed for establishing iron steam-boats on the Nile and Mahmoudie Canal, which continued to work for a short time', after which Mehemet Ali took the whole enterprise under his own control. One boat was Waghorn's *Little Nile* which Bevan recorded arriving about this time. The P&O Company also introduced the *Atfeh*, soon followed by the *Lotus* and the *Cairo*.[195] The Company faced difficulties because the Government mail remained under control of the Admiralty. Navy officers gave the mail priority, so ships would be ordered to sail as soon as it was on board, perhaps leaving passengers stranded for up to a month before being able to continue their journeys. Waghorn's mail service was a private concern so did not have this restriction. But he had other problems. In 1842 Waghorn was forced to sell his enterprise to Mehemet Ali by a murrain which broke out among Egyptian cattle and which also destroyed nearly the whole of Waghorn's stock of 300 horses kept for the Overland Route. This is the change of which Bevan speaks. The Pasha made an offer for Waghorn's stock and thereafter controlled the Route.[196]

---

194 British Library, Add. MS 43239, f. 241 (to Dawkins) and f. 243 (to Lord Aberdeen).

195 See David and Stephen Howarth, *The Story of P&O*, London, rev. edn., 1994, 42.

196 Information from *The Illustrated Australian Magazine*, vol. 1 (1850-1), 225-6.

The devastation of the cattle was mentioned by Waghorn in a letter to *The Times*, dated 10 April 1844 from his offices at 34 Cornhill:

> Sir,—In your columns this morning is a letter from 17 gentlemen connected with the civil and military services en route to India, complaining of the bad arrangements made for their transit through Egypt, more particularly over the desert; and really it is a source of great regret to me to hear complaints made, while, on the other hand, the greatest possible credit is due, even under the chief circumstance complained of, viz., the fatigue and exhaustion of the horses, arising from a course of nature, over which human means can have no control.
>
> In September 1842—eighteen months ago—that fearful mortality, the murrain, visited Egypt, as it occasionally ever has done since the time of the departure of the Israelites from it. It was one of the standing plagues inflicted by the Almighty upon Pharoah, for "refusing to let the children of Israel go." This fearful mortality has taken away ten-twelfths of the whole of the cattle of Egypt since that time. In October 1842, out of the number of horses in the desert for the transits of passengers, upwards of 100 died by murrain in that month, and its ravages not only continue in various parts of Egypt, but deprive the cattle that remain of their usual stamina and strength.
>
> The Pasha has lost upwards of 1,000,000l. sterling in camels, dromedaries, and horses, without mentioning sheep, goats, and other cattle, since September 1842. His ships have been constantly going to Tunis, Syria, Trieste, and other parts of the Mediterranean, to purchase cattle for the common purposes of husbandry, and many of them die a few days after their arrival.
>
> Under circumstances like these, had the passengers been aware of them, such complaints as have been made could never have emanated from them against the Transit Company. 80 passengers arrived at the Alexandria end to India, and upwards of 100 at the Suez end from India, on the same day; consequently, the cattle on the desert had to do double work; and it should have been a matter of thanks, instead of complaints, that they all got over that desert and embarked to and from India without one being left behind.
>
> Sir, I think enough has been said to exonerate the Transit

> Company, who are doing their utmost, under the Pasha's soul-stirring influence, amidst heavy losses, to give satisfaction to all who pass through.
>
> Regarding the provisions, the murrain will not allow the cattle that remain to gain fat or strength, and therefore their meats are lean, and do not look so well as otherwise, and this will account for the ordinary looking state of the provisions: also, the great influx of passengers at Alexandria and Suez (more than 180) would not allow of sufficient time to get them better; for it never can be known until the arrival of the steamers, whether there are 50, or 100 to provide for. …[197]

The Egyptian correspondent of *The Times* acquired a copy of a somewhat repetitive letter from Waghorn to the Pasha, written in October 1844, urging the construction of a railway from Cairo to Suez:

> TO HIS HIGHNESS THE PASHA OF EGYPT
>
> You asked me for a letter last evening. This is the letter promised to your Highness in my interview with you.
>
> The time is now come: the British Government require the shortest route to the East. This is only to be got at through your country, Egypt, being the centre and high road between China to the East, and America to the West. Eleven years ago, your Highness projected a railroad over the desert of Suez—the time has now arrived to execute it.
>
> Let no political object stop its execution; do it, through the highest auspices and you will make Egypt the emporium, as it was of old.
>
> This I write confidently—Messrs. Rosthchilds, the most extensive financiers of Europe, can find you the money either in London, Paris, or Vienna. Should you doubt it, I have been assured by them it can be done. The railroad through Egypt must come. I beg your Highness to reflect on this, in order to hand your name to posterity as a greater man, beyond any sovereign, in any European country.
>
> Political, commercial, and domestic relations between the East

197 *The Times*, 11 April 1844, 7.

and West call upon you to do this work. Egypt has already become the high road for Governor-General, officials, and their dependants, also of letters, valuable merchandise, &c., between Europe and the East and West.

Let a railroad be consolidated, by acquiring information from the first-rate engineers of Europe—Messrs. Stephenson or Brunell [sic]. Your country is destined to rise. The views of Russia, Austria, Prussia, England, America, and all other nations, except France, now wish for this railroad. Because France knows, if it be done, that Trieste will become what Marseilles now is. Look to the map of Europe for the truth of these observations, and if your Highness will place yourself or me in communication with both the financiers and engineers, you will have ample proof it will pay your country, and be the means of more wealth and commerce than now is foreseen.

The diplomatists would keep your Highness from the execution. Reason calls you to do this work. By it you will attract the whole world to this country; destined, I believe, to rise among nations.

Whether your Highness makes a railroad between Cairo and Suez, or not, it will come to pass by time as certain as the sun rises.

Seize the opportunity at once, and effect it. In your dynasty of Egypt it will come, as certain as these lines are written.

Money, if wanting, is to be had, and the execution of a railroad from Cairo to Suez will send your name to posterity greater than any act that I can remember in modern history.

I seek no emolument, no credit.

Your Highness stands forward among rulers for what you have done. Complete this railroad from Cairo to Suez, and Egypt is sure to become greater; and who can predict the benefits it may not produce?

I am only a humble man in telling you these ideas: I feel that every word here expressed comes from my heart, as I hope it may carry conviction to your own feelings.

With humble respect,

Your Highness's humble servant,

THOMAS WAGHORN[198]

Snodland

---

198 *The Times*, 5 November 1844, 3.

The British had been keen to establish a railway for the Overland Route and, as Waghorn states, the Pasha had initially agreed to this. In November 1834 he instructed Thomas Galloway, an engineer who had worked for him, to survey a route between Cairo and Suez. Costs having been approved, the Galloway brothers were directed to carry out the work. But John Galloway writes

> Unfortunately the agents of foreign powers, who were opposed to this work, in a political point of view, used every possible exertion and means to dissuade His Highness from proceeding with it, alleging, among other reasons, that the traffic, the extent of which was then doubtful, would not repay so large an outlay, and the necessary expenditure for working the line. These objections, strongly and constantly urged, with the sudden death of my brother, and the subsequent political events in Turkey, have hitherto prevented this important work from being carried out.[199]

He records that in September 1843 the Pasha 'resumed the order for the execution of the railroad to our establishment, and directed my brother to proceed to England to carry out the necessary arrangements.' Locomotives, rolling stock and track were delivered to Alexandria, but in the event the equipment was used just to build two small lines from quarries to the Nile, one in Cairo and one in Alexandria. The Nile remained the principal artery for Egypt's transport needs. In spite of letters from Galloway to British politicians, they failed to confirm any support for the scheme, in particular the rates for carrying mails once it was completed. It may have been the publication of Galloway's 1844 pamphlet which prompted Waghorn's letter—he was ever keen to jump on a band-wagon, but again the Pasha declined to proceed. It was not until 1851 that a contract was signed between one of the Pasha's successors and a representative of Robert Stephenson, the English railway magnate, and the Alexandria-Cairo line was opened in 1855. The Cairo-Suez one followed between 1856 and 1858. But

199 John Alexander Galloway, *Communication with India, China, &c. Observations on the proposed improvements in the overland route via Egypt, with remarks on the ship canal, the Boulac Canal, and the Suez railroad*, London 1844, 4.

after the opening of the Suez Canal in 1869 the latter line was largely useless and was torn up in 1879.[200]

The Pasha's acquisition of the Overland Route caused concern, and *The Times* thought 'All this is the work of French intrigue, for it has been their study to effect this object for the last five years'. The Pasha's grandson was put in charge of the Transit Company 'with subordinate Turks and Egyptians to assist him'. The paper also remarked that the Pasha 'has not been himself' since August 1844, but they were awaiting news 'of the steps our Consul-General at Alexandria, Colonel Barnett, has taken in this dilemma to maintain English interest in Egypt.

> This English Transit was made by Mr. Waghorn and his late partner Mr. Hill, who built all the stations on the desert on account of the Bombay Steam Committee and themselves. They are now taken possession of by the Pasha—this will annihilate the whole of the English interests in the overland route, if Lord Aberdeen does not immediately instruct Colonel Barnett what to do forthwith. A panic regarding this measure will have already reached Bombay by the *Semiramis*, which left Suez for that place 24th ult., and in the opinion of many will jeopardize the overland route, for the transit of mails, &c., so they cannot be safely confided to Turks. … We are also informed from Egypt that Mr. Waghorn anticipated this three months ago, and forthwith despatched his partner to the Committee of the Bombay Steam Fund, again to obtain the station-houses, which are still their property, in order to counteract this unfortunate interruption to our communication with India.[201]

The P&O Company also held talks with the Pasha and decided to transfer their interest in the Overland Route to him:

> The Peninsular and Oriental Company have determined on giving up to the Pasha, for the use of the transit service, their steamers, tugs, and track-boats on the Nile and the Mahmoudish Canal, which they have been using in this country for the past five years,

200 On the early history of Egyptian railways see Amr Nasr El-Din, *Railroads in the Land of the Nile* at <http://*www.aucegypt.edu/researchatauc/rc/ebhrc/news/documents/egyptian_railroads_historybyamrnasreldin*>.

201 *The Times*, 9 February 1846, 5.

for the conveyance of the goods which their steamers bring to and from England and India, and for facilitating the transit of passengers through Egypt.

This complete resignation of the privilege of the navigation of the Nile, on the part of the Peninsular and Oriental Company, has no doubt been brought about by Sir John Pirie, who, when here last March, on account of the company, seemed inclined to submit to the Pasha's views of a monopoly of the transit through Egypt, and in fact, sold to his Highness the small steamer Delta, which had been sent out by the Peninsular and Oriental Company for the purpose of plying on the Nile, and which Mahamet Ali would not permit to be taken round to the river.

It is possible that the Peninsular and Oriental Company may expect that, by present submission to the Pasha's wishes, they may at a future period obtain from his Highness some great advantage, and it is not unlikely that they anticipate that the Viceroy will get tired of the transit administration, when the company would come forward and make proposals by which they would get the transit through Egypt entirely into their own hands … The transit through Egypt will henceforward be a strict monopoly in the hands of Mehemet Ali, and the Peninsular and Oriental Company will pay to this Government at the rate of £8. sterling per ton for the conveyance from Alexandria to Suez, and *vice versa*, of the goods brought by their steamers in transit to and from India.[202]

An English home

For some twenty years Waghorn had been rushing from country to country and a permanent home would have been difficult to establish. Although there is a mention of 'a small cottage at St. Margaret's', Rochester, as the home of Thomas and his wife in 1836,[203] this might have belonged to his brother Edward or sister Mary, and which the couple used as a lodging when in the area. 'Holboro' in the parish of

202 *The Times*, 26 October 1846, 7, quoting a letter from Alexandria dated 9 October.

203 See p. 83.

Snodland often appears as an address on Waghorn's letters, so again at times they would appear to have lodged with his mother or grandfather, or even at the mill with Harriet's parents. In contemporary directories between 1837 and 1850 Thomas is listed as a Snodland resident.

It would appear that Harriet was in Egypt helping her husband between May 1839 to July 1841 at least—she is mentioned by Emma Roberts in September 1839 as recommending a servant for the journey to Suez and for supplying equipment, so she was familiar with the people and organisation. On 20 July 1841 Thomas and Harriet sailed for England from Alexandria on the P&O ship *Oriental*, arriving at Falmouth on 3 August. Thomas must have had a home in London where he stayed during the week. The address where he died: 'Golden Square, Islington', is difficult to trace, but was somewhere in Barnsbury Road, perhaps in the fine terrace still on the west side. However, just a single 1850 directory lists him there in 1849-50.

The Waghorns were still abroad when the 1841 census for Snodland was taken, but by the end of the year a new and substantial house had been built for them in the upper High Street. With the Egyptian agency flourishing this was the time of Waghorn's greatest success. He perhaps had a house-warming event soon after his house was completed. However the description of it in *The Maidstone Gazette* of 23 November is from Islington, so casts doubt on whether or not the event took place there or at Snodland. A later report in *The Albion* of New York must have been copied from a different Kent newspaper and gives Snodland as the venue:

> A most interesting meeting of scientific gentlemen, travellers, and others interested in Egyptian antiquities, took place on Saturday … at Snodland, at the house of our enterprising and distinguished countryman Captain Waghorn, of whom every man of Kent is justly proud.[204]
>
> This interesting opportunity was given to a party of Mr. Waghorn's friends on Saturday last on the occasion of a mummy being

204 This paragraph from *The Albion*, 26 February, 1842; the rest from *The Maidstone Guardian*.

opened, which had been brought to this country from Alexandria by Mr. Waghorn. The mummy was originally from Thebes, and in many respects agreed with the accounts of embalming, handed down to us in the works of Herodotus. The outside sarcophagus, or coffin, was of the acacia or sycamore wood, of the common flat and plain long case shape, without external adornment of figures or colours. On opening the coffin it as found that much violence had been down to the body on its transit to this country, or perhaps long before, as the head was separated from the body, and this accident at once gave evidence that the method of embalming in this instance had been that of steeping in boiling asphaltum or black balm, and that it would be impossible to unroll the bandages entirely, as so great a portion had become burnt and mixed up with the asphaltum. Mr Waghorn wishing, however, to gratify his friends' curiosity and love of investigation in a matter so new to many of them, allowed the mummy to be broken up, and during this operation I made the few following observations.

The body was covered with an entire envelope of coarse cloth, covered with many bands of *zig zag* and plain upright strokes in various colors on a flat white ground, but no hieroglyphic writing could be discovered. This outer covering was much destroyed by damp. Underneath this, the bandages appeared to be of the usual kind of coarse and fine linen, and of different lengths and widths, until within a few layers of the first wrappers applied to the body, when it was discovered that the bandages were so peculiarly fine as not to exceed a quarter of an inch in width, and so placed as to form the most beautiful work, in appearance like basket work, and wrought into shapes of the lozenge and diamond; some portions of this have been preserved. The limbs were separately bandaged, as also each toe and finger, but I was struck with a difference in the mode of covering the toes compared with other mummies in this country, and the difference consists in a representation of the toes being formed distinctly from the members themselves, and placed on the toes, having the figures of the nails formed by thread, and the whole artificial configuration of the foot and toes thereby much more neat than could be made in the common method of bandaging; the nails were not guilt [gilt], but the face had been entirely covered with a *gold wash* or by gilding, but not by *plates* of gold, as is the case with the external marks sometimes used. The teeth were perfect, but the whole head had suffered much from the heat of the bitumen or asphaltum, which had destroyed the entire flesh. The orbits of the eyes were quite empty, and the ears were apparently nearly reduced to a cinder in appearance. The nostrils were filled with neat rolls of linen; and the nose readily broke off the face, yet the internal bone or cartilage was perfect, and I have no doubt the brain had been extracted through the nostrils; there is every reason to suppose, from the general style of bandaging and the envelope covering the body, together with the form of the coffin, that this mummy was of the Graeco-Egyptian period, about two centuries before the Christian era. If you think these remarks are worthy insertion in your *Gazette* they are quite at your service, and I beg to subscribe myself

Your most obedient servant, C. J. MAJOR
Islington, 15th Nov., 1841

After about 1842 the antiquarian Charles Roach Smith used to visit Waghorn at Snodland, as he recorded in his *Retrospections, Social and Archaeological*:

Not unfrequently, I accompanied him on Saturday afternoons to his residence at Snodland, staying with him and Mrs Waghorn until the Monday mornings, when we returned together to London. In everything he was scrupulously methodical, but not fussily so. The chaise was always ready waiting for him at The Bull's Head at the corner of Cuxton Road at Strood. He drove rapidly, quite as fast as the horse, which was a swift one, could canter or gallop, calling for five minutes at the White Hart at Cuxton, and for one minute, on his mother, who lived in a neat cottage, on the right, near the brook at the entrance to Snodland. He would often say "These are my only times of real enjoyment" – which they unquestionably were.

In his own house, a neat comfortable habitation, he was reflective; cheerful he always was, his conversation ever taking a somewhat serious turn; but never touching on his own eventful life. He was deeply benevolent without the slightest ostentation. I had many opportunities of knowing his warmth of heart and his deep attachment to his mother, wife and sister. Usually I met at his house a few of his neighbouring friends, specially invited. The evenings were always agreeable, as the conversation ever took an intellectual turn, and instead of being trite and commonplace, usually ranged to character and men and manners. He adored Shakespeare.

In later years Charles Roach Smith was a frequent visitor to Snodland to give dramatic readings, at which he excelled, and perhaps these visits were the more appreciated because of his former friendship with Waghorn.

Waghorn's friendship with Roach Smith was also noted by the Strood writer, Henry Smetham,[205] who added other local stories:

> There was a turnpike gate at the junction of High Street—North Street, Strood. [...] Returning' from Rochester one night he [Waghorn] found this gate closed. He jumped his spirited horse over it with the chaise attached, the result being the death of the horse !

205 Henry Smetham, *A History of Strood*, Rochester, 1899.

He used to obtain his particular brand of (green) China tea from Mr. George Stevens, chemist, whose shop was near this gate. The packet of tea had to be ready and tossed into the carriage as he passed—he never stopped—arrived to the minute, and if the package was not there his custom was lost.

The Church Family Newspaper, July 1901, gives an amusing account of Waghorn. The writer states that our hero had "a genius for quarrelling with people"—very probably. He continues by stating that Waghorn arrived quite early one morning at his Cornhill office, "travelstained and dirty." "Anybody here who can run ?" he enquired. Being so early, only the secretary was present; a ticket-porter was fetched from outside; like Falstaff, this porter was short, fat and scant o' breath. "Can you run ?" asked Waghorn. "Yes, sir, if I'm paid for it," said the man. Waghorn handed him a packet and said, "Run with this to the Foreign Office." He watched this fat messenger waddling down the street at a pace that simply enraged him. Uttering a series of unprintable expletives, Waghorn ran after the panting porter, and seizing him by the coat tails, rent that astonished person's outer raiment into two pieces almost up to the neck! He then snatched the packet from his hands and rolled him in the gutter, having done which he ran off with it himself! His secretary helped the prostrate messenger from the gutter, and to avoid legal consequences, paid for the damaged coat, and with an added solatium and some soothing words calmed his troubled spirit.

The late Mr. Samuel Dove of Rochester—a retired officer of the Customs—worked for Waghorn in his younger days. Mr. Dove was a native of Snodland; later on he left Waghorn's service for the Customs, feeling probably that it was the wiser course before he had broken his neck.

Driving one day to Rochester. they had reached Wickham Hill. This old road has a sharp gradient with a short abrupt curve to the east at its foot. Waghorn was driving with his customary vehemence. Mr. Dove implored him to be careful. "We're all right, 'Sam, hold on tight," he replied. They soon were, for on turning the corner, over went the chaise, up the bank, over the low hedge into the field, the four wheels spinning round in the air. Up jumped Waghorn, "Are you all right, Sam ?" "Yes, Sir," replied Sam. "Then help me with the horse and to turn the chaise over !" said Waghorn, and off he went again as if nothing had happened.

Waghorn once reached the turnpike gate which then stood in Cuxton Road within a stone's throw of Temple Place; it was late at night and the gateman had gone to. bed; the effort to arouse him was more noisy and prolonged than Mr. Pickwick's friend experienced at the Royal Crescent, Bath. Waghorn fumed, roared, and swore as profanely as did Exciseman Gill; at last the door opened and the gateman appeared. Waghorn knocked him down! Later he said to Mr. Dove: "Sam, I'm really sorry I lost my temper with that gateman; you go and tell him so and give him this sovereign." Off went Mr. Dove and duly discharged his mission. The gateman pocketed the money, saying, "You tell your guv'nor he can d—n well knock me down every time he passes if he'll give me a quid each time he does it !"

Roach Smith's elocutionary abilities have already been mentioned. While attending to his business in Lothbury one day there came an urgent message from Waghorn, asking him to see him at a neighbouring hotel. C.R.S. went at once. What was his astonishment to find Waghorn at dinner with a company, of friends. He asked C.R.S. to oblige him with the recital of some piece, which he named. Roach Smith declined, saying that he had come from his shop as he stood and was quite unprepared for such a thing. Waghorn knew how to take him, "My dear friend," he said, "I have pledged my word of. honour to this company that I could absolutely rely on you both for your memory and that service." That did it, and C.R.S. gave the recital, to the pleasure of everyone present.

After his death Waghorn's house, The Lodge, Snodland, was put in the hands of William Day and Sons, auctioneers, of Maidstone. They advertised it to be let at £45 per annum, while a sale of the contents eventually took place on 27 April 1853. The auction catalogue has survived, but unfortunately it cannot currently be found among the un-catalogued archive of the firm at the Kent Library and History Centre. Fortunately Molly Proctor mentioned it in her book about Day

& Son and included two photographs and other remarks[206] which are gratefully copied here.

The property to be let comprised 'A pretty detached Residence containing large Dining Room, Breakfast Room, Drawing Room, Library, 5 Bedrooms, Water Closet, good kitchen and offices. Cellars, a back entrance with paved Court Yard, 4-stall stable, Coach House, Coachman's Rooms. Ornamental garden with handsome elevated Summer House commanding an extensive view of the surrounding countryside'. A plan to demolish the whole in 1950 fortunately came to nothing and the house survives as a Care Home.

The auction was of
The Dining Room
Brussels Carpet, Telescope, Dining Tables, Spanish
Mahogany Pedestal Sideboard, Indian
Japanned Work Table, Hooks, Musical
Box, Girandole, Barrel Organ;
CHINA, GLASS, AND PLATED GOODS;
Drawing Room
Brussels Carpet, Velvet Pile Rug, Pair of very
handsome Dragon Head genuine Chinese Vases,
Cabriole Rosewood Settee, Tables, Pianoforte,
Bisque China Figures, Paintings;
Breakfast Room
Tables, Chairs, Carpet, Engraving, very fine PROOF
ENGRAVING of Admiral Lord NELSON,
AUTOGRAPH LETTER OF LORD NELSON'S,
With Lady Hamilton's Signature attached;
THE FURNITURE OF FIVE BEDROOMS,
Including four-post French, iron, and tent
bedsteads and furnitures, goose feather beds,
Mattresses, palliasse, washstands, chairs,
dressing tables, carpets, &c.;
500 VOLUMES OF BOOKS; 100 FINE ENGRAVINGS;
A few Oil Paintings;

206 Molly G. Proctor, *"Day after Day" Wm. Day & Sons in Maidstone*, Maidstone, 2000, 14-16.

ANTIQUITIES FROM POMPEII;
HEATHEN DEITIES;
Some war Instruments presented by the Pacha of
Egypt to the late Lieutenant Waghorn; R. N.
VASES CARVED IN STONE;
Gardening Tools; the usual Wash-house, Kitchen,
and Pantry Requisites; and various Effects.

This is the collection of a man of some standing. Furthermore Mrs Proctor adds that William Day 'bought several curios for himself and acquired some interesting correspondence between Lieutenant Waghorn, his wife and notable people including the Duke of Wellington, Gladstone and the Lords Russell, Falmouth and Cardigan.' One wonders what has happened to these.

10

THE TRIESTE EXPERIMENTS

It is clear from Waghorn's letter of 29 June 1842[207] that he was already considering a plan to avoid France in transmitting the mails and that he favoured Trieste instead of Marseilles in seeking an alternative route. The Austrian Lloyd's Steam Navigation Company had been formed in Trieste in 1836 and had built up an impressive network of ships and routes in the eastern Mediterranean. An anonymous pamphlet, published in 1847 at 39 Cornhill, a very near neighbour of Waghorn's office, sang the praises of the Company and its capacity to serve the Overland Route.

> In the autumn of 1845, when complaints became universal that letters never arrived early enough to be answered by the next steamer, Lieut. Waghorn was induced to try the way of Trieste. He applied for assistance to the Austrian Lloyd's Steam Navigation Company, who placed one of its steamers at his disposal, and appointed Mr. Scheuer to accompany and assist him.
>
> Shortly after, the Government of Great Britain were indebted to the Austrian Lloyd's Steam Navigation Company, which dispatched one of their officers (Mr. Frigelmüller) to London, with the first tidings of the victory on the Sutlej.[208] So in the beginning of last year, advices from the East Indies arrived twice in London, quite unexpectedly, some days quicker than they were wont to do by way of Marseilles. In consequence of this success, Government, in conjunction with the East India Company, gave directions to Lieut. Waghorn for six experimental voyages via Trieste, who was again enabled by the aid he received from the Austrian Lloyd's to

207 See p. 202.

208 Victory on 28 January 1846 in the First Anglo-Sikh War.

> accomplish this difficult undertaking, the Company sending Mr. Scheuer to effect the necessary arrangements with the respective Governments and post-administrations.[209]

Waghorn had made a preliminary trial of the route earlier than this, for already on the 12th May 1845 the *Times* reported that

> Mr Waghorn left Dover yesterday (Sunday) at 7 a.m., per *Princess Mary* steamer, for Ostend, on his way to Trieste, to test the times between England and Trieste that mails could be sent to and from India and the East by that route instead of Marseilles. He expects (with his usual rapidity) to accomplish the distance expeditiously, yet it will not be so rapid as it might have been, as the special railway train he applied for from Ostend to Cologne cannot be granted, owing to an impediment at one of the tunnels on the line, and therefore he necessarily has to go that part of the journey by the ordinary train, thereby subjecting himself to the various stoppages to Cologne.

Later in the year the Trieste experiments were revived. *The Times* was very supportive:

> The topic of the day in commercial circles has been the extraordinary journey performed by Lieutenant Waghorn, in bringing the overland mail via Trieste. The complete success of the experiment has been everywhere a matter of conversation, and the projector has added fresh importance to his name by the masterly manner in which he has achieved his undertaking. Mr. Waghorn has now placed beyond a doubt the possibility of effecting a shorter route for overland communication than that at present carried on through France. Temporary obstacles may prevent the service from being performed with certainty throughout the year, but when these shall have been removed, and the advantages of railways in Germany be properly secured, then there is every reason to expect that even further advances may yet be made in shortening the period occupied in the transmission of the despatches. The dates

209 Anon., *The Overland Mail and the Austrian Lloyd's*, London, 1847, 4.

> of the advices from India have already appeared in *The Times* with the news, which was given at an early hour. In addition to this, we have ascertained that the journey from Trieste, made by Lieutenant Waghorn personally, consumed only 90 hours and three-quarters, that gentleman leaving the last named city on the 27th, and reaching London this morning about half past 4 o'clock. On his passage he passed through Niederndorf, Innspruck, Kempten, Meiningen, Stutgard, Cologne, Ostend, and Dover. After a service of this description done to the mercantile public of this country, we may fairly hope that the subscription in aid of awarding a testimonial to this enterprising man will not lack support either from the Government or the public. As the intelligence received by this opportunity was four days in advance of the anticipated arrival of the mail via Marseilles, it will in all probability be in Paris tomorrow, and be read before the Marseilles mail has arrived. The intelligence was published exclusively in the first edition of *The Times*.[210]

Further details of the journey emerged in the columns of the *Times* two days later:

> We received at 11 o'clock last night [2nd November] via Marseilles our express in anticipation of the ordinary Indian mail, which had been anticipated by the despatch brought on Friday morning by Mr. Waghorn via Trieste. [...] He arrived at our office at half past 4 o'clock on the morning of the 31st.

210 *The Times*, 1 November 1845, 6.

THE RACE FROM ALEXANDRIA TO LONDON—ALEXANDRIA, Oct. 22.—Mr. Waghorn started from this port at 10 minutes past 11 o'clock on the morning of the 20th inst., in a steamer placed at his disposal by the Austrian Government, and he hopes by that route to anticipate the arrival in London of the regular Bombay mail which will go through France. The Hon. Company's steamer *Semiramis* arrived at Suez with the Bombay mail on the morning of the 19th, and Mr. Waghorn received a private India despatch from Suez by express courier in the remarkably short space of 21 hours. The *Iberia* leaves this morning with the Bombay mail, which will be sent via Marseilles, thus Mr. Waghorn will have had from Alexandria the start of the mail by 17 hours, and although it cannot be expected that a heavy mail of 60 or 70 boxes can be conveyed from Suez to Alexandria in a short a time as a single despatch, still if Mr. Waghorn does anticipate the arrival of the mail in London by

> more than two days, it will prove that the Trieste route is shorter than that through France.[211]

The Morning Chronicle gave further details: mail from the *Semiramis* was conveyed on horses from Suez to Cairo (7 hours), then on Waghorn's own boat *The Little Nile* to Atfeh (10½ hours), Atfeh to Alexandria (5 hours), where it was anticipated that the journey to Trieste in the Austrian steamer *Emperor* would take a further five days.[212]

Waghorn on the 'Emperor' 24 October 1845

The French were not impressed with the experiment:

> The *Semaphore de Marseilles* after copying our article on the journey of Lieutenant Waghorn from Alexandria to London, observes:—"The English were ambitious of late to make a trial of the communication via Trieste, and congratulate themselves on the result of Lieutenant Waghorn's voyage, a result which the *Times* has every reason to be pleased with; for no other journal has made greater sacrifices to obtain correct and speedy information. Nevertheless we believe that the Marseilles road will not be abandoned. The experiment tried by Mr. Waghorn during the fine season, will stick in that storms are

211 *The Times*, 3 November 1845, 5.

212 *The Morning Chronicle*, 4 November 1845, 4.

> frequent in the Adriatic during the winter, and in the snows covering the roads of Germany, impediments to the progress of the mails which they do not encounter in their passage through France. Besides, at no very remote period, the railroad between Marseilles and Calais will greatly shorten the distance. England will no doubt be impressed by the above considerations with the necessity of making no change in her present communications with India, since that new road opened by Mr. Waghorn is only available when the state of the sea and the fine season combine to insure success.[213]

A couple of months later *The Standard* began to question the motives and authorities behind the Trieste route, following letters to *The Times* from Waghorn which included thanks to the 'spontaneous and, we will add, the gratuitous and wholly *unexpected* kindness of the Austrian Government.' Waghorn described the difficult journey:

> The Austrian Lloyd's steamer *Imperatrice* left Alexandria on the 22nd of January, at noon, soon encountered heavy storms, and having disabled some of her machinery, and run short of coals, was obliged to put into Corfu, and only arrived at Trieste at 6 p.m. of the 29th of January. [...] The dispatches were cleared by the Board of Health, at 8, and Mr. Frigelmüller left Trieste soon after.
>
> Here it must be remarked that no preparations were made on any part of the route ... there were nowhere horses ready, and in many instances the courier was obliged to wait for them. Rain or snow prevailed the whole journey, and in some parts the snow was from between three and four feet deep, and the roads in the worst condition that could be imagined during any winter. The journey therefore was from Trieste to Inspruck, Inspruck to Ulm, Ulm to Stutgard, Stutgard to Carlsruhe. The courier having arrived at Carlsruhe at night, and no preparation having been made for a special train on the railway to Manheim, and there being no steamboats on the Rhine, on account of the floods, the whole journey from Carlsruhe to Cologne was performed in a carriage, over roads that were much flooded. From Cologne to Ostend the journey was by railway.

213 *The Times*, 11 November 1845, 7.

Arrived at Ostend, Mr. Frigelmüller was obliged to wait five hours, no special steam-boat being available; and then he came, not to Dover, but to the Thames. He left Ostend at three o'clock a.m., and arrived in the river at half-past five p.m. on the 4th of February.

The Standard adds

> This is at least curious. In the one place, the express belongs to the *Times*; it brings *our* dispatches. In another place it is the Austrian Government that has paid homage in the *Times*, and has shown its gratuitous and unexpected kindness. Then comes Mr. Waghorn, next day, to claim the merit of his own work, and he thanks the *Times*, "on behalf of the Austrian Lloyd's Company," for the liberal present made to the messenger; that is to say to the person sent by Mr. Waghorn's agent from Trieste, with the Bombay journals, through Germany and Belgium.
>
> We call attention to these contradictions simply for the purpose of placing the saddle on the right horse. The Austrian Lloyd's Company, backed by the Austrian authorities, wish to cry up the German route, and they make Mr. Waghorn their agent. We give all possible credit to the energy and enterprise of this gentleman; but it is clear that he has an eye to number one, and that the merit of the *Times* consists in this—it purchases that which is brought

> to it.. The question of the superiority of the two routes, however, is still an open one, but will, no doubt, be *settled* in the course of the spring, by a really decisive experiment. ... But we have already shown that, by the aid of efficient steamers, and proper management, the journey may be made through France in a shorter time than it can be made through Germany.[214]

The 'race' to find the shortest route for the overland mail even prompted a correspondent in Spain to suggest that a journey from Alexandria to Barcelona via Malta might be worth considering, although some difficulties were pointed out. The *Times* published it 'as a curiosity in its kind'.[215]

Clunn's biography, quoting from *Old and New London*, notes how Waghorn helped the Times couriers, which was perhaps one reason why that newspaper always gave him support in his endeavours:

> In 1845, the jealousy of the French Government threw obstacles in the way of the Times couriers, who brought their Indian despatches from Marseilles. What was sea and deserts to Walter?[216] He at once took counsel with Lieut. Waghorn, who had opened up the Overland Route, and proposed to try a new route by Trieste. The result was that Waghorn reached London 2 days before the usual mail—the usual mail aided by the French Government. *The Morning Herald* was at first 48 hours before the *Times*, but after that the *Times* got a fortnight ahead, and although the Trieste route was abandoned, the *Times*, eventually, was left alone as a troublesome and invincible adversary.[217]

Waghorn did not accept defeat from the *Morning Herald*'s 'win' and wrote to the *Times* from 34 Cornhill on 30 December:

> Sir, ... The *Morning Herald* of this day claims considerable credit for having done a great feat, as it supposes, in getting the overland

214 *The Standard*, 7 February 1846, 3.
215 *The Times*, 25 November 1845, 3.
216 John Walter (1776-1847), second editor of *The Times*, who succeeded his father, the founder.
217 Clunn, *op. cit.* 13-14.

despatch which left Bombay on the evening of the 1st of December to London in 28 days.

I beg to point out, for general information, where the gain was arrived at. It was in the simple fact, which nothing can contradict, of the rapid voyage of the *Ackbar*, belonging to the Hon. East India Company, in 13½ days from Bombay to Suez. (That vessel two years ago was the first steamer that ever made a passage against the south-west monsoon in the China Seas to Suez.) The passage from Bombay to Suez has never before been done under 16½ days; and here was the unprecedented gain of three days for which the *Herald* claims credit, whereas it is due to my friend Robert Napier of Scotland, whose firm built and made the engines for the *Ackbar* that the real credit is due. There is no steamer like her in adverse weather in the Bombay line that I know of. If the *Ackbar* had brought the mail which I got by way of Trieste, and accomplished the passage in the same space of time (13½ days), I should have been in London in 26 days; and I am as positively sure as I write this, that the route of Trieste being 300 miles nearer to Alexandria, and having 400 miles of railway on it already besides, the route via Marseilles will stand no chance against that of Trieste, which I positively feel sure only requires the energy of our Government, the East India Company, and the continental states to bring India so much closer than now, that really I am almost afraid to say in how short a number of days it may be done.

Trieste is the proper way to India, for no man can persuade me it is better to go 300 miles round, via Marseilles, when we can get a better, shorter, and straighter route via Trieste. I hope, ere a year passes, there will not remain a doubt as to which is the most rapid; however, to make it so there is work to be done, and if I am favoured with health and the requisite assistance, Bombay will be within 22 days of London before this day next year.[218]

Even Wilson acknowledged Waghorn's merits in this venture:

In 1843, he [Waghorn] published a pamphlet, advocating the extension of the communication by the Peninsular and Oriental

218 *The Times*, 30 December 1845, 6.

Company to a bi-monthly one. The monthly communication by the Peninsular and Oriental Company had been established about two years, and the desirableness of this extension had already been suggested by other parties.

After this, he proposed the substitution of the route via Trieste for that via Marseilles, and performed several journeys, displaying indefatigable energy, expressly to prove its superiority. The formation of the Austrian Lloyd's Company has been the only result; but the Trieste route has not yet been taken up by our government, and that via Marseilles, and by the Peninsular and Oriental Company, is still the only conjoint one carried on under its auspices. I believe this route via Trieste is the only really original suggestion made by Mr. Waghorn throughout his career in the advocacy of steam between India and England, and whatever its merits may be, it has not yet superseded that of Marseilles.[219]

On 9 January 1846 *The Times* took care to state that it had not paid any money to Waghorn for his endeavours (apart from the contribution to his testimonial):

Mr Waghorn's Express.—We have been requested to contradict one of the numerous misrepresentations on this subject. We believe the experiment was made by Mr. Waghorn at his own expense. He offered to bring the despatches for all the morning papers, and he did so. He certainly was not employed by us, or paid by us, for the experiment, or for the carriage of our despatch. We subsequently subscribed to the testimonial on his behalf, but that subscription was in no way connected with the express, and only is acknowledgement of the great services he has performed in bringing one of our most important colonies within a month's journey.[220]

A meeting was convened at the British and Foreign Institute, 13, George Street, Hanover Square, on 16th January 1846 when members were given the opportunity to hear and question Waghorn on

219 Wilson, *op. cit.*, 69.
220 *The Times*, 9 January 1846, 5.

comparing the Trieste and Marseilles routes, but the report notes that 'although it was termed a "discussion", the proceedings seldom extended beyond desultory conversation, for the greater part of the auditors were solicitous to hear Lieut. Waghorn's experiences and to accept whatever opinion he laid down without dissent. It may be easily inferred that he advocated the Trieste line with the greatest zeal; and the enquiries which were made bore chiefly upon the features of this new and hardly-tried route, rather than upon any other.'[221]

Later on the *Times* copied *Allen's Indian Mail* as reporting that the East India Company had presented Waghorn with £300 'in consideration of his zealous and useful services in the establishment of steam communication between Great Britain and India'.[222]

Still the British Government were wary of committing themselves to Waghorn's scheme and he faced further frustration when their insistence on six trials of the Trieste route led to more delays. He wrote to Sir Robert Peel about this on 13 April 1846:

> H. M. Treasury and East India Company have consented to pay for six experiments via Trieste, that I might prove these, as I did in my last trip, 3 days and 4½ hours superior to that via Marseilles.
>
> These experiments have been delayed 3 months for want of a steamer from the Admiralty. The Austrian, Russian, Bavarian, Wurtemburg and Belgian Governments are all anxious for these experiments to come off.
>
> May I beg of you, Sir Robert, to speak to Lord Ellenborough (to whom I send copy of this) on this subject, that I may not trespass on your time, by troubling you for a personal interview. H.M. Steamer 'Trident', now in the East India Dock Basin, would be most effective for the service.[223]

Waghorn next appears in the columns of *The Times* on 8 July 1846, in a report from Vienna written on 26 June. It revealed that he had been

221 *The Times*, 17 January 1946,4; *Morning Chronicle*, 19 January 1846.

222 *The Times*, 26 February 1846, 5.

223 British Library, Add. MS 40589, f.354.

in the city for several days working on details of a route from the port of Dwino to the North Sea.[224] Two days later further information was added:

> Mr. Waghorn was treated with the greatest consideration when at Vienna. It was stated that the English Government had, in the question of the Indian transit, requested that six successive experiments should be made previously to deciding in favour of Trieste. Mr. Waghorn had received from Prince Metternich the assurance that the railroad of Salzburg will be finished in three years. Mr. Waghorn was about to leave for Trieste.[225]

While at Malta in August his volatile temper got him into trouble again, perhaps inflamed by drink:

> On the 28th of August Lieutenant Thomas Waghorn ... was placed at the bar of the Malta police court, charged by Sergeant-Major Carnana, on the complaint of Lieutenant John Osborne Barnett, of the 42d Royal Highlanders, with threatening to kick this latter wherever he might fall in with him in the street, and otherwise provoking him to fight a duel.
>
> The only witness called to substantiate the complaint was Lieutenant Alexander Ramsey of the 42d, who deposed that he, being in charge of the main guard, had asked Lieut. Barnett and Lieut. Waghorn to dine with him. That this latter had grossly insulted both Lieut. Barnett and the witness, had called the colonel of the 42d a fool and a liar, and after boasting that he (Lieut. Waghorn) had done more for his country than either Nelson or Wellington, had proceeded to provoke Lieut. Barnett to fight a duel, calling him opprobrious names, and swearing that he would shoot him through the brains.
>
> Lieutenant Waghorn admitted that he used these threats, but stated that he had been the party insulted and provoked, and that the witness had only told one side of the story, but that he would nevertheless, not lower himself by cross-examining him.

---

224 *The Times*, 8 July 1846, 5.

225 *The Times*, 10 July 1846, 5.

> The magistrate bound Lieut. Waghorn over to keep the peace towards her Majesty's liege subjects in general, and Lieut. Barnett in particular, for two years, under the bail of two friends, in the sum of £100.
>
> This matter has created some stir at Malta, and the prevailing opinion is, that it should never have been carried into a police court, arising as it did out of an after-dinner conversation, which, notwithstanding the offensive words made use of, was allowed to go to great lengths before being in the least degree checked.[226]

Waghorn was keen that the Navy's *Trident* would be used for the experiments rather then the *Ardent* since it had more power, and the ship left Woolwich for Malta on 12 August. Unfortunately a steam pipe failed on 21 August and *Trident* had to be rescued and towed for repairs. Various details of the early experimental trips appeared by degrees. On 4 September it was reported that the sea voyage from Alexandria to Trieste was accomplished in 80 hours,[227] the substituted *Ardent* was at Alexandria ready for the first trip on 19 September,[228] and a further report from that city on 25 September detailed the journey from Suez:[229] Suez to Cairo 16½ hours, using a relay of horses every five miles across the desert, Cairo to Atfeh 9 hours, Atfeh to Alexandria 4½ hours. The trials continued:

> Ramsgate. Lieutenant Waghorn left this harbour this morning [13 October] at five minutes past 10 o'clock, in the South East and Continental Steam Company's packet the Princess Maud for Ostend, on his way to Trieste, for the purpose of making arrangements for the conveyance of the next overland despatches for India.[230]

He was back in London on 31 October at the end of the second experiment.[231]

---

226 *The Morning Chronicle*, 24 September 1846, 5.
227 *The Times*, 16 September 1846, 7.
228 *The Times*, 3 October 1846, 5.
229 *The Times*, 8 October 1846, 4.
230 *The Times*, 13 October 1846, 4.
231 *The Times*, 21 November 1846, 4.

Meanwhile the French were not standing idle and set in motion a series of journeys between Alexandria and Marseilles to provide evidence that their route was still to be preferred. In this they were assisted by the P&O ship *Ariel*, much to the displeasure of *The Times* who felt that this was unpatriotic and a snub to Waghorn. At the end of the year a resumé was made following the first three experiments and *The Times* quoted *The Augsburg Gazette* in summarizing the trials:

Preliminary Trials

France.—From Alexandria to Marseilles, 190 hours; from Marseilles to London, 85 hours—total, 275 hours.
Germany.—From Alexandria to Trieste, 156 hours; from Trieste to London, 99¾ hours—total, 255¾ hours.

First Trial Trip

France.—From Alexandria to Marseilles, 196 hours; from Marseilles to London, 79 hours—total, 275 hours.
Germany.—From Alexandria to Trieste, 130 hours; from Trieste to London, 167 hours—total, 237 hours.

Second Trial Trip

France.—From Alexandria to Marseilles, 152 hours; from Marseilles to London, 77½ hours—total, 229½ hours.
Germany.—From Alexandria to Trieste, 133 hours; from Trieste to London, 120½ hours—total, 253½ hours.

Third Trial Trip

France.—From Alexandria to Marseilles, and from Marseilles to London, 246 hours.
Germany.—From Alexandria to Trieste, 156 hours; from Trieste to London, 97 hours—total 253 hours.

Totals of the above Trips.—France, 1,025½ hours; Germany, 999¼ hours.

It was further pointed out that the *Ariel* sailed at 12 knots an hour while the *Ardent* 'seldom upwards of 10, and very often only 8 knots, [so] the superiority of the German route cannot remain doubtful another moment.'[232] But the French continued to be dismissive of the scheme and the *Journal des Débats* printed a report from Ancona dated 5 November:

> Mr. Waghorn, having failed in his attempt to convey the Indian mail via Trieste, now proposes to bring it through Ancona, Lombardy, and the Splugen. The trial of this new road will be made at the close of December. Mr. Waghorn arrived here the day before yesterday to prepare for its execution, and, after having had a long conference with the British Consul, he repaired to Rome. It appears to be in contemplation to establish a railroad along the Adriatic coast, in order to favour the conveyance of the Indian mail through the states of Italy and Germany.[233]

The Navy's steamer Ardent 1846
(© National Maritime Museum, Greenwich, London)

232 *The Times*, 22 December 1846, 3.
233 *The Times*, 18 November 1846, 6.

At this point the press seems to lose interest in the experiments and no further reports are made about them, except it was noted they had concluded in March 1847. Waghorn himself submitted the results of the six trials to the Post Office on 28 April 1847:[234]

	Left Bombay	Arrived at East India House, London	
		Via Trieste	Via Marseilles
1st trial	27 Aug 1846	3 Oct 1846, 5.10 a.m.	7 Oct 1846, 10.30 a.m.
2nd trial	1 Oct 1846	31 Oct 1846, 3.45 a.m.	4 Nov 1846, 6 a.m.
3rd trial	2 Nov 1846	2 Dec 1846, 7 a.m.	2 Dec 1846 (evening)
4th trial	2 Dec 1846	2 Jan 1847, 5 a.m.	3 Jan 1847, 9.45 p.m.
5th trial	2 Jan 1847	4 Feb 1847, 3 a.m.	6 Feb 1847, 2 p.m.
6th trial	2 Feb 1847	4 Mar 1847, 7.20 p.m.	4 Mar 1847, 1 p.m.

The Standard continued to support the French route, noting that the 'new and splendid' *Ariel* of the P&O Company would add advantage (although noting on 4 January 1847 the complaint in the *Morning Herald* of the Navy rather 'employing … a wretched crazy old vessel'), and the promise of a rail connection from Marseilles to Paris 'in the next two or three years' would further strengthen the French claim.[235]

A key element in the development of communications between England and India resulted from the election of a new Pope, Pius IX, on 16 June 1846. He succeeded the very conservative Gregory XVI, who had been against technological developments and who had actually banned railways in the Papal States, calling them *chemins d'enfer* [roads of hell], rather than *chemin de fer* [iron road]. Pius IX was welcomed as one open to innovation and he soon strove to make social and economic improvements. Already in November 1846 four railways from Rome were authorised, including one to Ancona and Bologna.

234 G.P.O. records quoted by Sidebottom, *op. cit.*, 108.

235 *The Standard*, 31 October 1846, 3; 3 November 1846, 3; 4 January 1847, 3. In fact it took until 1856 before all the connecting sections of the Paris-Marseilles railway were completed.

Furthermore the British Government learned that companies approved of by the papal authorities would be able to bid for contracts and 'the Roman government would place no obstacle in the way of an English Engineer examining and reporting upon the practicability of the line decided upon for the purpose of conveying the mail from India.'[236]

Not surprisingly Waghorn was part of the action and the *Augsburg Gazette* reported from their Rome agent on 12 April 1847

> During his residence in our city, Mr. Waghorn had several conferences with the superior employees of the Government. His wish is to have the Indian mail brought from Egypt to Brides [Brindisi], as soon as the railroad from that place to Naples and form Naples to Ancona, shall be completed. From the latter port the mail will be carried by a steamer to Trieste.

Elsewhere there were other reports:

> The line of railway communication through Italy, to its furthest accessible limits in the south-east will, if accomplished, reduce the time between London and Brundisi to three days; and by first-rate steamers from Brundisi, the time between London and Alexandria will be reduced to six days. His Holiness the Pope has manifested his desire for the accomplishment of improved means of communication, by offering a gold medal of a thousand dollars value to him who will present the best plan for crossing the Appenine barrier between Ancona and Rome.'[237]

> Mr Waghorn had an interview with the Pope and was most graciously received. His Holiness expressed his high sense of the importance of the attempt, and presented Mr Waghorn with a gold medallion of himself, complimenting him on his great exertions. Mr W. then started for Naples, by invitation of the King, to arrange for the examination of the best route through his dominions, and intended afterwards to proceed northwards, to determine the most

236 Letter from Cardinal Antonelli to John Freeborn, quoted in Saho Matsumoto-Best, *Britain and the Papacy in the Age of Revolution, 1846-1851* (Woodbridge, 2003), 34-35.

237 *South Australian Register*, 9 June 1847, 2 [news left England on 24 February]

> practicable line through the Alps, having possessed himself of all the most feasible points.[238]

> Accident to Mr. Waghorn. This indefatigable traveller, while crossing the Alps with Mr. Austin, the engineer and surveyor, was upset in his carriage. An avalanche had fallen across the road, which had been cleared away only from half the breadth of the road. It being night, the postillion did not see it, and he drove one wheel up the slope of the bank, and overturned the carriage. Fortunately, neither Mr. Waghorn nor his companion was in the smallest degree hurt.[239]

Matsumoto-Best writes that 'representations were made by the British *chargé d'affaires* in Naples, Mr. Waghorn, who had persuaded the Neapolitan king of the benefit of a railway from Brindisi,' but the newspaper accounts suggest that Waghorn had no official position. On 11 December the British ambassador in Vienna informed Metternich that the British wanted permission to link the railway from Brindisi to the Austrian railway system.

Three reports were made by the civil engineer Mr. H. Austin for the Foreign Office, who wrote:

> According to the instructions which I had the honor to receive from you through Lieut. Waghorn that I should accompany that officer to Italy, to examine and report upon the Plans of the lines of Railway proposed through the Neapolitan and the Papal States which might be most available for the purposes of the Overland Route for the conveyance of Mails and traffic between England and India, Lieut. Waghorn and myself started for those countries on the 9th December last [1846].

All three reports are particularly concerned with the engineering required for the lines, the first from Brindisi through the Neapolitan and Papal States, the second on crossing the Alps via Mont Luckmarier, and the third on an aborted scheme from Trieste

238 *Adelaide Observer*, 12 June 1847, 4 [news left England on 24 February]
239 *Observer*, March 22

to Bavaria and that through Trieste, Vienna, Berlin, Hanover and Ostend to London.[240]

On 7 January 1847 Pope Pius IX personally presented Waghorn with his gold medal. It appears he was in the right place at the right time to benefit from the Pope's promise and that it was not originally specifically intended for him, but as a general inducement for someone to tackle the difficulties of the route. An engraved page was made comprising a copy of Sir George Hayter's portrait of Waghorn with an illustration of the medal beneath. On 16 September Waghorn proudly sent a copy to W. E. Gladstone:

> Pray do me the kindness to accept and keep this likeness of myself; it is a faithful copy of a picture painted by Sir George Hayter, H. M. Portrait Painter, presented to me by The London East India & China Association, with the addition only of the Gold Medal presented to me by the Pope, and which I believe is the first ever given by a Pope (his own likeness) to a Protestant.[241]

The medal was said to serve 'as a mark of approval of his [Waghorn's] efforts to promote international intercourse.'

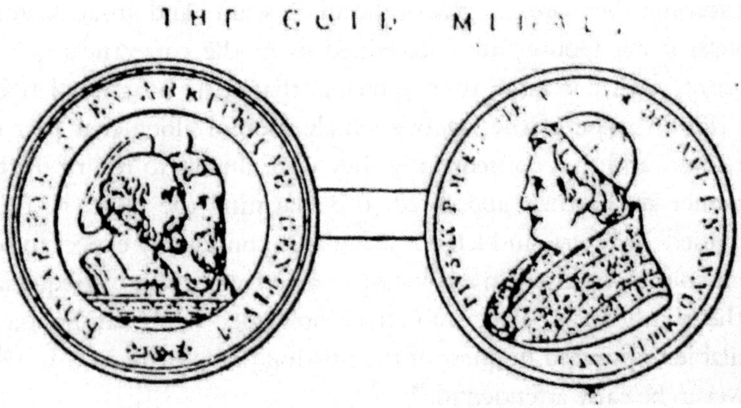

The image of the medal as it appears beneath the engraving of the Hayter portrait.

240 Sidebottom, *op. cit.*, 109.

241 British Library, Add. MS 44,366, f.104.

In an eerie premonition of 21st century unrest, the correspondent for the *Times* in Aden reported that 'a fanatic, [Sheik Ismail], from the neighbourhood of Algiers, on a pilgrimage to Mecca with a large retinue, was seized with a fit of religious enthusiasm, and made a vow that he would drive the English out of Aden or perish in the attempt. On his way from Mecca he continued to preach extermination to all Feringees [foreigners] in Arabia.' About 7000 well armed men were believed to be under his command, 'whom he has taught to believe that he is destined to restore the true religion in all its purity.' The report mentioned that coaling of the *Hindostan* had to be done by Government workmen because all the Arabs had joined Sheik Ismail, and also

> The English schooner *Higflyer*, belonging to Messrs. Waghorn & Co., returned [to Aden] from the African coast on the 15th [August], in charge of the mate, who made the following statement:—that the Captain, A. Alcock, and Mr. Wheatley of the house of Waghorn & Co., had gone on shore at a place on an island called Sad ul Deen, seven or eight miles distant from Zeyla, belonging to a tribe of Somalles, named Eassa, and that they had both been murdered by the natives, and that he got alarmed and left the coast. [...] This is all the account the mate can give of the affair, scanty and unsatisfactory though it be. Doubts are entertained as to the correctness of the account, and it is more than probable that their boat was left by the tide in some of the lagoons which abound along that part of the coast, and that consequently they were unable to return to the schooner at the time appointed; this alarming the mate, he only remained 24 hours, and left for Aden. We confidently expect to see them coming over safe in a few days in a native boat. In consequence of the hourly anticipated Arab attack no armed vessel can be made available to proceed in quest of the missing party at present. It will, however, be early attended to.[242]

Why was Wheatley making this journey? Was it an opportunity to get away from his desk in Cornhill and discover something of what

242 *The Times*, 12 September 1846, 5. Also the later report on 24 September 1846, 5.

his customers were experiencing? Two further reports, the last on 1 September, confirm the men were still missing, but no more is heard of the event. They must have returned safely, since Wheatley took over Waghorn's agency in May 1848. The uprising also came to nothing because some of those who had appeared to join the insurrection had done so out of 'curiosity' rather than religious fervour. It is interesting to find that Waghorn and Company had a vessel operating on that side of the isthmus, to match *Lady Emily* working in the Mediterranean and the *Little Nile* travelling to and from Cairo. In spite of subsequent hardships, there was a time when his agency must have provided Waghorn with a comfortable income.

11

STEAM TO AUSTRALIA

In the meantime, while all these journeys were being made, Waghorn had also turned his attention to extending the steam service to Australia. The P&O Company was growing in size and influence and its first regular mail ship to Singapore arrived there in August 1845. A route was established by the Company between Point de Galle (Ceylon), Singapore, and Hong Kong, soon extending to Chinese ports (and fuelling the opium trade). Waghorn's idea was to create a line from Singapore to Sydney. It is in the nature of the man that he would not have proposed his scheme without first trying it out. In 1845-6 he was far too busy with the Trieste experiments to have undertaken a journey to Sydney, but there is a clue in a newspaper article in the *Sydney Morning Herald* of 23 September 1846 that Waghorn may have tried the trip in 1838. 'The Indian Islands' is an account of the journey from Singapore to Sydney made by (or based on) one by George Windsor Earl in that year and which the newspaper presumably revived because of renewed interest in the proposal. It is clear that the fixed points for coaling and refreshment which Waghorn proposes in his pamphlets were not then firmly established, and indeed never did become fully operational:

> Our steamer has now arrived at the tenth parallel of south latitude, and has passed the 130th meridian east of Greenwich; and our captain has been these two hours in consultation with Mr. WAGHORN, Captain KING, Sir Gordon BREMER, Sir EVERARD STOKES, Mr TYERS, Mr DRURY, Captain STANLEY, Captain BLACKWOOD, Mr. EARL, and a number of others, who have been before in these parts, and are now our fellow passengers. We shall learn, as soon as they have finished their wine and fruit (the former European, the latter Arafuran) whether we are to steam it right slick away through Torres Straits, or, for

> more, abundant caution, take the steam off during the night; also whether we are to coal at Port Essington or at Wednesday Island.[243]

An extract from an undated letter from Waghorn printed in August 1838 strengthens the idea that he was then exploring the Far East: 'I shall visit Canton via Calcutta, and see if sufficient interest and capital cannot be realised for the extension of Indian steam to China.'[244] Yet there is no mention in his pamphlets of his making a journey to Australia, which surely would have been the case had he done so, and he rather draws attention to the work of others who had surveyed the route.

The Times reported that with Mark Boyd and Samuel Browning, Waghorn had a meeting with Lord Palmerston at the Foreign Office. This must be the meeting mentioned by Boyd in his *Reminiscences of Fifty Years* 'in reference to a postal communication from Pointe de Galle to our Australian and New Zealand Colonies'. Boyd makes much of the fact that Palmerston was always kind to Waghorn and that those waiting to see the Lord that afternoon were told by an official that 'I shall take up your names to his lordship; but I think it as well to apprise you … that the overland route, or rather its author, always takes precedence at the Foreign Office.' However Waghorn was advised by Boyd

> strictly confine yourself to receiving the letters for the Austrian Government promised you by his Lordship, *but on no account whatever* enter upon the Australian question [to prevent delays]. … As he was to start that night for Vienna and Trieste, he followed my advice and the interview was over in two minutes. … Waghorn occasionally spent a day or two at Vienna on postal arrangments, and was always kindly received (thanks to Lord Palmerston) by Prince Metternich the Prime Minister, who asked him to dinner and paid him other attentions.

Waghorn complained light-heartedly to the Prince about official obstructions day and night. '"I tell you, Prince, it won't do; your empire is dreadfully behind the rest of Europe; and if I am to take

243 *Sydney Morning Herald*, 23 September 1846, 2.

244 *Manchester Courier and Lancashire Advertiser*, 4 August 1838, 2. He was in Suez on 11th July and Cairo in late October, but his movements between those dates are not documented.

charge and expedite the British and continental correspondence to the East, you must remove those absurd interruptions I complain of, and that pretty sharply." The Prince promised me that he would do so, and like a good man kept his promise, as I never had anything to complain of afterwards.'[245]

Waghorn's friendly working relationship with Metternich, as well as his flamboyant attire, were demonstrated during his last visit to Vienna when he was reported to have 'waltzed with Princess Metternich in a volcano waistcoat of such preternaturally alarming colours that it is incredible the Austrian revolution was not precipitated a year in advance.'[246]

William Ewart Gladstone (1809-1898) in 1843; engraving after George Richmond
(© National Portrait Gallery, D20650)

245 *The Times*, 12 October 1846, 5; Mark Boyd, *Reminiscences of Fifty Years*, London, 1871, 275-7.

246 *Liverpool Albion*, 14 January 1850.

To increase interest in extending the shipping route to Australia, in typical fashion Waghorn wrote to the mercantile groups in Manchester, Liverpool, Glasgow and Leeds seeking support and he also badgered Members of Parliament. Mark Boyd seems to have been the person who suggested a public meeting to promote the scheme and he helped draw up an advertisement for it, noting that Waghorn 'put [it] in his pocket, and with the aid of a hansom cab—it was midnight when he left me—he drove round to the newspaper offices, for next morning the Waghorn advertisement appeared in the papers. This was a slight specimen of the "go ahead" principle with which he wished to indoctrinate the Austrian Government'.

> STEAM to AUSTRALIA.—A PUBLIC MEETING will take place on Friday the 17th inst., at 12 o'clock at the London Tavern, Bishopsgate-street. Mr. Waghorn will attend, and will explain the benefits to be derived from steam communication between England and Australia. The friends of Australia and New Zealand are earnestly requested to attend.[247]

Waghorn published an open *Letter to the Rt. Hon. Wm. Ewart Gladstone, M.P. Secretary of State for the Colonies, On the Extension of Steam Navigation from Singapore to Port Jackson, Australia* which, according to the *Liverpool Albion,* was published on 23 May 1846. In addition to the 'letter' itself, the pamphlet includes newspaper reports of the public meeting held the previous month. That of the *Daily News* the next day was by far the most extensive. Waghorn wrote:

> My most earnest and unqualified thanks and duty are herewith tendered to Sir George Larpent, Bart.; to the Hon. Francis Scott, M.P.; to Joseph Hume, M.P.; to Captain Barber; to Mark Boyd, Esq.; and the other gentlemen of the Committee for their kindness of manner and the assistance each has given me in bringing the plan in question before the public after the London Tavern Meeting called by me on Friday, 17th April, 1846; the proceedings of which, copied from the *Daily News,* are as follows :-Proposed Steam Communication with Australia and New Zealand.

247 Boyd, *op. cit.,* 278-80; *The Times,* 15 April 1846, 4.

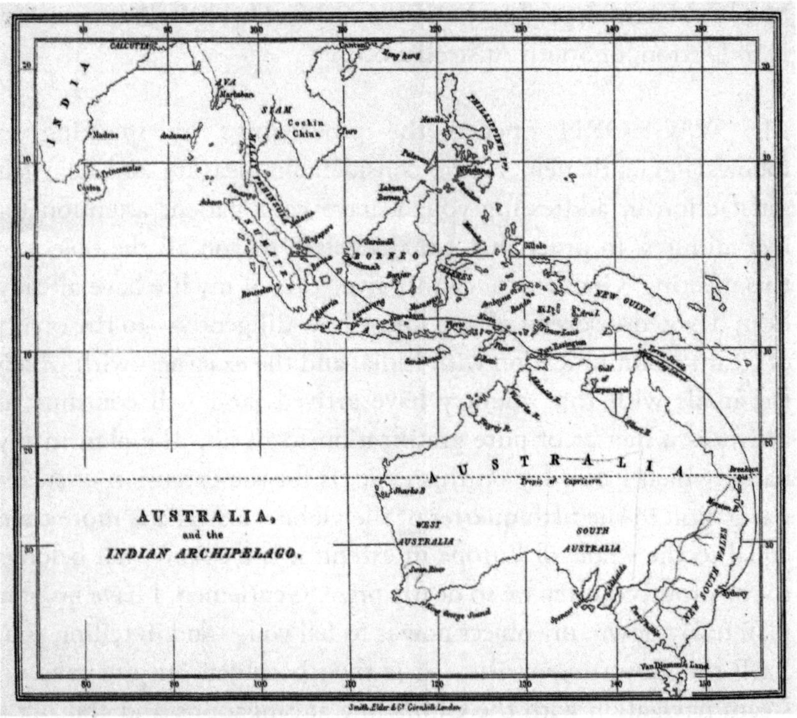

The plan in the 1846 pamphlet addressed to Gladstone.

A public meeting was held yesterday, at noon, at the London Tavern, Bishopsgate-street, for the purpose of hearing from Mr. Waghorn an explanation of the benefits to be derived from steam communication between England and Australia. There was a numerous attendance of highly influential gentlemen, amongst whom we noticed—Sir G. Larpent, Bart.; the Hon. F. Scott, M.P.; Mr. J. W. Sutherland, Mr. Mark Boyd, Mr. J. O'Connell, Mr. S. Browning, Mr. R. Brooks, Mr. Boyd, sen., Capt. E. Robinson, R.N., Mr. L. Boyd, Mr. H. Wise, Mr. D. Brown, Capt. Barber, Mr. A. Robinson, Mr. J. Crawford, Mr. D. McLaren, Mr. G. Capper, Mr. G. H. Wray, Capt. Bushby, R.N., Mr. T. R. Todd, Mr. F. Maitland, Mr. H. Buckle, Mr. G. R. Donaldson, Mr. J. Lambert, Capt. Henderson, Mr. W. Scott, Mr. J; C. Lyall, Capt. H. Bavarne, Mr. Serjeant Mereweather, Mr. S. J. Capper, Mr. J. Gore, Mr. D. Hagen, Mr. T. Sutherland, Mr. A. Fleming, Major Alcock, 95th regt., Mr. A. Maclaren, Mr. J. Smith, Mr. J. Macguire, Mr. Reynolds, Mr. J. Livingston, Mr. G. Borradaile, Mr. D. Cooper,

Mr. W. Merrithorpe, Mr. J. A. Smith, Mr. H. H. R. Aikman, Mr. F. S. Dutton, of South Australia, &c.

Mr. WAGHORN opened the proceedings by speaking as follows —Gentlemen, I have considerable pleasure and heartfelt satisfaction in addressing you. I crave your patient attention for five minutes, in order that I may explain to you all the object of this meeting. Gentlemen, twenty-five years of my life have already been devoted—several of you know how diligently—to the object of steam communication with India; and the exactness with which the mails with that country have arrived (and will continue to arrive) is a matter of pure gratification to us all. The plan in my hand, which I now lay on this table, is for the extension of steam navigation to the fifth quarter of the globe. Australia is more than equal to the whole of Europe in extent; it is a colony that belongs to the proud country we so dearly prize. Gentlemen, I have no new plan to lay down; my object now is to tell you—and in telling you, I tell the Government also—it is their bounden duty to take up steam navigation with the China line at Singapore, and concoct a mail system from thence to Port Jackson. The distance from Singapore to Port Jackson, within 50 miles, is 4450; the stoppages may be altered when this matter comes into detail. For the present, I would go from Singapore to Batavia, in the island of Java; thence to Port Essington; thence to Wednesday Island, on the east coast of Australia; and from thence to Port Jackson; thus dividing this 4450 miles into four stages, every way embracing the benefits of trade: and gentlemen, mark the fact, that by this measure we stretch steam to the furthermost parts of the British possessions in the east, not forgetting New Zealand and Van Diemen's Land. Gentlemen, in speaking of this scheme, I can hardly yet call it a plan. A member of her Majesty's Government told me yesterday, that the Government have a two-fold interest in this matter; viz., it was putting Australia in possession of a steam navy, should that island ever have to act on emergency; and it is this particular fact you should keep before her Majesty's Government, in order to get the greatest possible grant of money for connecting Australia with the Straits of Singapore by steam, and I believe they would lend a two-fold power for that purpose. Gentlemen, it is not for me to

> attempt to dilate upon the benefits in every point of view, that such an establishment, in course of time, would create for yourselves, or for your common country. Here is a letter from Manchester, in which the whole of that most remarkable town is with the object of this meeting. Here is another letter from Liverpool; here is another from Leeds. A letter from Glasgow will be with me this afternoon to the same purport. A spontaneous combination from every part of the British empire will respond to the same purport: and why, I ask the Government, shall they give the benefits of steam to every colony, and debar Australia from it? Gentlemen, each of our lives is numbered; and it is our bounden duty to connect Australia with this country as soon as we are able. I do confidently trust this will not be a meeting of mere words, but a meeting of action, by bringing that gigantic power of steam to connect Australia with Singapore. It is time that will prove the results. Each of us cannot appreciate it; and none of us would have conceived the benefits we enjoy from steam, were it not before our eyes; and pray do not let the next generation say that we debarred the present from the fruits of sociality between England and Australia. (Hear, hear). I beg pardon for trespassing so long; and I will now move that Sir George Larpent do take the chair, in order to explain this scheme, and afford each gentleman who may wish to speak a patient hearing. I shall be most happy, if called upon, to answer any questions that may be put to me.

Sir George Larpent then took the chair and letters were read out from Manchester Commercial Association, Liverpool and Leeds, all expressing the view that the scheme would be beneficial. One from Bischoff and Co. sounded a note of caution:

> So few are directly interested in the trade to China or Australia, that those houses whom we consulted were of opinion that the attendance would be so small, no good would arise from calling a meeting of merchants; nor can we send you a document with a number of signatures. We are therefore sorry we cannot find you a more powerful testimonial for the accomplishment of your object.

The chairman, responded by approving the scheme, but asked 'who is to bear the expense, and what will that expense be?' He hoped that 'we shall be able to obtain, to a moderate extent, the assistance of her Majesty's Government, and also of the Colonial Government' in being able to 'graft this communication, as it were, on the main trunk of the steam communication with India and China'.

> The Hon. Francis Scott, M.P. proposed the resolution "That this meeting highly approve of the scheme for a steam communication being continued from Singapore to Sydney, in New South Wales, by the plan laid upon the table by Mr. Waghorn." and went on to produce a mass of economic data supporting the venture. The proposition was seconded by Mr. Mark Boyd who 'said that himself, Mr. Scott, and another gentleman, had taken a great interest in the subject; and they naturally turned to a gentleman who, having brought Bombay within twenty-six days of London, might be expected to bring New South Wales within fifty-six days' sail of this country. (Loud cheers.) To this most adventurous gentleman, the commercial public were eminently indebted (Hear, hear.)

This is the first of several tributes to Waghorn heard at the meeting—and which the man himself was not at all abashed at printing, but a note of caution was introduced by the next two speakers. Mr Henderson believed the route 'via the Isle of France and Bass's Straits' was preferable and he called for a committee to decide the matter, while Mr. S. Evans said that 'while recognising the great merits of Mr. Waghorn, the meeting ought not to overlook the services of Mr. Wheelwright, who had done much for the trade to the Pacific. It would be necessary, before the object could be carried out, to secure the assistance of government, as the colony itself could do little; and the best way of securing this would be to select the best route.' In view of these objections the meeting modified the resolution to the form 'That this meeting highly approves of a scheme for a steam communication to Sydney, New South Wales.' Mr. Wise moved 'That a committee be formed, to bring the subject as forcibly as possible before her Majesty's Government; and that the committee do use their endeavours with the colonial government of New South Wales, to induce them to pay their portion of such an establishment as soon as it may be equitable.' It was then decided that the committee should comprise the chairman and the movers and seconders of the resolutions, with power to add to their number. The list of The London Committee for the extension of Steam Navigation to Australia as printed at the end of Waghorn's pamphlet comprised 33 names, including Waghorn's—and this in spite of the chairman's remark that 'a small committee would probably perform the work best'!

The remainder of the meeting was taken up with thanks to Waghorn. What is interesting about the shorter accounts in the *Evening Sun*, and *Morning Advertiser* (18 April), *Observer* (19 April), and *London Mail* (24 April) is their unanimous support of Waghorn and condemnation of the Government's indifference towards him. *The Evening Sun*:

> It is impossible to estimate too highly the advantages, social, national, and commercial, which must accrue both to the colonies and to the mother country, from the carrying out of the propositions of Lieutenant Waghorn. Already he has brought India within one month of England. It is owing to the exertions, the almost unaided exertions, of Lieutenant Waghorn, that we are aware of the successful termination of the campaign on the Sutlej, at a time when, according to the old system, we should have hardly received information of its commencement. It was entirely owing to his exertions that we were enabled to repair the disasters of Caubul [Kabul]; for had there been no overland mail, the summer … would have elapsed before the destruction of Elphinstone's army could have reached England,[248] and orders have been transmitted out to India; and the Affgans would have had twelve months in which to concentrate and discipline their forces. And what has been his reward for services which are above all praise? The Government have given him the rank of a lieutenant in the navy; that is absolutely all that has been done for him. Now this is really disgraceful to us as a nation; and we call upon the Government to wipe out this disgrace, by recommending to her Majesty to bestow upon Lieutenant Waghorn some substantial mark of favour. But if it is disgraceful to us as a nation generally, still more deeply disgraceful is it to the commercial body of the

248 Mount Stuart Elphinstone (1779-1859).

nation. That body has derived immense pecuniary advantages from the facility of communication with India, which has been opened by Lieutenant Waghorn, and as yet they have not shown their gratitude to their benefactor in a manner befitting either him or themselves. Still he continues his career of usefulness, and is now about to add to the obligations under which he has laid his country, by opening for her a safe and speedy communication with her magnificent Australian colonies. Should he succeed, he may with truth say, that he, too, like Canning,[249] has called a new world into existence. But while he does his duty, let us not neglect ours; and it is our bounden duty to present Lieutenant Waghorn with such a testimonial of our gratitude as shall be worthy a great nation, and which, while it discharges a small portion of the debt due to him from his countrymen, shall, at the same time, act as a stimulus to others to follow his example. For our own sakes we should do this, and do it quickly, for there cannot be a doubt but that our ungrateful neglect of the services of Lieutenant Waghorn has already operated as a "heavy blow and a great discouragement" to enterprise in other quarters.

The *London Mail* of 24 April continues in the same vein:

> The restless energies of Lieut. Waghorn have taken a fresh direction. He is now agitating for the establishment of steam intercourse with our Australian colonies, and with every prospect of success; for the route he proposes appears the most feasible that has yet been suggested for communicating with those distant possessions … let us … remark, that though endeavouring to promote a line of intercourse with Australasia, this officer is not relaxing one iota of the exertions he has been making, for improving the overland intercourse between this country and India. On the contrary, to that object he is devoted. He is as sanguine as ever, and fully determined upon demonstrating, by a series of experiments, the advantages of the Trieste line over the route via Marseilles. Lieut. Waghorn is the man to accomplish this, provided only it can be

249 George Canning (1770-1827) was instrumental in promoting the New World (the Americas) 'to redress the balance of the Old'.

> done. He does not hesitate at ordinary difficulties, nor will he permit himself to be influenced by either public indifference or official apathy. Despite discouragements of all sorts, and opposition in every shape, he has the moral courage to persevere, and hence is to be attributed his success. Really such men are invaluable in their day and generation, and yet none are more frequently neglected by those who should be anxious to reward merit—by the very persons who enter upon their labour, and reap the full fruits of their exertions. Lieut. Waghorn's case has been no exception to the general rule. What has the Government done for this officer? Nothing. What the East India Company? We are ashamed to say how little! What the public? Let the subscription to the Waghorn Testimonial declare that; and yet the committee must acknowledge that as far as the public is concerned, a more anxious disposition has recently been evinced to acknowledge Lieut. Waghorn's merits, and to reward his many services.

The *Observer* (April 19) noted the meeting, concluding with the words 'To Waghorn we would say, "go on and prosper"', while the *Morning Advertiser* (April 18) remarked 'Mr. Waghorn was of course, as usual, the "great card," and entered into a plain and lucid exposition of his views upon this very interesting subject.'

The title page of Waghorn's pamphlet notes him as 'F.R.A.S., etc.' Membership lists of the Royal Asiatic Society did not appear on a regular basis at this time, but Waghorn is not mentioned in 1845 or earlier and appears only in the lists for 1846 and 1847.[250]

In August 1847 The India and Australia Mail Steam Packet Company was formed with the aim 'to authorise the Company to establish communications to and from the United Kingdom, East Indies, Australia and New Zealand' with a route via Ceylon, Singapore, and the Torres Islands. Thomas Waghorn was named as one of the committee and communications were to be addressed to his offices at 34 Cornhill.[251]

---

250 I am indebted to the Royal Asiatic Society's librarian, Michael Pollock, for searching for me. Two of Waghorn's pamphlets are in the Society's library: *Particulars of an Overland Journey* (1831), and the *Second Letter to Earl Grey. On the extension of Steam Navigation from Singapore to Port Jackson* (1847).

251 *The Morning Post*, 16 August 1847, 1.

All the Australian newspapers reported on Waghorn's proposed route and debated if there were better alternatives, but his idea was generally well received and supported. A meeting was held in Sydney on 27 August 1846 to petition the Governor to do all in his power to establish the route.[252]

The *Liverpool Albion* Waghorn obituary makes much of the amusement created in Earl Grey by the antics of Waghorn in arguing for his schemes.

> But the thing that most surprised certain of Waghorn's friends was his mesmerism of the sleepless irritability of Earl Grey. This time three years, when steam to Australia was being agitated, there were many deputations to the Colonial Office, the "Pioneer" being generally of the party. Here, while all others, overpowered with a sense of the great Satrap's presence, hardly dared to take their eyes off the ground or open their lips for fear of giving offence, Waghorn would walk up and down the room, as if parading the quarter-deck of the *Akbar* steamer in the monsoon, rattling on incessantly about all manner of men and things that might, could, would, or should be met along the proposed line, "shotting his discourse" with an occasional sea oath, and keeping up a species of row polka, by way of accompaniment, on the crown of his hat. The "Crotchety One", instead of loftily resenting this audacious indecorum, would be hugely tickled thereat, and would make a noise in his throat, as if he should like to try, for the first time in his life, what sort of thing a laugh was—that was more astonishing to those who know the proprietor of Howick than all the lieutenant's enterprise.[253]

252 *Sydney Morning Herald*, 28 August 1846, 2.

253 *The Liverpool Albion*, 14 January 1850. Accounts suggest that Waghorn was never overawed by visits to those in authority and his appeals to them for help would generally add a sailor's oaths to enliven the topic under discussion.

Earl Charles Grey (1764-1845), engraving after John Jackson.
(© National Portrait Gallery)

It is interesting that Waghorn's means of addressing his superiors involved mixing salty expletives with making his points; perhaps this was the vulgarity which disturbed Captain Escourt on his return from the Euphrates expedition., although it caused amusement in the former Prime Minister. Earl Grey was now in the twilight of his years, spending most of his time at Howick Hall, Northumberland, but even this did not dissuade Waghorn from pressing his claim. The newspapers report two meetings: on 16 February 'Sir George Larpent and Lieut.

Waghorn, accompanied by Messrs. Boyd, Sutherland, Browing, G. H. Donaldson, and Wise (merchants), had an interview with Earl Grey at the Colonial Office.' Later in the year 'Lieut. Waghorn has returned to town from an interview with Earl Grey at Howick Hall, on the subject of steam with Australia'.[254]

Both Waghorn and the Government were clear that the P&O Company would be the only one able to provide the ships for the Australian route, but that the project would be expensive. At their meeting on 8 December 1847 the Directors issued the following statement:

> Reference having been made in former reports to the probability of a line of steam communication being established under Government contract, for the conveyance of goods between the mother country and Australia, the directors on the present occasion have merely to repeat that the subject still continues to receive their attentive consideration. To carry out such a service which would embrace a distance of 115,000 to 116,000 miles annually of steam navigation between Singapore and Sydney, would, doubtless require considerable Government aid to render it remunerative. At present comparatively little intercourse exists by this route with England. The establishment of a steam communication would, unquestionably, confer a great boon upon those rapidly improving colonies, and, whether the service may fall into this company's hands, or into those of other parties who are desirous of obtaining it, the directors will be prepared to afford every facility in their power, so far as the connecting link between Singapore and England is concerned, to promote the passenger intercourse with those colonies.[255]

Debates and arguments continued for some ten years, but eventually the Singapore route was created and the first regular P&O service to Sydney arrived in the city in August 1852.[256]

---

254 *The Times*, 17 February 1847, 6 and 11 September 1847, 6; [also *The Standard* and *Morning Post*]

255 *The Times*, 9 December 1847, 6.

256 See David and Stephen Howarth, *The Story of P&O*, London, rev. edn., 1995, 82-5.

The Testimonial

Waghorn was part of the bustle of London life and it was here that he honed his connections with the merchants, who supported him in his aim to speed their mail and produce across the globe. Evidently the Jerusalem Coffee-house was a hub of his empire where he was frequently to be found and where deals could be done. Wilson's remark that 'He told me, among other things, that the London houses in the East India trade at this time gave him each a salary' was noted earlier.[257] The *Liverpool Albion* obituary records that all those from 'his old haunts, Garraway's, Tom's, Lloyds, the North and South, the Baltic, &c., has some tale or other of his eccentricity and restlessness.' It goes on

> He has been a thousand times sketched in pen and ink … but the following, which occurs in a notice of the Jerusalem Coffee-House, is the best:
>
> That small but firmly-built, drab-complexioned, and dark whiskered man, whose manner and gait are so rapid, whose eye scans ye boldly but not rudely, whose brow is the tablet of honesty and industry, whose attire marks him for a private gentleman, although the walk, the step, and the attitude of the naval officer are not easily to be disguised by the formal costume of the civilian. That is a sea captain of the right sort; not such a sea captain, such a water-maniac as Bulwer once painted, but a downright and upright good seaman—a strong man physically, a sound one mentally, with true spirit and energy, active in every limb, sinew, and tissue—body and brain alike. He whom we have been describing is a leading man in commerce, a popular man everywhere—it is Lieutenant Waghorn, the enterprising originator of the overland route to India, one of the most daring and courageous and uncompromising of British seamen. Waghorn is a pretty regular attendant at the Jerusalem when in London. He is the head of a house in which an East Indian agency is efficiently carried on; Mr. Wheatley being the active factotum of this erratic, half-sailor, half-merchant employer. Though the latter be Mr. Waghorn in Cornhill, he is dubbed Captain Waghorn at

257 p. 85.

> Grand Cairo. He started his life as an apprentice on board one of the East India Company's steamers belonging to the flotilla of the Indian navy. We find him now in the service of the company; now out of it; now sailing on the broad ocean, studying navigation; now careering along the Haymarket, and wrenching knockers at night time; at one time traversing the lonely desert; at another smoking a cigar at the American stores; on board ship; in affairs of business; a leading speaker at a public meeting on receiving an honoured testimonial; then a quiet man of business in Cornhill, attentively posting his ledger! Such is Waghorn. He is now, of course, steadied by years; the most honoured and the worst paid public individual the city can at present boast of.[258]

Another very similar description comes from a book about the city, which notes that the Jerusalem 'numbers between three and four hundred subscribers, who reckoning among them the first of the traders connected with India and Australia, must return a good revenue to the proprietors.'

> The chief subscribers to the Jerusalem, are the East India and Sydney merchants, and the captains, with some few of the highest brokers connected with the produce markets; the latter of whom desire the earliest information or the arrival of vessels with cargoes likely to pass through their hands at public auction. The wealth of the parties who meet here together, including, as it does, our first ship-owners and builders, and Government contractors, must be immense.
>
> But before going further with a description of this place, one person frequenting it deserves to be especially noticed, and that is the indefatigable gentleman, Lieut. Waghorn; by whose exertions and plans the overland route was first adopted. He has now started an Agency for the conveyance of parcels overland, and is in some small degree benefitting by the undertaking, since he is well supported by the majority of the merchants, who knowing they can rely on his punctuality, patronise him in preference to numerous other firms who are following the same description of business.

258 *Liverpool Albion, 14 January 1850*, quoted in *The Maitland Mercury and Hunter River General Advertiser*, 1 June 1850, 3.

> Lieutenant Waghorn is rather an eccentric man, and though excitable, is undoubtedly an honest British seaman. A story is current that "Tom Waghorn", as he is familiarly called, can do nothing without the Pascha of Egypt, and the Pascha of Egypt nothing without him. This statement, it is commonly understood, originates from the strong friendship existing between them. … Every reason exists for believing, that the influence the one possesses over the other has done much to ensure the safety, and facilitate the passage of the mail across the desert. …
>
> This eccentric individual is about fifty years of age, he is, we should say, five feet six, with a robust constitution and intelligent countenance, the latter much tanned by his frequent voyages to, and excursions in, Asiatic countries. He is a regular attendant at the Jerusalem when he is in town, and has large connections with many of the first merchants in the city. The only remuneration Mr. Waghorn is understood ever to have received from government for the interest he exhibited in promoting and directing the route of the overland mail, was the concession of the title of "Lieut. R. N.", for which he sought several years before it was allowed. The merchants, in the year 1839-40, however, very handsomely subscribed a considerable sum, and presented it to Mr. Waghorn, to enable him to push his agency, both at home and in India, which then required more capital than he could readily command. Since that date, although competition has made a dead set against him, he has gone on pretty successfully, and so continues up to the present time. Within the last two months the merchants have commenced a subscription for a testimonial to Mr. Waghorn, which promises to be liberally supported.[259]

In due course the response to the 'Public Testimonial to Lieutenant Waghorn, R.N.' was published as a small pamphlet. A copy survives among the papers of Sir Robert Peel, which includes some manuscript additions to the printed list:[260] The Committee comprised 60 members(!), including four Earls, four Lords and 13 MPs. More than

259 *The City, or the Physiology of London Business: With Sketches on Change*, London, 1845, 144-7.

260 British Library, Add. MS 40593, ff.96-103. The whole is printed as Appendix IV below.

230 subscribers are listed and the principal benefactors were the Bank of England (£100); 'From Bombay' (£500); Madras Chamber of Commerce (£100), 'The Times' (£200), with £50 or £25 subscriptions from a number of commercial firms and banks who were benefitting from the quicker mail service. The subscription seems to have been kept open until 1 February 1848.

12

FINAL YEARS

In a letter to *The Times* dated 15 February 1847, from 34 Cornhill, Waghorn attacked the *Morning Herald* for implying that delays in the progress of mails and passengers were due to the Navy steamers rather than the P&O Company. He accused the latter of taking 11 and 10 days from Southampton to Gibraltar,

> the ordinary time being 6 days, and it is often done in 4½ days. … This, Sir, is the way the mails are continually delayed at Alexandria, and not from the insufficiency of Her Majesty's steamers, although I do not say they are first-rate; but, as the Admiralty are intent on bettering that service, surely the Admiralty should not be the butt of the Peninsular and Orient Company in the columns of the Herald.[261]

The Times of 24 February 1847 reported that 'Lieutenant Waghorn left Hiscock's Royal Hotel, Ramsgate, per Princess Maude, for Ostend, on Monday morning at half-past 9 o'clock for Trieste.[262] Brief notices later showed that the sixth and last Trieste trial began when the *Ardent* left Alexandria for Trieste on 21 February and that it had arrived at Malta on the return trip on 15 March. Another letter from Waghorn acknowledged that the actions of the P&O Company had hit his business very hard:

> Sir- I deeply regret to give notice to the public of England, India, Egypt, &c., who have continued to patronize my firm in its parcel department from the existence of the overland route, and to state it without fear or untruth, that in consequence of the grasping and

261 *The Times*, 15 February 1847, p.6.
262 *The Times*, 24 February 1847, p. 5.

> improper monopoly of the Peninsular and Orient Company, by which I am made to pay them double freight directly and indirectly for the said parcel business, and which was clearly intended to effect my ruin therein, it becomes my duty, out of honesty to the public at large and in justice to myself, to state that after the 1st of July next my firm will not receive parcels in connexion with the Peninsular and Orient Company, of 51, St. Mary Axe; for it was all along legitimately felt by the world generally that as I was the pioneer of the overland route, no company, much less that one, whose very existence has been built upon my labours, would have been found to carry so sweeping a measure, dishonourable to me and disgraceful to themselves.
>
> I leave England once more with Mr. Austin, the engineer, in pursuit of more facilities in the land communication of the overland route, towards which so many years of my life have been so constantly devoted, and on my return I have in view to be able to appeal to the public for its continued support independent of that company.[263]

No more is heard of Waghorn until the autumn when two advertisements in *The South Eastern Gazette* of 7 September 1847 show that he was facing hard times:

> Forty pictures (collected by Lieutenant Waghorn, R.N., in two visits at Rome) are now placed in the County Assembly Rooms, Maidstone. For inspection and sale, apply to Mr. Day, 23, High Street, Maidstone, from whom particulars may be known.
>
> An Arab stud horse (imported from Egypt by Lieutenant Waghorn, R.N,) 6 years old, which has not yet been used. To be seen at Mr. Waghorn's Stables, Snodland.

In October he announced that his business at Cornhill was to be closed on 24 December 1847, much to his dismay, with the P&O Steam Packet Company taking the whole of the overland business into its own hands. Soon after the announcement he made his will, perhaps uncertain how his estate would fare in the future.

---

263 *The Times*, 27 February 1847, p.8.

> I Thomas Fletcher Waghorn of Cornhill in the City of London and of Snodland in the County of Kent Esquire a Lieutenant in Her Majesty's Royal Navy do hereby revoke all former and other wills Codicils and Testamentary dispositions made by me at any time heretofore and I do declare this to be my last Will and Testament I give devise and bequeath All and every the Real and personal Estate to which I shall be entitled at the time of my decease unto my dear wife Harriet Waghorn absolutely but as to Estates vested in me Upon trust or by way of mortgage subject to the Equities affecting the same respectively and I appoint my said wife Harriet Waghorn the executrix of this my will In witness whereof I have hereunder set my hand this 16th day of Novr in the year of our Lord One thousand eight hundred and forty seven Thos. F. Waghorn signed by the said testator in his last Will and Testament in the presence of us present at the same time who at his request in his presence and in the presence of each other have subscribed our names as Witnesses – Philip Smith Coxe Coleman S^t^. Sol^r^. Geo: Wm Wheatley 34 Cornhill.[264]

Wheatley decided to carry on with the business and placed an advertisement in *The Times* on 22 May 1848:

> NOTICE:—Mr. G. W. WHEATLEY RESUMES the BUSINESS of an EAST INDIA and GENERAL AGENT, ay 156 Leadenhall-street, heretofore carried on at 34, Cornhill under the firm of "Waghorn and Co.;" and hopes for the support of all who favoured that firm, of which Mr. Wheatley has for many years been an active member.
>
> Mr. WAGHORN calls the attention of his friends to the above notice, and adds his unqualified recommendation of Mr. Wheatley.

264 TNA, PROB 11/2110; proved 5 March 1850 by Harriet Waghorn.

Business card used by Wheatley's firm until well into the 20th century

On 29 February 1848 Waghorn was present when a deputation of Army and Navy officers had an audience with Prince Albert, the reason for which is not stated.

It was Waghorn's obsession with proving that the Trieste route was quicker than one via Marseilles that caused his financial ruin. Rivalry between *The Times* and the *Morning Herald* fuelled the competition,[265] with *The Times* supporting Trieste and the *Herald* supporting Marseilles. This in turn somewhat heightened tensions between the French and the Germanic countries, each of whom were anxious to reap the benefits of charges they could make for the transit of the Indian mail. As early as April 1846 Waghorn had confirmed that the Treasury and East India Company had 'consented to pay for six experiments via Trieste, that I may prove these'. He would receive £3000 at the end of the series and was given an advance of £500. In the course of the trials it became clear to Waghorn that his expenses would be £6000. He actually received £4000, but it was not enough.

A 'Memorial of Mr. Waghorn's claims on his country' is dated 3 January 1848, although it was not submitted until 28 March following, apparently to Lord John Russell, then Minister for Foreign Affairs. Together with the covering letter Waghorn annexed a number

265 See pp. 219-229.

of testimonials from eminent members of the Government supporting his claim for restitution of £2000 he felt he was owed for his 'great and important services'.[266] They were from

(a) Lord Palmerston, Foreign Secretary, 10 January 1848
(b) Earl of Aberdeen, late Secretary of Foreign Affairs, 31 January 1848
(c) Earl of Ellenborough, late Governor-General of India, 21 January 1848
(d) Earl of Harrowby, Secretary of the India Board, 29 January 1848
(e) Sit John Cam Hobhouse, President of the India Board, 29 January 1848
(f) Joseph Hume, M.P., 23 January 1848
(g) Sir Robert Gordon, H.M. Ambassador at Vienna, 1 November 1846
(h) Lord Combermere, Commander-in-Chief in India, 24 February 1848
(i) Earl of Ripon, President of the India Board in 1846, 28 February 1848

Waghorn now gave his total costs as £8000 and the Memorial was submitted to the Government on 12 July. The Treasury awarded him £1500 and a pension of £200 a year and they expected that the Directors of the East India Company would make an equal grant. However the latter decided instead to give Waghorn a life pension of £100 a year, first revealed by a 'mole' to *Allen's Indian Mail* and reported in the Times of 27 July 1848:

> The Court of Directors of the East India Company have granted a pension of £100 per annum for life, to Lieutenant Waghorn, R.N., as an acknowledgment for the services he has rendered the cause of steam communication between this country and India. We understand Mr. Waghorn, after a long and laborious public career, has retired into private life; we trust he may long be spared to enjoy the fruits of his perseverance and zeal. His agency business will in future be carried on by his late partner, Mr. Wheatley.[267]

This was the first Waghorn himself had heard of the pension and he responded the next day to record that he had had no official notice of

266 The Memorial is transcribed in full at Appendix C. The supporting letters are printed in Sidebottom, *op. cit.*, 112, 119-123. Only Ellenborough, Hume and Combermere appear in the printed list of subscribers to Waghorn's testimonial

267 *The Times*, 27 July 1848, p. 4.

the intentions of the Court of Directors, adding: 'I deeply regret that I cannot retire into private life—I wish I could. I have sacrificed all my own means towards accomplishing the great object to which my past life has been devoted, and must now seek employment for the future.' Somewhat snootily the Mail told Waghorn that 'we are not in the habit of making statements of this kind at random' and advised him that if he 'will give us credit for a short time, he will probably find that that statement which he has "distinctly contradicted" is correct.' Sure enough, on 4 August Waghorn asked *The Times*

> to insert the accompanying letter I have had the honour to receive from the Honorable East India Company:
>
> East India House, July 28, 1848.
>
> Sir,—I am commanded to acquaint you that the Court of Directors of the East India Company, adverting to your merits and services in the establishment of steam communication with India, and the great benefits derived therefrom, have granted you, as a further mark of the same entertained by The East India Company of those services, an annuity of one hundred pounds (£100.)
>
> This annuity takes effect from the 12 inst., the date of the resolution by which it was granted.
>
> I am, Sir, your most obedient humble servant, J. D. Dickson.[268]

Under normal circumstances such an annuity would have been very welcome, but the heavy debts which Waghorn had incurred made it a mere drop in the ocean so far as his requirements were concerned. There was an inadequate attempt to do something on his behalf, as Waghorn reveals in a letter to Richard Cobden, M.P.:

> Snodland, near Rochester
> 14th August 1848
> My Dear Mr Cobden,
>
> My Lord John Russell will (I believe) this week propose to Parliament the grant of £1500) for my services & losses in opening up the "Overland Route" to India. – Altho' duly appreciating Lord

268 *The Times*, 4 August 1848, p. 5. The letter was written at Snodland on the 3rd.

John's kindness for even that sum, tho' it is only One Fifth, will pay my debts arising, from having had to work (unaided & alone) it, induces me to ask you, and a few other Members of the House to try & persuade Lord John to increase it, now the E. I. Comp^{y} have only given me an annuity of 100^{ls}, for doing the greatest benefit "India has yet received". Honestly feeling I have deserved well, is my best excuse for asking you to do me this favor, in token of the great service, I have rendered to our country – I remain

Yours faithfully,

Thos Waghorn

NB. My papers relative to this were sent you some months since TW.[269]

A second letter to Cobden a few weeks later gives a hint that the depression which blighted Waghorn's last years was already taking hold:

34 Cornhill 22 Sept. 1848

My Dear Sir,

May I solicit your good Offices in sending the Enclosed to Mr Boothman, & to take any steps you deem necessary to the object it has in view.

I have been in Eng^{d} about six weeks & when I can find time I will call at your residence in London to pay my respects to you.

Mrs Waghorn also returned with me this last time. She will not return whatever I may do – I have had a sad time out in Egypt this last trip in all clases[?] except that I stand as high with Mah^{t} Ali as ever.[270]

The 'sad time' presumably reflected the illness of Mehemet Ali, who had recently passed rulership of Egypt and Sudan to his son Ibrahim. This was compounded soon after Waghorn's letter, when Ibrahim died on 10 November. His father lapsed into senile decay and himself died on 2 August 1849.

On 20 October 1848 Joseph Hume assured Waghorn that he too

269 West Sussex RO, Cobden Papers, Cobden/2, No. 109.

270 West Sussex RO, Cobden Papers, Cobden/1, No. 41.

was trying his best to secure the extra money which still remained unpaid and regretted that he

> had not been in the H. of C, when the £1500 was voted for you at 1 o'clock in the morning that I considered that you ought to be repaid the expense and out of pocket charge for the Trieste Route, and further that the £1,200 to you for meritorious service should be considered with a pension for you.[271]

He advised that the claim could not be re-submitted by the Treasury and suggested that Waghorn should therefore contact Sir John Russell directly. Evidently Waghorn's creditors were clamouring for their money and on 10 January 1849 he asked the Directors of the East India Company for further help. They increased his pension from £100 to £200, but both this and the Government pension were seized to offset his debts. On 8 June 1849 he submitted a second Memorial, supported by the same men as before. The tone is truly bitter and desperate:

> Once in the enjoyment of the Pasha's friendship I was enabled to establish mails to India; and to keep that service in my own hands for four years. On one occasion I succeeded in getting letters from Bombay to England in forty-six days, by means of a fast French brig, hired by me from Alexandria lying in ballast, and ready to start at a moment's notice to Marseilles; and immediately after, the Government and the East India Company, at the pressing solicitations of the London East India and China Association (the then Mr., now my friend, Sir George Larpent, chairman), started mails of their own, taking from me the conveyance of letters, without a sixpence compensation for the loss from that time to this—these authorities having, till then, repeatedly declared that they had no intention of having mail by that route at all. Had this additional deprivation of my income been adjudicated upon by any commercial tribunal in the world, £20,000 is the lowest sum that could be in fairness awarded me and this without taking into the estimate the fact that I had put to rest the 'North-westers in

271 Sidebottom, *op. cit.*, 124, from a letter formerly in his possession. A page from it is shown in Rudi Jeidel, *The Waghorn Story*, slide 64.

the Red Sea,' the 'Monsoons in the Indian Ocean,' the 'Plagues of Egypt and the sands of the desert' that were to have swallowed up the adventurous wayfarers by the dreaded Overland Route.

Next, in conjunction with my partners, I took up the carriage of passengers, planted hotels at Alexandria, Cairo, etc., etc., and familiarised the desert with the spectacle of horses, vans, and all the usual adjuncts of English travel, instead of the unchanging Arab and his primeval camel.

These, with packet boats on the Nile and Canal, duly provided with English superintendents, and afterwards steamers, rendered Eastern travel as facile to the most timid as a journey of the same length in this country; and I had every prospect of finding this hitherto undreamt of novelty as lucrative to myself as it was agreeable to those vast numbers of my countrymen who availed themselves of it. But, unfortunately, just when my enterprise, industry, capital, and my possession of Mehemet Ali's friendship were beginning to produce their natural results, Her Majesty's Government and the East India Company gave the monopoly of a chartered contract to an opulent and powerful Company [P&O], for I had coupled with the passenger system the carriage of overland parcels—a source of great profit, and through it there was a constant accession to the comfort of the passengers in transit. This company, already extensive carriers by water, gleaned from my firm the secret of conducting my business, with an alleged view to supply it on a much more comprehensive scale, and to employ us in so doing; and when nothing more remained to be learned from us we were forthwith superseded, though with a useless and utterly unproductive expenditure on the part of our successors of six times the money we should have required to accomplish the same end. Overwhelmed by the competition of this giant association, I was entirely deprived of the advantages of this creation of my own energy, and left with it a ruin on my own hands, though to have secured me at least the Egyptian transit would not only have been but the merest justice to an individual, but would have been a material gain to the British public politically and otherwise. In my hands the Egyptian traffic was English, and I venture to say that English it would have continued to this day had I not been interfered with. But my successors gave it all up to the Pasha, and under the altered and the altering circumstances of Egypt, it will be fortunate indeed if the circumstances of that act do not bitterly atone for the hardships so inconsiderately and wantonly inflicted upon me. … I will only add that on the commencement of my career I was possessed of, property by inheritance. This has been sacrificed, and I am still left in debt to the extent of £5,000.

The immediate origin and cause of my embarrassments was a forfeited promise on the part of the Treasury and the India House, whereby only four instead of six thousand pounds relied on by me were paid towards the Trieste Route experiments in the winter of 1846-7 when, single handed and despite unparalleled and wholly unforeseen difficulties, I eclipsed on five trials out of six the long organised arrangements of the French Authorities specially stimulated to all possible exertion and supplied with unlimited means by Monsieur Cinzot. On the first of these six occasions there arose the breaking down on the Indian Ocean of the steamer provided for me, thereby trebling the computed expenses through the delay; and, when startled by this excessive outlay, I hesitated to entail more and the Treasury and the India House told me to proceed to do the service well and make out my bill afterwards. I did proceed. I did the service, not only well, not only to the satisfaction of my employers, but in a manner that elicited the admiration of Europe. […]

I presented by bill. *It was dishonoured.* I had made myself an invalid and sown the seeds of a broken constitution in the performance of that duty. The disappointment occasioned by the non-payment of the two thousand pounds has preyed incessantly upon me since; and now a wreck alike almost in mind and body, I am sustained alone by the hope that the annals of the Insolvent and Court will not have inscribed upon them the Pioneer of the Overland Route because of obligations he incurred for the public, by direction of the public authorities.'

This plea too went unheeded, but as a sop to Waghorn the P&O Company later gave him £300 and offered him a free passage to and from Malta, when it was hoped his health would be improved by the voyage. A letter to Charles Roach Smith from Harriet Waghorn[272] at Barnsbury Road shows that her husband had availed himself of the offer and *The Times* reported that he had sailed there from Southampton on 20 October 1849 on the *Euxine*:

> My dear Sir,
>
> I thank you very much for your kind enquiries of Mr. Waghorn. I am hourly expecting a letter. The first from Gibraltar November 4th made me exceptionally anxious, but the last, dated Malta, November 13 more relieved my feelings, as he writes of being a little better.
>
> I cannot tell until the mail is in, if he remains or returns to England till the unpleasant season has passed away.
>
> I am hoping he will send for me to join him there.

But various newspapers reported that 'Lieut Waghorn, who is residing at Malta for the benefit of his health, is so much enfeebled, that those who formerly knew him could scarcely recognise him'.[273] Waghorn returned at the end of the year, landing on Christmas Day, and an Australian recalls journeying with him:

> I remember being a fellow passenger in the *Indus* from Malta to London in December 1849. He [Waghorn] had made a proposition to [the Australian] Government, and told them that if they would grant him the contract, he would deliver the mail from London to Sydney in fifty days, and he was sanguine of getting up a company. Poor fellow, he died ten days after we landed, a strong body destroyed by too energetic a mind.[274]

Ever optimistic Waghorn it seems was still hoping to set up schemes. But it was too late, for on 9th January 1850 *The Times* told its readers:

---

272 Sankey, op. cit., p. 120. She gives 'Barnsbury Road' as in Strood, which is an error; this must be the house in Golden Square, Pentonville, in which Waghorn later died. I have not been able to trace the original letter. *The Times*, 30 October 1849.

273 *Royal Cornwall Gazette*, 21 December 1849, 7.

274 *Sydney Morning Herald*, 23 March 1855 (the letter written on the 19th).

'We regret to announce the sudden and unexpected death of the gallant pioneer of the overland route, at his residence, Golden-square, Pentonville, on Tuesday [8th], in the 49th year of his age. Mr. Waghorn had returned only on Christmas-day from Malta, where he had been residing a short time for the benefit of his health, which had been considerably impaired by anxiety of mind, arising chiefly from pecuniary engagements, contracted in his prosecution of the Trieste experiments in 1846, and which liabilities the devotion of all his means and the sacrifice of his entire property were inadequate to liquidate. Of the pensions lately awarded him by government he lived to receive only one quarter's payment. … His death was occasioned not so much by any specific disorder as by the general break-up of the system, though the wreck of his iron constitution, and his irrepressible energy, offered so great a resistance to the inroads of debility that it was thought to the last he would rally, and his dissolution was attended with great pain and suffering.

Waghorn was buried in the churchyard at All Saints, Snodland, on 14 January 1850 from 'Pentonville', aged 49, near his Fletcher, Goodhugh and Gorham ancestors and his sister Frances. A couple of months later an advertisement was placed in the *Times* in England and in *Allen's Indian Mail* in India inviting subscriptions for a 'memorial window proposed to be erected in the church of Snodland, Kent, to commemorate the valuable services rendered to the country by the late Lieut. Thomas Fletcher Waghorn, R. N. ... The friends and admirers of this enterprising officer are respectfully invited to subscribe to the proposed object.'[275] A list of six early subscribers, headed by the Rector, was appended, but evidently not enough support was received for the project and it seems likely that the money was rather channelled into paying for the substantial stone memorial now on the south wall of the nave.

Conclusion

Much is made in the accounts of Waghorn of the fact that he was shunned by the government and authorities of his day and that he was not given proper support by them. Is this true? Yes it is, but we ought to consider the situation as they saw it. In the East India Company Waghorn held a lowly position as First Class Volunteer, being promoted merely to Second Mate (at the same wage) after his return from the First Burmese War. Having been granted leave in 1828 by the Company to promote his scheme they were nevertheless loath to risk putting money into the venture; the problems of establishing a route had not then been properly addressed—could a steam ship sail to Suez? Could coal depots be established, and at a reasonable cost? Could the Overland Route be secure?—still less, ought he to have the authority to run it? No doubt relations between Waghorn and the Company became increasingly difficult. Here was an employee with undeniable energy and enthusiasm who constantly pestered them concerning the development of a steam route to India and beyond. He clearly was obsessive in pursuit of his aim and seemed to have a bee in his bonnet. Waghorn's service in the navy was honourable,

275 *The Times*, 1 April 1850, 4; *Allen's Indian Mail*, 1850, p.245.

but relatively unproductive and for a long time the authorities found technical reasons why he should not gain his promotion to lieutenant. Again, then, he remained a minor figure in the service.

Why too should the Government bow to his wishes? Certainly Waghorn had gained support from some of their number, but the Government was cautious when it was eventually decided to establish the Overland Route. For all his enthusiasm and expertise, rather than link up with a private entrepreneur like Waghorn, it surely was safer for them to employ a large company like P&O, which is what happened. That Waghorn could not compete with their size and money was unfortunate, but in this he was merely a victim of commercial competition. They also questioned whether his complaints of being ignored were entirely justified, pointing out that he had been given 'rewards' of money and plate by mercantile organisations. He can hardly have endeared himself to them either when constantly singing the praises of Mehemet Ali and Egypt, where they preferred to keep the Pasha at a diplomatic distance. In short Waghorn was probably looked upon as something of an upstart, with ideas above his station.

Nevertheless, he had his supporters, some in the mercantile business, some in India and Australia, and some among the newspaper proprietors. A few in Government supported his efforts. *The Times* in particular had reason to be grateful to him when he helped speed their dispatches through Europe by new routes when the French were proving difficult. All these certainly did their best for him. Waghorn himself, perhaps because the posts he held in the navy and in the East India Company were relatively insignificant, took every opportunity to promote himself in the numerous pamphlets he published, seeking testimonials from anyone who would care to supply them. Undoubtedly the newspapers played their part in boosting his ego, for from the first they described him as 'intrepid', 'zealous', 'enterprising', 'enduring', 'indefatigable', 'energetic', and such like. In the end his descent into debt and despair resulted from his realisation that he was unable to compete with the enterprise set up by the Government and P&O and that all the money he had invested in the hope of overseeing the Overland Route and the mails was lost, since the Government would not reimburse him. After much pressure from newspaper publicity he was granted two small pensions, but these were immediately swallowed up by his creditors and came too late to be of help.

To his friends and acquaintances he was something of a *Boy's Own* hero, constantly battling to overcome all opposition; to officialdom he was a persistent nuisance, constantly goading them to venture into unchartered waters. With hindsight we can admire his vision that new technology could be harnessed to make a great leap forward in communication with the East, and we can admire his energy, enterprise and enthusiasm in establishing the Overland Route through Egypt. In the event advances in technology were so rapid that all his efforts were eclipsed after a few years. Nevertheless, his achievement was increasingly recognised after his death: indeed pressure continued to ensure that his widow and sisters were granted pensions, statues were erected at Suez and at Chatham,[276] and remembrances were made in 1900 and 1950 (but none in 2000). Remembrances took many forms. Members of Waghorn's wider family, and some outside it, proudly used 'Waghorn' as a middle name for their children. The most celebrated show was a *Diorama of the Overland Route to India*, compèred by

276 See Appendix D.

Joachim H. Stocqueler (1801-1886), which opened in Regent Street on 1 April 1850 and was an enormous success.[277] For some years it led to imitations by others in numerous cities. The *Sydney Morning Herald* advertised 'The Game of the Route to India, or the Juvenile Waghorn, in red mahogany case, with counters, etc.' on 20 December 1851. And the playwright Tom Taylor (1817-1880) had success with his play *The Overland Route* in 1860. When the Suez Canal was opened Ferdinand de Lesseps, the builder, said of Waghorn:

> He it was who first conceived the idea; it was his indomitable courage and perseverance that led me on to prove its practicability. I am pleased to have the opportunity to proclaim the noble qualities of that much underrated gentleman; but he was in advance of his age, and the very plans that were scoffed at when first mooted were those which, in my position as engineer of the works, have enabled me to carry them through.

277 He contributed a guinea to Waghorn's testimonial, but no doubt made considerably more from this show. The paintings from the show were collected and preserved and are now part of the P&O Heritage Collection. Two are shown in chapter 8.

APPENDIX A

Waghorn family: Ann Goodhugh's ancestors and her children

Thomas GOODHUGH = Margaret Pountain
marr. 9 Jan 1713, Birling

John FLETCHER
[born c. 1685]
bur. 26 Feb 1752,
Snodland

= (1) Ann Scultup
bur. 29 Nov 1727
Birling
= (2) Margaret
[born c. 1697]
d. 20 Aug 1748,
Snodland

John GOODHUGH = Elizabeth Seamark
marr. 29 June 1742, Birling 1724-
1715-1801 1723-1780

John FLETCHER = Elizabeth Gilder
bur. 7 Oct 1803 at Snodland
bur. 16 Nov. 1803 at Snodland

John GOODHUGH = Elizabeth FLETCHER
marr. 10 July 1771, Birling
bap. 21 Apr 1745 Birling; bur 4 Jan 1835 at Snodland
bur. 24 May 1782, at Snodland

Thomas WAGHORN = Ann GOODHUGH
marr. 28 July 1794, Snodland
(c.1770-1826) 1773-1859

Children of Thomas and Ann Waghorn:
(1) John, baptised 9 September 1795, St Mary the Virgin, Chatham. He was still alive on 28 March 1821, when he wrote to his mother from Aldgate, London, with news that he had gained a position in a slaughter-house; he married Harriet Buck at Hoo St Werburgh on 15 September 1818.[278]

278 See Andrew Ashbee, 'A Waghorn Discovery', *The Clock Tower*, 15 (Aug 2009), 27-31.

(2) Elizabeth, buried 14 February 1797, St Mary the Virgin, Chatham. (an infant.)

(3) Ann, baptised 3 March 1798, St Mary the Virgin, Chatham; married Robert Munday at All Saints, Snodland, 28 June 1824, when Thomas Waghorn, senior, was a witness. Robert was then of the parish of St Nicholas, Rochester. He is named as a plumber in 1826, as plumber and glazier in 1828, and innkeeper between 1835 and 1839. Their children were Mary (bap. 18 Jan 1826),[279] married [?Christopher James] Campbell [?18 Feb 1847, St James, Clerkenwell]; Ann (no details); Robert Thomas (born 26 Dec 1828; bap. 28 June 1829 [died young]); Robert [Thomas] (bap. 30 May 1830); Fanny (bap. 19 Feb 1832, married Robert Comyns in Sydney, 6 June 1854, died at North Carlton, Melbourne on 6 Sep 1914); John Goodhugh (bap. 2 Oct 1833 [died young]); Sarah (bap. 25 June 1837, died unmarried at North Carlton, Melbourne in 1924); Hannah (bap. 31 Mar 1839 [died young]).[280] Wright's 1838 directory of Rochester notes Robert Munday as a licensed victualler at the City Coffee House, High Street.[281] He was in Cairo from around 1839 to perhaps 1847[282] as manager of Waghorn's hotel there, but was dead by 1853. In 1843 he sued Waghorn in Chancery and the case was renewed in 1850 with Ann Munday and Robert Thomas Munday as plaintiffs and Harriet Waghorn, Ann Waghorn and Robert Munday as defendants.[283] Ann Munday is listed in Land Tax records at Island Cottage, Holborough, between 1849 and 1852, and as an 'annuitant' in the 1851 census. The latter also records her daughter Sarah, born in Rochester, aged 13, as a 'scholar at home'. The mother and children left Southampton in the *Meteor* on 17 March 1853 and arrived at Sydney on 3 July 1853: Ann described as aged 55, domestic servant, born at Chatham, father dead, mother living at Rochester; daughter Fanny, aged 20, nursery governess,

279 Baptisms are at St Nicholas, Rochester.

280 Details from parish register of St Nicholas, Rochester, kindly supplied by Mrs. Robin Handley.

281 I. G. Wright, *Wright's Topography of Rochester, Chatham, Strood, Brompton, &c. and Directory of the Clergy, Gentry, Tradesmen, &c.*, Chatham, 1838 (facsimile, Baggins Book Bazaar, Rochester, 1995).

282 Snodland Poll Book, 1847, shows him there, but Samuel Shepheard seems to have taken over by then.

283 TNA, C14/118/M4 and C14/1160/M50.

born at Rochester, father dead; Sarah, aged 16, nursery maid, born at Rochester; another daughter, Mary Campbell, living in Sydney. Ann died on 20 April 1889 at 115 Raglan Street, South Melbourne, and was buried at Boroondara General Cemetery on 3 May.[284]

(4) Thomas Fletcher, baptised 16 July 1800, St Mary the Virgin, Chatham.

(5) James Goodhugh, baptised 29 December 1802, St Mary the Virgin, Chatham; buried there, 14 October 1804.

(6) Mary Jane, baptised 27 June 1804, St Mary the Virgin, Chatham; unmarried; died in Strood Union after a fall at her home, 18 May 1883; buried at All Saints, Snodland, 25 May 1883. Mary Jane acted as witness at the marriages of her sisters Ann and Sarah, was present at the deaths of her mother and her sister Frances and acted as executrix for her brother Edward. A letter from Harold R. Owden Stedman[285] gives first-hand accounts of some of the Waghorn family, including Mary Jane. She was

> frequently to be seen in the streets of Rochester attired in a long red plaid coat and poke-bonnet. She was a handsome woman, tall, and of fine personality, living at 11 Boley Hill, afterwards at Union Street, Rochester, and finally at a house opposite St Nicholas' Church, Strood. There in 1883 or 4, advanced in years and infirm, she had a fall, striking her head on the fender, causing a very serious wound. Her sad plight was discovered by a little girl who used to run errands for her. She was removed to Strood Union, where death quickly ensued. The late Messrs. John Ross and William Foord kindly arranged and attended the burial at Snodland, as did the writer, his father and mother. She lies adjacent to the resting place of her brother, the pioneer. Mary Jane was a frequent visitor at the writer's home, when she would talk hour after hour on her own and brother's life. I well remember on one occasion she remarked: "When I die, my name will go forth throughout the length and breadth of the land." As assuredly it did! For both London and

284 *The Age*, Melbourne, 2 May 1889, 8.

285 Unidentified newspaper cutting, with *Rochester, Chatham and Gillingham News*, 22 October 1948. Stedman (*b.*1867) claimed descant from John Boyer of Cuxton, who married Elizabeth Goodhugh, sister of John, Waghorn's grandfather, at Birling on 1 November 1769.

provincial papers strongly commented on the deceased's poverty and ultimate end in the poor-house.

In 1883 *The Daily Telegraph* had intended launching a subscription to support Mary Jane, but she died before it could be realised. On 19 May that year the paper published the following:

Sir—I have read with much pleasure your interesting article in to-day's issue, upon Lieutenant Waghorn, the pioneer of the overland route to India and the East, and as it was your intention to have received subscriptions on behalf of the sister bearing his honoured name, but who has passed away before your generous offer could meet with, what I hope, would have been a hearty response, will you allow me to make the same appeal on behalf of the two surviving sisters—Sarah Ranson [sic], aged seventy, and Ann Munday, aged eighty-five, now living in Melbourne in anything but affluent circumstances. They receive the same pension (£25 per annum) as the sister referred to, and which has been paid to them, through me, as trustee since it was granted in 1873, but, if this amount could be supplemented by a few pounds quarterly, it would at least show the survivors that, although late, their brother's noble efforts have at last been recognised by a portion of the English public.—I remain, sir, your obedient servant, William W. Foord.
Rochester, May 19.

P.S.—I may add that Miss Waghorn will have a respectable funeral, as Mr. R. Prull [Prall], Mr. C. R. Foord, and myself have arranged to bury her in the same vault as her brother, at Snodland, near Rochester, and shall remove her body from the workhouse as soon as the inquest has been held.

Yesterday morning, Mr. W. H. Bell, Deputy Coroner for the City of Rochester, held an inquest in the infirmary of the North Aylesford Union Workhouse, upon the body of Miss Mary Ann Waghorn, sister to the late Lieutenant Waghorn, R.N., the originator of the Overland Route to India.

Kate Jones deposed that the deceased was a distant cousin of hers, and was seventy-six years of age.

Arthur Meadows, a youth, said that on the evening of Monday, the 14th instant, he saw the deceased sitting on the doorstep outside her house. She was too weak to get inside, and she asked him to assist her. He did so, and sat her upon her bed, and afterwards lighted a candle for her. He afterwards got a jug of water, which she asked for, and stood it upon the table, and, after closing the shutters, he left the house. The deceased did not appear to be ill, but very infirm.

Mr. H. Tronah, an hotel keeper, stated that he had known the deceased all his life. She had no occupation, but had a pension of £25 a year from the Government, and received a little help from a few friends in India. Witness had known the deceased to have suffered several falls. She was very eccentric, and had delusions. On Sunday week she had three falls, and afterwards sent for witness. He went to her, when she handed him in key of her sitting-room, saying there was some one in the room. He unlocked the door, but could see no one, when she said they were hiding behind a screen which was in the room. As he had seen nothing of the deceased from last Monday until Wednesday evening, he got his son to force the door, and then found the deceased lying upon the floor. She had a large bruise on the forehead, the table was overturned, and a water jug was lying on the floor broken. She was in a helpless state, and her mind was wandering. She shouted out, "Thieves!" and "Murder!" Witness sent for Dr. R. R. Brown, the workhouse doctor, who ordered her removal to the workhouse. Witness believed the bruise on her forehead was caused by her falling against the table.

Charlotte Madle, a girl, said she had been in the habit of going errands for the deceased. She had fallen very often. She had food in the house, but ate very little. It appeared to witness that she would not eat.

Dr. Browne deposed that he ordered deceased into the infirmary, as she had no one to look after her. She was then insensible. She had a bruise on the forehead, which had caused extravasation of blood on the brain, and which was the immediate cause of death, but some of the organs of the body were diseased, including the heart. In his opinion death was the result of natural causes, accelerated by the bruise on the forehead, which was probably produced by a fall.

The jury returned a verdict in accordance with the medical evidence.

(7) Edward, baptised 14 May 1806, St Mary the Virgin, Chatham. He was a butcher trading in St Margaret's Street, Rochester, by 1838, but does not appear in Bagshaw's directory of 1847. He acted as witness at the marriage of his sister Sarah in 1834. Edward emigrated to Australia [details not yet found] and died, unmarried, on 18 July 1868 at Queen Street, Melbourne, still named as a butcher.[286]
(8) Eliza, baptised 12 July 1809, St Mary the Virgin, Chatham; buried there, 29 August 1809.
(9) Frances, baptised 1 August 1810, St Mary the Virgin, Chatham; died, unmarried, 8 December 1848 at Maidstone Road, St Margaret's [Rochester]; buried at All Saints, Snodland, 14 December 1848, from 'Birling', aged 38. In the 1841 census she was living with her uncle James Goodhugh at Rookery farm and this may have become her usual home.[287] The memorial reads: Sacred / to the memory of / Frances Waghorn / who died December 1848 / aged 38 years / This stone was placed here / by her affectionate brother / Lieut. Waghorn R.N.
(10) Sarah, baptised 9 June 1813, St Mary the Virgin, Chatham; married William Ransom at All Saints, Snodland, 8 December 1834; died of 'senile decay', 14 February 1887 at Prahran, Melbourne. The pair lived in Rotherhithe until at least 1847, and then moved to 11 Cardington Street, Hampstead-road, Middlesex. William, like his father, was a mastmaker and a 'proprietor of houses'. Waghorn acknowledges that William Ransom gave him considerable financial help. Ransom died before 1855; his widow and family emigrated to Melbourne, Australia, on the *Stebenheath* on 17 May 1855; arriving in December 1855. A son, Thomas Waghorn Ransom, b. Rotherhithe 3 April 1845, was a merchant seaman.

286 Information from Mrs R. Handley and Edward Stock. Edward's administration is among the PCC records at the Public Record Office.
287 The farm was in Birling, although only a few yards from the Snodland boundary.

*****

A plea for financial assistance for Ann Munday and Sarah Ransom was made in Australia in 1872:

> The attention of the public was directed in our issue of yesterday to the indigent circumstances of the two aged sisters of the late pioneer of the overland route to India (Lieutenant THOMAS WAGHORN, R. N.). The facts of the case are that Mrs. ANN MUNDAY and Mrs. SARAH RANSOM—whose ages are respectively 85 and 70 years—have been in receipt for a few years of the beggarly pension of £25 each per annum from the Imperial Government. This is how England rewards the immediate relatives of her heroes and best men! The majority of the public are no doubt aware of the vicissitudes of Lieutenant Waghorn's career: how he initiated the overland route, and, in spite of tremendous opposition from the Government of the day, carried it to a successful issue. The work of the overland route was carried on, not at the expense of the Government, but at the expense of his family, who, we are told, at various periods of the last years of his life advanced him between £30,000 and £40,000! Poor WAGHORN was confident that there would be a permanent retention on the part of the Crown of his services; but he was doomed to disappointment. The monopoly of a chartered contract was given to a wealthy and influential company, and WAGHORN, ruined in mind and body, went to his grave with a broken heart. Her Majesty's Government, not content with swallowing up the large fortune which WAGHORN inherited (besides the £40,000 referred to), actually allowed him to die £5000 in debt. There is scarcely a man of the present generation who has conferred such benefits on the civilised world. Why, therefore, should his immediate relatives have occasion to beg for assistance? We do not hesitate to say that it is a crying disgrace to this boasted age of civilisation that the two elderly ladies referred to should be living amongst us in penury and want. England has forgotten WAGHORN—one of her greatest heroes—but is eager to worship men like Lord WOLSELEY and Lord ALCESTER, who get paid handsomely for simply "doing their duty!" The former received a grant of £25,000, and the latter £30,000, for slaughtering the

> Egyptians. The case is one demanding the immediate attention of the Government, who can even now, at the eleventh hour, recognise the services of one who did more for the advancement of the Australian colonies than any one individual of the present generation. The Premier is in possession of the facts and actual positions of the two sisters of WAGHORN, and no doubt the matter will be fully discussed in the Cabinet. If necessary, probably Mr. Service will make representations through the Governor to the Imperial Government.[288]

Harriet Waghorn was placed on the Navy pension list on 1 February 1850, where it was noted that her private income was £91.[289] A Bombay merchant, Sir James-jee Jujobhoy gave her a further pension of £20 a year.[290] She moved away from Snodland following her husband's death and made her will on 17 May 1851 at Bark Place, Bayswater,[291] although she lived on until 19 January 1856 and died at Ashton Lodge, Tunbridge Wells, presumably the 18th century listed building in London Road..

> This is the last Will and Testament of me Harriett Waghorn of Bark Place, Bayswater, widow of the late Lieutenant Thomas Fletcher Waghorn of the Royal Navy. I direct my Executors shall order my funeral in an inexpensive unostentatious manner. I also direct that all my just debts, funeral and testamentary expenses shall in the first place be paid and satisfied. I give and bequeath unto Joseph Matthews my Executor hereinafter named my painting of a favorite horse called Jack. I give and bequeath unto Susannah Matthews, sister of the said Joseph Matthews, my pianoforte and a daguerreotype likeness of my late husband. I give and bequeath to my Godchild Harriett Matthews my watch and portrait. I give and bequeath to my friend Mr. George Wheatley the portrait of my late husband by Sir George Hayter. I give and bequeath to Mrs. William Ransom, the sister of my late husband, all the articles of

288 Newspaper cutting, but date of edition not ascertained. Mr Service was Premier of Victoria in 1884 only.

289 TNA: ADM 23/106.

290 *Royal Cornwall Gazette*, 17 January 1851, 2.

291 See Appendix.

his clothing remaining with me at my decease, together with his watch and ring. I give and bequeath to my friend Mrs. Mountjoy my mourning brooch with pearls containing hair of my late husband and also nineteen guineas for a mourning ring and … All the rest, residue and remainder of my Estate, Property and Effects, real and personal in possession, remainder, or expectancy, plate, jewells, wine, linen, rents in arrear, pensions in arrear, dividends, interest, stocks, funds, securities and money of and to which I shall be seized, possessed, or entitled at the time of my decease, I give and bequeath the same unto my friend Thomas Matthews of Snodland in the county of Kent, farmer, his heirs, executors, administrators and assigns, according to the respective natures thereof, for his and their own absolute use and benefit and I appoint the said Thomas Matthews and his son the said Joseph Matthews Executors of this my will, hereby revoking all former wills. In witness whereof I the said Harriett Waghorn the Testatrix have hereunto set my hand this seventeenth day of May one thousand eight hundred and fifty one – Harriett Waghorn. Signed and acknowledged by the said Harriett Waghorn the Testatrix as the last will and testament in the presence of us present at the same time who at her request, in her presence and in the presence of each other have subscribed our names as witnesses – Saml. Piercy 15 Three Crown Sq^{re}, Southwark – Wm Kilby of the same Place his Clerk.

She was buried at Snodland on the 23 January 1856 from 'Tunbridge Wells'. She left most of what estate she had to the family of Thomas and Susannah Matthews.[292] The estate duty record[293] confirms the bequests recorded in the will:

1) Piano forte & likeness to Susannah Matthews
2) Watch, Ring, & articles of Clothing of Test^{rix} late husband to Mrs William Ransom
3) Watch and Portrait to Harriet Matthews

292 Thomas Matthews' estate had passed to Susannah, his widow, of Milton next Gravesend, by 1865. Joseph Matthews was then described as of Southwark, hop factor. The daughter Susannah had married Henry Solomon at Holy Trinity, Milton by Gravesend, on 16 October 1860; they were 'of Cliffe' by 12 April 1865: KHLC: U2102/T13.

293 TNA: IR26

4) £19. 19s. 0d & mourning brooch to Mrs Mountjoy
5) Real Estate charge
6) Portrait of Testrix last Husband by Sir G Hayter to George Wheatley
7) Residue to Thomas Matthews
8) Painting of a horse to Joseph Matthews

Thomas Matthews (c.1785-c.1861) seems to have come to Snodland around 1816 and by 1818 was established at Covey Hall, one of the principal farms of the parish. No doubt he was a good customer of the mill at Holborough—only a quarter of a mile away—and Harriet's brother Edward, miller there in succession to their father, calls Thomas 'my friend' in his own will. Susannah, Thomas's wife, was much younger and this may have been a second marriage. The baptism of their son Joseph took place at All Saints, Snodland, on 25 May 1835, followed by two daughters: Susannah on 11 Sep 1837 and Harriet (Harriet Waghorn's god-child) on 13 December 1847. In the estate duty record Joseph's address is given as No. 11 Northumberland Terrace, Regent's Park Road, Middlesex, and he is already described as a hop factor. Harriet's estate was valued at under £200 and duty of £2. 16s. 10d. was set.

The Standard summarized the pensions paid to Waghorn's female relatives: Harriet initially received a pension of £40 a year, increased after 12 months to £100. £50 was granted to his mother in 1856 (she died in 1859) and in 1872 pensions of £25 a year were agreed for his three sisters Ann, Sarah, and Mary-Jane.[294]

294 *The Standard*, 3 March 1884.

APPENDIX B

Some time in 1845 Waghorn's friends in the mercantile trade and in government moved to set up a testimonial to him in gratitude for his work in establishing speedier links between India and England (see p. 148), having felt that this was insufficiently acknowledged by those in Government and the East India Company who could have rewarded him financially. The testimonial eventually closed on 1 February 1848 and a small pamphlet was produced recording subscriptions. This is the text.

The Testimonial

The services of Lieutenant Waghorn are well-known, and the daily-increasing importance of the relations of England with India renders the Overland Route between the mother Country and her magnificent dependency, of which he was Pioneer, one of the most remarkable improvements of the time. In fact, not only England, but Europe, and even America, participate in the advantages which MR. WAGHORN'S services have secured.

Before MR. WAGHORN stepped forth to devote himself to a task of such magnitude, no part of India could be reached in less than four months. The mails from Bombay now reach England in about thirty-four days, and the regularity with which the Overland Communication is conducted is the practical demonstration of his original views on the subject.

His last trip by way of Trieste gives further proof of his zeal for still further shortening the time between India and this country. It is unnecessary to dilate further on the subject, but reference can be had at all times to MR. J. STIKEMAN, the Honorary Secretary to the Committee, Cowper's Court, Cornhill, London.

AT a Committee held at the London Tavern, Bishopsgate Street, to take into consideration the services of Lieut. WAGHORN, R.N.,
It was unanimously agreed,

1st.—That Lieutenant WAGHORN, with great personal and pecuniary risk, and by indefatigable perseverance and exertion, first led the way to placing upon its present footing the system of rapid communication between Great Britain and India.
2nd.—That in order to mark the sense so universally entertained of the immeasurable advantages derived by the British Empire from the establishment of the Overland Route to India and China, by way of Egypt, and of the benefits it has conferred upon all those who have political, social, or commercial relations with the East; and to acknowledge, by a pecuniary reward, the eminent services of Lieutenant WAGHORN in the attainment of those important results, a subscription be immediately opened, and that the following Noblemen and Gentlemen form a Committee to carry the same into effect, with power to add to their numbers.
3rd.—That the following Noblemen, who have kindly given their consent, be Presidents of the Committee, viz.

THE RIGHT HONORABLE THE EARL OF AUCKLAND, G.C.B., and
THE RIGHT HONORABLE THE EARL OF ELLENBOROUGH, G.C.B.
(Formerly Governors-General of India).

Committee
The Right Hon. EARL AMHERST,
EARL OF CARDIGAN,
EARL OF CORK AND ORRERY,
EARL OF DERBY,
LORD ASHBURTON
LORD VISCOUNT COMBERMERE, G.C.B.
LORD SIDMOUTH,
LORD SANDON, M.P~
DAVID BARCLAY, Esq., M.P.
WILLIAM BAGGE, Esq., M.P.
JOHN BAGSHAW, Esq.
JAMES BLYTH, Esq.
ALEXANDER BEATTIE, Esq.
SAMUEL BRIGGS, Esq., of Alexandria.

Major-General CAULFIELD, C.B.
BAZETT D. COLVIN, Esq.
WM. CRAWFORD, Esq., Barrister, Bombay.
Col. The Right Hon. G. D. DAMER, M.P.
WM. DALLAS, Esq.
R. DURANT, Esq.
WILLIAM EWART, Esq., M.P.
THOMAS ELLIOTT, Esq.
J. MINET FECTOR, Esq., late M.P. for Maidstone
WILLIAM FEILDEN, Esq.,M.P.
W. E. FERRERS, Esq.
HARRY G. GORDON, Esq., Messrs. Ritchie Stewart, & Co., Bombay.
SAMUEL GREGSON, Esq.
JOHN GURNEY FRY, Esq.
Sir JOHN GUEST, Bart., M.P.
JAMES GARDNER, Esq.
J. H. GLEDSTANES, Esq.
Professor GOODEVE, M.D.
Sir GEORGE HAYTER, R.A.
FREDERICK HODGSON, Esq., M.P.
JOSEPH HUME, Esq., M.P.
CHAS. JOYCE, Esq., of Alexandria.
CHARLES KERR, Esq.
Sir GEORGE LARPENT, Bart.
WILLIAM LYALL, Esq.
JAMES MATHESON, Esq. M.P.
JAMES MACKILLOP, Esq.
J. R. MARTIN, Esq., B.M.S.
JAMES PATTISON, Esq., M.P.
THOMAS POYNDER, Esq.
Sir JOHN RAE REID, Bart., M.P.
CAPT. P. A. REYNOLDS.
LEITCH RITCHIE, Esq.
JOHN ABEL SMITH, Esq., M.P.
JOHN SCOTT, Esq.
ROBERT SMALL, Esq.
THOMAS SMART, Esq., Agent to Austrian Lloyd's Company,
between Alexandria and Trieste

BABOO DWARKANATH TAGORE
R. THURBURN, Esq.
W. H. THOMAS, Esq.
General J. S. WOOD, Lieut.-Gov. Tower.
Major-General M. WHITE.
C F. WEBER, Esq.
B. B. WILLIAMS, Esq.
THOMAS ALLSOP, Esq.

4.—That Mr. JOHN STIKEMAN, Secretary to the London East India and China Association, be Honorary Secretary to the Committee; and that Sir GEORGE LARPENT, Bart., be requested to act as Treasurer to receive Subscriptions, and that Subscriptions be also received in his name at the following Banking-houses.

Messrs. BARCLAY, BEVAN, and Co., 54, Lombard Street.
COCKBURNS and Co., 4, Whitehall.
COCKS, BIDDULPH, and Co, 43, Charing Cross.
COUTTS and Co., 59, Strand.
GLYN (Sir R. C., Bt.), HALIFAX, MILLS, and Co., 67, Lombard Street.
HERRIES, FARQUHAR, and Co., 16, St. James's St.
SCOTT (Sir Claude, Bt.) and Co., 1, Cavendish Sq.
SMITH, PAYNE, and SMITHS, 1, Lombard Street.
TWININGS, 215, Strand.
WILLIS, PERCIVAL, and Co., 76, Lombard Street.

Also at Messrs. GRINDLAY and Co., 16, Cornhill, and 8, St. Martin's Place, Charing Cross ; Messrs. SMITH, ELDER and Co., 65, Cornhill; Messrs. W. H. ALLEN and Co., Leadenhall Street; J. M. RICHARDSON. Esq., 23, Cornhill; and CHARLES ROACH SMITH, ESQ., F. S. A., &c., &c., Honorary Assistant Secretary.

Gentlemen in all parts of the country, who are willing to form Local Committees, are requested to co-operate with the London Committee, and communicate with their Secretary, who will supply afford every information and assistance.

The following Subscriptions have already been received.

	£.	s.	d.
The Rt. Hon. Earl Amherst	10	10	0
The Rt. Hon. Earl Auckland, G.C.B.	10	10	0
The Rt. Hon. Lord Ashburton	10	10	0
M. W. Attwood, Esq.	20	0	0
Col. T. Alcock	1	1	0
Major T. Alcock	1	1	0
W. H. Allen, Esq.	5	5	0
Thos. Allsop, Esq., Stock Exchange	5	5	0
John Alves Arbuthnot, Esq.	5	0	0
Messrs. Ashmore and Sons	5	5	0
Bank of England	100	0	0
Messrs. Baring, Brothers, and Co.	50	0	0
Barclay, Brothers and Co.	25	0	0
David Barclay, Esq. M. P.	10	10	0
Messrs. Barclay, Tritton & Co.	20	0	0
Messrs. Barnett, Hoare & Co.	20	0	0
John Bagshaw, Esq.	5	0	0
Messrs. John Baker and Co.	10	10	0
H. J. Baldwin, Esq.	2	2	0
F. A. Balmaine, Esq. (St. Leonard's)	1	0	0
Messrs. James Barber and Co.	10	10	0
Rev. J. N. Barron	0	10	0
Messrs. Bathe and Breach	1	1	0
W. T. Baxter (Bengal Marine)	2	2	0
Messrs. Beattie and Co.	15	0	0
W. Wilberforce Bird, Esq.	5	5	0
W. W. Bird, Esq., late Deputy Governor of Bengal	5	5	0
Messrs. Bischoff and Coxe	10	10	0
H. Blanchard, Esq.	5	5	0
J. Blyth, Esq. (Austin Friars)	10	10	0
From Bombay	500	0	0
Messrs. J. W. and A. Borradaile	2	2	0
Boyd and Thomas	10	10	0
Samuel Briggs, Esq. (of Alexandria)	10	10	0

John Brightman, Esq.	2	2	0
Messrs. Frederick Bryant and Davis	10	10	0
J. S. Buckingham, Esq.			
William Buckmaster, Esq.	5	5	0
Miss Butterworth	1	1	0
General the Rt. Hon. Earl of Cork and Orrery, K.P.	5	5	0
Lady Compton	2	2	0
Messrs. Cockerell and Co.	50	0	0
B. D. Colvin, Esq.	10	10	0
Messrs. J. Cockburn and Co.	5	5	0
W. R. Collett, Esq, M.P.	10	10	0
C. A. Cahill, Esq.	1	0	0
C. S. Catrill, Esq.	1	0	0
Major-Gen. Caulfield, C.B.	3	3	0
Messrs. Cheape and Leslie	10	10	0
C.Chubb and Sons	3	3	0
Cook, Sons and Co.	5	5	0
Coutts and Co.	25	0	0
Messrs. I. and H. Cox, Brothers	5	5	0
Coxe and Sons	5	0	0
Crawford, Colvin and Co.	50	0	0
Cruikshank, Melville and Co.	5	5	0
W. F. Cumming, Esq. M.D.	1	1	0
Messrs. Curtis and Harvey	5	5	0
Dallas and Coles	10	10	0
Proprietors of the Delhi Gazette	10	0	0
W. Dent, Esq.	5	5	0
Messrs. Charles Devaux and Co.	2	2	0
Ditchburn and Mare	5	5	0
W. Dixon, Esq., Brixton	1	1	0
Messrs. Durant and Co.	10	10	0
The Rt. Hon. the Earl of Effingham	5	5	0
The Right Hon. the Earl of Ellenborough, G. C. B.	10	10	0
Messrs. Edwards and Son	2	2	0
R. Eglinton and Co.	21	0	0
Thomas Elliott, Esq. (London Mail)	21	0	0

Messrs. L. J. Enthoven and Co.	10	10	0
John Entwisle, Esq.	10	10	0
Capt. Elliott, 2nd W. I. Regt.	1	0	0
J. M. Fector, Esq.	10	10	0
Messrs. Fletcher, Alexander and Co.	50	0	0
John Follett, Esq.	1	1	0
Messrs. Forbes, Forbes and Co.	25	0	0
Frith, Wallace and Co.	10	10	0
J. Gurney Fry, Esq.	10	10	0
Messrs. Fry, Griffiths and Co.	10	10	0
Gardner and Urquhart	10	10	0
General Steam Navigation Company	25	0	0
Messrs. Gledstanes and Co.	25	0	0
J. H. Gledstanes, Esq.	10	10	0
Messrs. Gobby, Haines and French	2	2	0
Professor Goodeve	2	2	0
General Goodfellow	2	2	0
H. G. Gordon, Esq. (late of Bombay)	10	10	0
Geo. Gordon, Esq. (late of Madras)	10	10	0
Messrs. A. A. Gower, Nephews & Co.	10	10	0
Gregson and Co.	25	0	0
Grey and Coles	5	5	0
G. F. Griffith, Esq.	3	3	0
Archibald Griffith, Esq.	2	2	0
Messrs. Grindlay and Co.	10	10	0
Grissell and Peto	10	10	0
Sir John Guest, Bart., M.P.	10	10	0
Messrs. Frederick Huth and Co.	20	0	0
Joseph Hume, Esq., M. P.	5	0	0
Henry Hance, Esq.	1	1	0
Messrs. Harvey and Co.	2	2	0
B. B. Haydon, Esq.	0	10	0
Messrs. Hayter and Howell	5	5	0
Andrew Henderson, Esq.	3	3	0
Rowland Hill, Esq.	10	10	0
H. J. Hinchcliffe, Esq.	2	0	0
J. L. Hodges, Esq.	5	0	0
Frederick Hodgson, Esq., M. P.	10	10	0

Messrs. Holtzapffel and Co.	3	3	0
Hunter and Edwards	1	1	0
Hyde, Lenox and Co.	5	5	0
J. Johnson, Esq., 6,Winchester Street	5	5	0
John Jones, Esq., 6, Regent Street	10	10	0
Messrs. Jones, Lloyd and Co.	10	10	0
Charles Joyce, Esq. (of Alexandria)	10	10	0
Charles Kerr, Esq.	10	10	0
Messrs. Thomas Kilby and Co.	1	1	0
Sir George Larpent, Bart.	10	10	0
Messrs. Landon and Co.	10	10	0
John P. Larkins, Esq.	5	0	0
Alfred Latham, Esq.	5	5	0
Edward Lawford, Esq.	5	5	0
Messrs. Laurence, Phillips and Sons	5	5	0
Lawson and Anderdon	2	2	0
W. Lerro, Esq.	0	10	6
W. Lerro, Jun., Esq.	0	10	6
Geo. Lerro, Esq.	0	10	6
Messrs. Lewis and Allenby	1	1	0
H. H. Lindsay, Esq., New East India Chambers	1	1	0
Lloyds	25	0	0
Messrs. Lyall, Brothers and Co.	25	0	0
William Lyall, Esq.	10	10	0
Messrs. Magniac, Jardine and Co.	50	0	0
Mackey, Holt and Co.	10	10	0
James Mackillop, Esq.	10	10	0
J. Mackenzie, Esq.	1	1	0
Messrs. Madden and Malcolm	2	2	0
Madras Chamber of Commerce	100	0	0
Messrs. Manning and Anderdon	5	5	0
Frederick Mangles, Esq.	5	5	0
James Matheson, Esq., M.P.	10	10	0
Messrs. Maudslay, Sons, and Field	10	10	0
L. N. A. Maxwell and Co.	2	2	0
Maynard and Harris	2	2	0
Mc. Cabe and Co.	2	2	0
T. Milroy and Sons	2	2	0

Messrs. Morrison, Dillon and Co.	10	10	0
E. Moxhay, Esq.	2	2	0
Messrs. Palmer, Mackillop and Co.	25	0	0
Parbury, Thacker and Co.	5	5	0
James Pattison, Esq., M. P.	5	5	0
Messrs. J. & R. Pearce	10	10	0
H.&T.Peat	10	10	0
Peppercorn and Co.	5	5	0
Samuel Phillips and Co.	5	5	0
Phillips and Tiplady	5	5	0
F. Place, Esq., Editor of the Delhi Gazette	5	0	0
Thomas Poynder, Esq., Deputy Lieut. for Kent	5	5	0
Messrs. Prescott and Co.	10	10	0
W. Price, Esq. Craven Street	5	5	0
Messrs. Reid, Irving and Co.	50	0	0
Messrs. Rawson, Norton and Co.	10	10	0
Captain Reynolds, 16, Cornhill	10	10	0
J. M. Richardson, Esq.	5	5	0
Alex. F. Ridgway, Esq.	5	5	0
Leitch Ritchie, Esq. (Indian News)	10	10	0
Messrs. Roberts, Mitchell and Co.	25	0	0
W. R. Robinson and Co.	2	2	0
W. H. Rolfe, Esq., Sandwich	1	1	0
Messrs. Ross and Sons	1	1	0
Rothschilds and Co.	25	0	0
James Russell, Esq.	5	0	0
Rt. Hon. Lord Sandon, M. P.	5	0	0
David Salomons, Esq.	21	0	0
Messrs. Scott, Bell and Co.	15	0	0
John Scott, Esq., Alderman's Walk	10	10	0
Messrs. Shaw, Maxwell and Co.	2	2	0
George Sherwood, Esq., Lime Street	5	5	0
Major Shiel	1	1	0
Captain C. L. Showers	1	1	0
Messrs. S. W. Silver and Co.	10	10	0
Robert Small and Co.	10	10	0
John Abel Smith, Esq., M.P.	10	10	0
Edward Osborne Smith, Esq.	1	1	0

John Smith, Esq. (per Coutts and Co.)	1	0	0
C. Roach Smith, Esq., F. S. A.	1	1	0
Messrs. Smith, Elder and Co.	5	5	0
Smith, Payne and Smith	10	10	0
South Eastern Railway Company	25	0	0
Messrs. Stilwell and Sons	21	0	0
J. H. Stocqueler, Esq.	1	1	0
Messrs. Story, Browne and Co.	5	5	0
John Straith, Esq.	5	0	0
Mrs. Suart, Tunbridge Wells, by P. Richardson, Esq.	2	2	0
Charles W. Tabor, Esq.	5	5	0
Mrs. Elizabeth Tabor	5	5	0
Baboo Dwarkanath Tagore	10	10	0
Col. H. Tennent	1	1	0
W. H. Thomas, Esq., 2, Moorgate St.	10	10	0
Messrs. W. J. Thompson and Sons	5	5	0
H. Thompson and Co.	5	5	0
Captain A. Thompson,	1	1	0
"The Times"	200	0	0
William Tindall, Esq.	5	5	0
Messrs. Joseph Travers and Sons	10	10	0
Trueman and Cook	10	10	0
Twinings, Strand	5	5	0
Tower Esq.	1	1	0
Messrs. Willis, Percival and Co.	50	0	0
J. Walker, Esq., Gt. George Street	5	5	0
C. F. Weber, Esq.	10	0	0
Charles Welstead, Esq.	1	0	0
Messrs. Whippy and Co.	2	2	0
Thomas White, Esq.	2	2	0
Joseph White, Esq. (Lloyd's)	2	2	0
B. B. Williams, Esq., Stock Exchange	10	10	0
A. T. Windus, Esq.	5	0	0
General J. S. Wood	5	0	0
Henry Wooler, Esq.	1	1	0
Col. Young	1	0	0
Mrs. Col.Young	1	0	0

Miss Young	1	0	0
Miss E. Young	1	0	0
[the following are added by hand]			
W. Fielden Esq M.P.	5	0	0
H. Sikes Esq	1	0	0
The Rt Hon of Derby	10	10	0
Frodsham & Son	2	2	0
L. W. Gilliard Esq	3	3	0
The Rt Hon Earl St Germans	10	0	
The Morning Chronicle	50	0	0

Mr C Roach Smith presents his humble respects to Mr Robt Peel and on the part of Lieu^t Waghorn's Committee forwards a receipt for his kind donation and the best thanks of the Committee.

5 Liverpool St City
June 6.th 1846

APPENDIX C

Waghorn's Memorial of Service, 1848

Waghorn's covering letter to ?Lord John Russell:[295]

London, 34 Cornhill,
28th March 1848

My Lord /

The enclosed Memorial of Service for, one Generation, with its influential Documents (of which I have ½ Cwt, of minor ones, will I trust, induce Your Lordship, in common with other Members of the House, to give it your instant support, and thus unite your feelings with the general sympathy (out of doors) which my claims demand from the Country in the House of Commons.

My Debts from having accomplished such benefits to the Country, are £8000.

The Overland Route was achieved by me without the assistance of H. M. Govt, for truly as my Memorial states it grew into life, and to its present usefulness through my own unaided toils, and this I can say without egotism.

Trusting to Your Lordship's support in the House of Commons,

I remain With Respect
Yours Lordship's Thankful Servant
Thos Waghorn

295 Formerly in the 'Sidebottom Collection' and printed in Sidebottom, *op. cit.*, 113. An image is seen in Rudi Jeidel, *The Waghorn Story*, no. 62.

MEMORIAL OF MR. WAGHORN'S CLAIMS ON HIS COUNTRY

Page 141.-By the courtesy of Mr. Wheatley I here append to my notice of Lieutenant Waghorn one of several documents which, emanating from Waghorn himself, may be relied on for supplying facts not generally known.

His birth was in 1800, at Chatham. At twelve years of age he was a midshipman in Her Majesty's navy; and, sixteen days before he was seventeen, passed in navigation for lieutenant, being the youngest midshipman that had ever done so ; at the end of 1817, was paid off, and went third mate of a free-trader to Calcutta; returned home, and, in 1819, got appointed to the Bengal Marine (pilot service) of India, where he served till 1824 ; at which time he was asked by the Bengal Government to volunteer for the Arracan War, and then received the command of the Honourable East India Company's cutter `Matchless', and a division of gunboats, and repaired to the scene of action in Arracan with the south-east division of that army and flotilla; was five times engaged, and saw much service by land and sea, and was once wounded in the right thigh. On return to Calcutta, in 1827, after having received the thanks of all the authorities in that province (after two years and a half's service), with a constitution then undermined from the baneful fever of Arracan, where so many thousands died ; for, out of 19,000 men (army and flotilla) composing that division, not 100 are now alive. The pestilence of that climate reduced the forces, in six months, to two-tenths of their original number; but from the indomitable perseverance (without egotism he can faithfully say) that has marked his course, he rallied to the great project he had secretly at heart, namely, ' A steam communication between our Eastern possessions and their mother-country, England.' Ere his departure from Calcutta on furlough, in 1827, ill in health, harrassed from the Arracan fever, still, between its attacks, his energies returned. He communicated his plan to the officials, namely, the Marine Board at Calcutta, who forthwith advanced it to the notice of the then Chief Secretary to the Bengal Government, the present Mr. Charles Lushington, M.P. for Westminster; through whom he brought home letters of credence from Lord Viscount Combermere, then acting as Vice President in Council (Earl Amherst, Governor-General, being on a tour in Upper India), in consequence of his meritorious conduct in the Arracan War, for the Honourable Court of Directors of the East India Company in London, I as a fit and proper person to open steam navigation with India, via the Cape of Good Hope.

On arrival in England, he advocated the object at all points, particularly in London, Liverpool, Manchester, Glasgow, Birmingham, etc.; as he had previously done on his homeward voyage at Madras, Mauritius, Cape, and St. Helena. But Her Majesty's Post Office at that time, was opposed to ocean steam navigation; and so, unfortunately, were the East India Directors (except Mr. Loch), although he advocated its usefulness to all for two years. However, in October 1829, he was called on by Lord Ellenborough, then President of the India Board, and Mr. Loch, the then Chairman of the Court of Directors, to go to India, through Egypt, with despatches for Sir John Malcolm, Governor of Bombay, etc., and more especially, to report upon the practicability of the Red Sea navigation for the Overland Route. On that trip he got to Alexandria in twenty-six days; so extraordinarily rapid was that part of the journey to Trieste (done in nine and a half days, through five Kingdoms), that an enquiry was then made by the Foreign Office respecting it, for at that time, our Post Office letters occupied fourteen days to that place! His orders, also, were to join the 'Enterprise' (first steamer from England to India), at Suez, on 6th December 1829 ; she did not appear, and as he had important Government despatches, he had no resource, except, either to return to England, or go on in an open boat down the Red Sea. He preferred the latter, as a matter of duty; and sailed down the centre of that sea without chart, or compass, the North Star being his guide by night, and the sun by day. Suffice it to say, that he arrived at Juddah, 620 miles, in six and a half days, in that boat. The crew were six Arabs, who often threatened (through fear) to take the charge of the boat from him, but his firmness prevailed, assisted by the Pasha of Egypt's Firman, which he got, ere he left Cairo. On arrival at Juddah, he first learned the steamer had broken her machinery on the way from Bengal to Bombay, and was not coming. Thus baffled, a delirious fever came on him; and he was six weeks before he could proceed onward to Bombay by sailing vessel. On arrival at Bombay with the despatches, the thanks of the Government in Council, etc., were voted to him, for having, when disappointed of a steamer, proceeded with these despatches in an open boat, down the Red Sea, etc.' From what he observed in that trip, he felt convinced, for every purpose of interest, politically, morally, and commercially, between England and the East, that that was the route; and it were a waste of time to say with what ardour, perseverance, and firmness, he worked it to completion. He for many years sailed and travelled hundreds of thousands of miles between the two countries, from 1827 to 1835 most particularly, up and down the Red Sea with mails, before the East India Company had any steam system in that sea ; and on one most special occasion, on this side the Isthmus, he did, in October 1839, when the news arrived at Alexandria from Bombay of Sir John (late Lord) Keane's success at Ghuznee, one day after Her Majesty's steamer had left Alexandria, obtain the use of the Pasha of Egypt's own steamer ` Generoso', and personally command that vessel, and conveyed that mail to Malta, which was immediately sent on by the admiral there to England; indeed he could recount numerous instances of such extraordinary conduct, and usefulness to England, etc.

He has received the thanks of three-quarters of the Globe, namely, Europe, Asia, Africa, besides numberless letters of thanks and commendations from Mercantile Communities, at every point where eastern trade is concerned. Still, to make his claim more and more convincing, it is only justice to himself, that it should be known, that himself and his partners, unaided and alone (except the assistance of the Bombay Steam Committee), built the eight halting places on the desert, between Cairo and Suez ; also the three hotels established above them, in which luxuries even were provided and stored for the passing traveller; and that hitherto waste is now the wonder of every passer by. Iron tanks with good water were stored under them ; in fact it would take more space, and be tiresome here to dilate upon the means, the comforts, and the facilities that are now to be found in that once desert locality.

Fancy that desert, when he took it up, a precarious path beset with wandering robbers with their camels. Now see it: those wandering robbers are converted into faithful guides; even ladies, alone with their infants, pass to and fro with security as in Europe. Not an act of violence has been committed on that desert to them between England and India!!

Not one English individual has died of, or become infected with, the plague in passing over it, or at Suez; the violence of the south-west monsoon, added to the supposed dangers of the Red Sea, the Bugbears then set up against that route, are at an end, as well as the drifting sands of that desert, that were to swallow people up in passing over! The friendship arrived at by Mr. Waghorn, from Mehemet Ali, as well as his officers, were the main means by which he accomplished these benefits.

When he left Egypt, in 1841, he had established English carriages, vans, and horses, for the passengers' conveyance across the desert (instead of camels) ; indeed, be placed small steamers (from England) on the Nile and the canal of Alexandria. Every fraction of his money was spent by him in getting more and more facilities; and, bad the saving of money been one of the characteristics of his nature, the Overland Route would not be as useful as it now is-and this is acknowledged by all.

Mr. Waghorn claims for himself the merit of this work; be claims it without fear of denial ; and states, upon his honour, that no money or means were ever received by him from either Her Majesty's Government or the East India Company to aid it.

It grew into life altogether from his having, by his own energy and private resources, worked the 'Overland Mails' to and from India for two years (from 1831 to 1834) in his own individual person; and be summed it up by putting letters to England from Bombay in forty-seven days, in February 1834, without any steam from Alexandria to London, for none then existed between them. Will it be believed, that up to that time he (Mr. Waghorn) was thought and called by many, a `visionary', and by some a `madman'?

He made repeated application, from 1832 to 1842, to be made a lieutenant in Her Majesty's Navy, without avail; all spoke of his merits but none rewarded them. At length, in 1842, Lord Haddington, being head of the Admiralty, did grant that rank.

Had that rank been awarded him in 1832, how much greater would have been his position in Egypt as an officer, instead of a private individual. Yet he possessed secret influence enough with Mehemet Ali to be once sent as his confidential messenger to Kosshrew Pasha, grand vizier to the Sultan at Constantinople, in August 1839; as well as to Lord Ponsonby, the then ambassador from England there.

My Lords Palmerston and Aberdeen, as Foreign Ministers of England, Lords Ellenborough, Glenelg, and Ripon, and Sir John Hobhouse, as Presidents of the Indian Board (from 1827 to 1848), know his merits, in bringing about the Overland Route through Egypt, and thereby the stability of our English interests connected with our Eastern empire.

In this short history of himself, he passes from 1842 to 1846, when he began to show, against Guizot and the French power, that England possessed another way to India than through France.

He accomplished, patronised by Her Majesty's present Government and the Honourable the East India Company, in six successive months, across the Alps last winter, the gain of thirteen days odd hours, via Trieste, over the Marseilles route: and Mr. Trevelyan, of Her Majesty's Treasury, is referred to, to corroborate his services for the arduous and fatiguing duties in establishing the Trieste route, as a set-off against the route of Marseilles.

He has, moreover, secured the friendship of Pope Pius IX for a mail route through the Papal States, via Ancona, between England and India; as well as the friendship of the King of Sardinia, for another route through his dominions by way of Genoa. Each of these routes is now open (Trieste, Genoa, or Ancona) for such purpose whenever Her Majesty's Government may think proper to order him to carry mails to and fro between England and India by either.

He now craves Parliament to reward his past labours, hoping that services like his own, from 1827 to 1848 (one generation), may at once be compensated.

Mr. Trevelyan, of the Treasury, has been told by him of the loss of £2,000, which he last sustained in opening the Trieste route, and knows that there is no other means of compensation for the good he has done than by an honourable grant through Her Majesty's Government in the House of Commons. And he assumes to himself that there are few members of any party in that House who will not cheerfully respond thereto, in token of the great and important services, by establishing the 'Overland Route', he has rendered to his country, out of doors, in general opinion, second to none performed by any private individual to the existing interests between England and India, and tending by and by to be forthcoming to the whole Eastern world. And when it is further considered that all his energies, ability, and usefulness are still further extending steam navigation from Singapore to Sydney, thus forming the most direct steam way from London to Australia (considered the best in the opinion of Rear-Admiral Beaufort, hydrographer to the Admiralty), full surely, after the passing over of a whole generation of one uniform systematic line of conduct, without any regard to the slightest selfish consideration, it is not too much for him to expect the gratitude of his country by a good pecuniary grant, in order to enable him to pay his debts, and also possess an equivalent for his labours.

" He has not attached testimonials, thinking his claims sufficiently known; but, if wanting, they are forthcoming.

(Signed) THOMAS WAGHORN, Lieut. R.N."
34, Cornhill, 3rd January, 1848

APPENDIX D

The statues at Suez and at Chatham

Following the opening of the Suez Canal on 17 November 1869, which was built in spite of considerable opposition from the English, a bust of Waghorn was erected at Port Tewfik at the southern end of the canal. *The Illustrated London News* described it as 'a colossal bust in bronze, on a handsome marble pedestal, with a bronze bas-relief of Waghorn surveying the desert on a camel, attended by a train of Orientals'.[296]

The monument was destroyed in 1956 during the Suez Crisis.

It was much later, on 24 November 1883, that *The Times* recorded the first moves in England to erect a statue to commemorate Waghorn's endeavours, when a deputation of the High-Constable and Court Leet of Chatham had visited Lord Northbrook, First Lord of the Admiralty, to get his support for the venture. They also visited Ferdinand de Lesseps, the builder of the Suez Canal, then in London, who

296 *Illustrated London News*, 12 Oct 1872, 383-4.

> expressed himself much gratified at the scheme. He had known his old and esteemed comrade Waghorn at the time when the gallant explorer's views respecting the new route to India were looked upon as the acme of foolishness and as impracticable. It was to Waghorn alone that he was indebted for the original idea of forming the Suez Canal. He was a zealous, warm-hearted man, whose memory he would do anything possible to honour, and he would be only too pleased to take part in the scheme to perpetrate the memory of so eminently useful a navigator.[297]

Meetings were held at the Mansion House in London in March 1884 and again on 18 November that year, by which time it was reported that £1400 of the estimated £2000 cost had been raised. The commission for the statue was given to H. H. Armstead and it was hoped that the gun metal for it would be provided by the War Office.[298] The project was finally completed in 1888 and a ceremonial unveiling took place which was reported briefly in *The Times*,[299] but fully in *The Chatham and Rochester Observer*, 11 and 18 August 1888. Charles Roach Smith was among the invited guests.

297 *The Times*, 24 November 1883, p. 5; 26 November 1883, p. 6.

298 *The Times*, 4 March 1884, p. 3; 19 November 1884, p. 10. A letter of support for the enterprise from a W. P. Andrew was published in the newspaper on 15 March 1884, pp. 5-6.

299 *The Times*, 13 August 1888, p. 14.

BIBLIOGRAPHY

Books, Pamphlets and Articles

Anon., *The Bengal Obituary*, Calcutta, 1848 (repr. Calcutta, 1991)

—, *Report of the London Provisional Committee for promoting Steam Navigation with India via the Red Sea*, London, 1837. [Smith, Elder and Co.]

—'Mr Waghorn's Iron Express Coach for the Desert', *The Mechanics' Magazine, Museum Register, Journal and Gazette*, 1840, 223-4.

—, *The Overland Mail and The Austrian Lloyds*, London, 1847 [pamphlet].

—, *Letter addressed by the Directors of the Peninsula and Oriental Steam Navigation Company to the Secretary of the Admiralty*, London, 1848. [Smith, Elder and Co.]

—, 'Waghorn, The Overland Pioneer', *The working man's friend and family instructor*, 1850, 114-117.

Anderson, Arthur, *Communications with India, China, &c. via Egypt* ['not printed for sale', 1843]

Ashbee, Andrew, *Thomas Fletcher Waghorn 1800-1850*, Snodland Historical Society, pamphlet 12, 2000

—, 'In Search of Thomas Fletcher Waghorn (1800-1850)', *The Clock Tower* [Journal of the Friends of Medway Archives], 6 (May 2007), 11-15

—, 'Who was Waghorn's Father?', *The Clock Tower*, 7, (August 2007), 14-17

—, 'A Waghorn Discovery', *The Clock Tower*, 15, (August 2009), 27-31

Barber, James, *The Overland Guide-Book; a complete vade-mecum for the Overland Travller to India via Egypt*, London, 1850.

Barker, Edward B. B., *Syria and Egypt under the last five Sultans of Turkey*, London, 1876, reprinted New York, 1973.

Besumee, Hassenaine Al', *Egypt under Mohammad Aly Basha. A reply to the "Remarks" of A.T. Holroyd, esq., on "Egypt as it is in 1837."*

Addressed to the Right Hon. Viscount Palmerston. London, 1838 [Smith, Elder & Co.]

Bevan, Samuel, *Sand and Canvas, a narrative of adventures in Egypt, with a sojourn among the artists in Rome*, London, 1849.

Bird, Michael, *Samuel Shepheard of Cairo*, London, 1957.

Boyd, Mark, *Reminiscences of Fifty Years*, London, 1871.

Brown, David K., *Paddle Warships. The Earliest Steam Powered Fighting Ships 1815-1850*, London, 1993.

Chambers, William and Robert, 'Lieutenant Waghorn and the New Land Route from India', *Chambers Edinburgh Journal*, no. 102, New Series, 13 December 1845.

Chesney, Lieut.-Colonel Francis Rawdon, *The Expedition for the Survey of the Rivers Euphrates and Tigris [...] in the Years 1835, 1836, and 1837 [...]*, London, 1850 (R Greenwood, New York, 1969).

Clunn, P. E., *Lieutenant Waghorn, R.N., Pioneer of the Overland Route to India,* London, 1892 and 1894.

Comyns, Thomas Waghorn, 'The Pioneer of the Overland Route to India and Australasia, *Once a Month* [Australian Journal], 15 September 1885, 204-8.

Cooley, James Ewing, *The American in Egypt, with rambles through Arabia, Petraea and the Holy Land during the years 1839 and 1840*, [with appendix by George Robbins Gliddon], Philadelphia, 1842.

Damer, Mary Georgiana Emma Seymour Dawson, *Diary of A Tour in Greece, Turkey, Egypt, and the Holy Land*, London, 1841.

Doveton, F. B., *Reminiscences of the Burmese War 1824-5-6*, London, 1852.

[Evans, David Morier], *The City; Or, The Physiology of London Business: With Sketches on 'Change, and at the Coffee Houses* London, 1845.

Foreign Quarterly Review, Vol. XVIII, No. XXXVI (1937), 342-392.

Fuller, Michael J., *Snodland and Holborough Watermills*, Snodland Historical Society pamphlet No. 9, Snodland, 1998.

Galloway, John Alexander, *Observations on the proposed improvements in the overland route via Egypt ...*, London, 1844 [pamphlet]

Grindlay and Co., *Hints for Travellers to India, detailing the several routes*, London, 1847.

Guest, John S., *The Euphrates Expedition*, London, 1992

Havelock, Sir Henry, *Memoir of the Three Campaigns of Major-general Sir A. Campbell's army in Ava*, Serampore, 1828.

Holroyd, Arthur T[odd], *Egypt and Mahomed Ali Pacha in 1837; a Letter containing remarks upon "Egypt as it is in 1837" addressed to the Right Hon. Viscount Palmerston*, London, 1838.

Howarth, David and Stephen, *The Story of P&O The Peninsular and Orient Steam Navigation Company*, London, rev. edn., 1994.

Illustrated London News, 'Waghorn's Overland Route from India', 21 May 1842.

Jefferys, William, *An account of the fire [...] at Chatham ... June, 1800, [and] the money collected for the relief of ... sufferers*, Chatham, 1801.

Jefferys, William, *An Account of the Dreadful Fire at Chatham which happened on Friday the 3d of March, 1820*, Chatham, 1821.

Journal of the Belles Lettres, 1850

Joyce, Brian, *The Chatham Scandal*, Rochester, 1999

Kinross, Lord, *Between Two Seas*, London, 1968.

Lardner, Dionysius, *Steam Communication with India by the Red Sea advocated in a letter to the Right Honourable Lord Viscount Melbourne*, London, 1837

Low, Charles Rathbone, *History of the Indian Navy*, 1877, reprint 1989

Marshall, John, *Narrative of the Naval Operations in Ava during the Burmese War*, London, 1830.

Matsumoto-Best, Saho, *Britain and the Papacy in the Age of Revolution 1846-1851*, Woodbridge, 2003

Notes and Queries, 6th series, vii, 218

O'Byrne, William Richard, British Library, Add. MS 38,053 [collection of papers relating to the compilation of *A Biographical Dictionary of All Living Naval Officers*, London, 1861]

Parbury, George, *Handbook for India and Egypt*, London, 1842.

—, *Parbury's Oriental Herald and Colonial Intelligencer*

Pigot & Co. *Kent Directory*, 1826-7.

Proctor, Molly G., *"Day after Day" Wm. Day & Sons in Maidstone*, Maidstone, 2000

Pudney, John, *Suez, De Lesseps' Canal*, London, 1969.

Report of the Select Committee on Steam Navigation, 1834.

Report of the Select Committee on Steam Navigation, 1837.

Rhé-Philipe, George William Vittalli de, *A Narrative of the First Burmese War 1824-26,* Calcutta Military Dept., 1905.

Roach Smith, Charles, *Retrospections, Social and Archaeological*, London, 1883, vol. I

Roberts, David, *The Holy Land*, London, 1855.

Roberts, Emma, *Notes of an overland journey through France and Egypt to Bombay,* London, 1841.

Sankey, Marjorie, *'Care of Mr. Waghorn'. A Biography*, Postal History Society, Special Series, No. 19 (1964).

Searight, Sarah, *Steaming East*, London, 1991.

—, 'A Waghorn letter book for 1840', *Journal of the Royal Asiatic Society*, 3rd Series, vol. 7, part 2 (July 1997), 229-248.

Sidebottom, John K., *The Overland Mail. A Postal Historical Study of the Mail Route to India*, published for the Postal History Society, Allen and Unwin, London, 1948.

Smetham, Henry, *A History of Strood*, Rochester, 1899.

Smith, George Murray, 'The Life and Labours of Lieutenant Waghorn', *Household Words*, 1850, 494-501.

—, 'In the Early Forties', *The Cornhill Magazine*, IX, No. 53, N.S., November 1900, 577-585.

Stephens, J. L., *Incidents of Travel in Egypt, Arabia, Petrea and the Holy Land. By an American*, New York, 1837.

Stocqueler, J[oachim] H., *The Overland Route 1850* [pictorial souvenir book of the Diorama shown at 14 Regent Street], London, 1850.

[Thackeray, William Makepeace], 'M. A. Titmarsh', *Notes of a Journey from Cornhill to Grand Cairo…*, New York, 1845.

Tillotson, John, *Our Untitled Nobility*, London, 1856.

Waghorn & Co., *Messrs W[aghorn]. & Co's Overland guide to India, by three routes to Egypt*, London, 1842; 1844; 1846

Waghorn, Thomas Fletcher, *Steam Navigation to India, by the Cape of Good Hope, Mr Waghorn's accounts and papers relating to Steam communication with India* [London, 1829]. [C. Whittingham]

—, *Particulars of an Overland Journey from London to Bombay by way of the Continent, Egypt and the Red Sea* (privately printed, 1831).

—, *Address to the British public in India, Ceylon, the Sraits and China: on the best means of promoting steam navigation between India and England*, Bombay Gazette Press, Bombay, 1833.

—, *Steam Navigation to India, via Egypt and the Red Sea*, Liverpool, 1835. [Kaye]

—, *Egypt as it is in 1837*, London, 1837. [Smith, Elder & Co.]

—, *Egypt as it is in 1838*, London, 1838. [Smith, Elder & Co.]

—, *Truths concerning Mahomet Ali, Egypt, Arabia, and Syria: addressed to the five powers, or to their representatives in the contemplated congress*, [London, Smith, Elder & Co.], 1840.

—, *Overland mails to India, China etc: the acceleration of mails, once a fortnight, between England and the east Indies and vice versa*, London, 1843 [Smith, Elder & Co.]

—, *Letter to the Rt. Hon. Wm. Ewart Gladstone, M.P. Secretary of State for the Colonies, On the Extension of Steam Navigation from Singapore to Port Jackson*, Australia, London, 1846. [Smith, Elder & Co.]

—, *Lieutenant Waghorn's lecture at Bath, by invitation of General J S Wood, Lieutenant-General of the Tower*, H. E. Carrington, Bath, 1846.

—, *Second Letter to Earl Grey. On the extension of Steam Navigation from Singapore to Port Jackson*, London, 1847. [Smith, Elder & Co.]

—, *Waghorn on emigration to Australia: on the broadest possible principles, for the future emelioration and prosperity of Great Britain*, London [1848?] [George Mann and James Ridgeway]

Wheatley, George W., 'Some Account of the Late Lieut. Waghorn, R.N., the Originator of the Overland Route', *Bentley's Miscellany*, 27 (January 1850), 349-357.

Wilson, Henry Horace, *Documents Illustrative of the Burmese War*, Calcutta, 1827; London, 1852.

Wilson, John H., *On Steam Communication between Bombay and Suez: with an account of the Hugh Lindsay's four voyages*, Bombay, 1833.

—, *Facts Connected with the Origin and Progress of Steam Communication between India and England*, London, 1850.

Woolmer, John, *Historical Jottings of the Parish of Snodland*, Snodland, 1894.

Wright, I. G., *Wright's Topography of Rochester, Chatham, Strood, Brompton, &c. and Directory of the Clergy, Gentry, Tradesmen, &c.*, Chatham, 1838 (facsimile, Rochester, 1995).

London: British Library

Add. MS 36468, ff. 161, 318.	letters to Sir John Cam Hobhouse
Add. MS 36469, f. 3	the plan
Add. MS 36470, ff. 159, 167, 306-7	letters to Sir John Cam Hobhouse
Add. MS 38053, f. 361	letter to William Richard O'Byrne
Add. MS 40413, f. 348.	letter to Sir Robert Peel
Add. MS 40495, f. 187.	letter to Sir Robert Peel
Add. MS 40499, f. 67.	letter to Sir Robert Peel
Add. MS 40504	letter to Sir Robert Peel
Add. MS 40512, ff. 5-9	letters to Sir Robert Peel
Add. MS 40589, f. 354	letter to Sir Robert Peel
Add. MS 40593, ff. 96-103	printed Testimonial (1846)
Add. MS 43239, ff. 91-2, 100, 127, 129, 241, 243.	letters to Lord Aberdeen
Add. MS 44366, f. 104.	letter to William E. Gladstone

London: British Library: Asia Pacific and Africa Collections [APA]

Calcutta Annual Directory, 1821, 1823, 1824, 1831. (APA does not hold the 1825-30 editions.)

East India Register and Directory: 1821, 1822.

E/1/267, No. 1648 and 2020	letters to Waghorn from E.I.C. secretary
E/1/176	Wilson on journey of *Hugh Lindsey*
L/MAR/8/1	oath for Bengal Pilot Service

L/MAR/8/11: 1820; 1821	appointment to Bengal Pilot Service
L/MAR/B/12 G	Astell: log
N/1/12	marriage register: St John's cathedral, Calcutta
N/1/40/f16:	burial register: St John's cathedral, Calcutta
R/19/1.	correspondence with Col. Patrick Campbell
R/19/10	letter from Capt. John Lyons
SM155 (microfilm):	Calcutta Journal, November and December 1818.

London: The National Archives (TNA)

ADM 7/560-561	Admiralty records of ship movements
ADM 9/58	Waghorn's own summary of his career 1846
ADM 23/106.	Navy pension for Harriet Waghorn
ADM 35/4532.	*African* log book
ADM 37/9105	*Fire Fly* muster books
ADM 37/3918	*Bahama*, muster book
ADM 37/5462	*Tigris*, muster book
ADM 37/5816-18	*Tigris*, muster books
ADM 51/2183	*Bahama*, log
ADM 51/2904	*Tigris*, log
ADM 51/3048.	*African* log book 1831-2
ADM 51/3171	*Fire Fly* log book
ADM 52/3986.	*Firebrand* log book 1832
ADM 107/49	Naval College, Portsmouth: Waghorn's Navigation exam
C14/118/M14	Chancery: Munday v. Waghorn (1843)
C14/1160/M50	Chancery: Munday v. Waghorn (1850)
FO 841/3, No. 6.	Edmund Francis v Waghorn

FO 841/3, No. 8.	Henry Raven v Waghorn
FO 841/5	P. Anstruther v Waghorn
IR26	estate duty for Harriet Waghorn
PROB 11/1764	will of Edward Martin
PROB 11/2110	will of Thomas Fletcher Waghorn
PROB 11/2054	will of Harriet Waghorn

The British Postal Museum and Archive

POST 43/329	Correspondence written by Lt. Thomas Waghorn RN relating to the establishment of an overland route to India 1827-1837

Maidstone: Kent History and Library Centre (KHLC)

U2102/T12	Island cottage at Holborough
U2102/T13	messuages at Holborough
U2102/T34	1827 sale of Island Cottage to Waghorn
Uncatalogued	sale of The Lodge, Snodland, 1853

Medway Archives and Local Study Centre [MALSC]

Parish registers: from	Birling, All Saints (microfilm of P29 KHLC)
	Chatham, St Mary (P77)
	Snodland, All Saints (P342)
P342/2/4	marriage licence: Waghorn/Martin
P342/2/6	marriage licence: Ransom/Waghorn

University of Nottingham, Hallward Library: Portland Collection

Pw Jf 2166	Letter from Waghorn to Lord William Bentinck
Pw Jf 2167	Petition of Waghorn to House of Commons
Pw Jf 2168	Letter from Waghorn to Lord William Bentinck
Pw Jg 367	Letter and Plan from Waghorn to Sir James Carnac
Pw Jg 368	Letter from Waghorn to Lord William Bentinck
Pw Jg 369	Copy of letter from Waghorn to Col. Patrick Campbell

Pw Jg 370 Letter from Waghorn to Lord William Bentinck
Pw Jg 371 Plan for establishment of Overland Route
Pw Jg 372 Letter from Waghorn to Lord William Bentinck
Pw Jg 373 Printed announcement of formation of 'Waghorn and Co.'
Pw Jg 376 Letter from George W. Wheatley to Lord William Bentinck

University of Southampton, Special Collections, Wellington papers
WP1/1018/3 Correspondence between Waghorn and the Duke of Wellington: 15 May 1829
WP1/1156/14 Waghorn requests an interview with the Duke of Wellington: 20-12-1830

West Sussex Record Office
Cobden Papers, Cobden/1, No. 41.
Cobden Papers, Cobden/2, No. 109.

National Archives of India, Delhi [NAI]
Currently some 45 documents/files listed online in search for 'Waghorn'

Australian Newspapers and Journals

Sydney: State Library of New South Wales: Mitchell Library
Adelaide Observer
The Illustrated Australian Magazine, vol. 1, pp. 46-8, 225-6; vol. 2, pp. 46-7
Once a Month, September 1885.
South Australian Register
The Maitland Mercury and Hunter River General Advertiser

English Newspapers

Chatham and Rochester Observer
Kent Messenger and South Eastern Intelligencer

Leeds Times
Liverpool Albion
Maidstone Gazette
Manchester Courier and Lancashire Advertiser
Morning Chronicle,
Morning Post
Rochester, Chatham and Gillingham News
Royal Cornwall Gazette
The Standard
The Times

Indian Newspapers and Journals

(Alexander's) East India and Colonial Magazine
Allen's Indian Mail
Bombay Courier
Calcutta Annual Directory
Calcutta Magazine and Monthly Register
Parbury's Oriental Herald and Colonial Intelligencer, vols. I-IV